Improving organizational performance

A Handbook for Managers

Philip Baguley

McGRAW-HILL BOOK COMPANY

London · New York · St Louis · San Francisco · Auckland
Bogotá · Caracas · Lisbon · Madrid · Mexico · Milan
Montreal · New Delhi · Panama · Paris · San Juan
São Paulo · Singapore · Sydney · Tokyo · Toronto

Published by
McGRAW-HILL Book Company Europe
Shoppenhangers Road, Maidenhead, Berkshire, SL6 2QL, England
Telephone 0628 23432
Fax 0628 770224

British Library Cataloguing in Publication Data
Baguley, Phil
   Improving Organizational Performance:
   Handbook for Managers
   I. Title
   658.4

   ISBN 0-07-709006-3

Library of Congress Cataloguing-in-Publication Data
Baguley, Phil
   Improving organizational performance: a handbook for managers /
   Philip Baguley.
      p.   cm.
   Includes bibliographical references and index.
   ISBN 0-07-709006-3
   1. Organizational effectiveness.   2. Performance.   3. Management.
   I. Title.
   HD58.9.B34   1994
   658–dc20   94-30158
                                                                      CIP

12345 BL 97654

Typeset by BookEns Ltd,
Printed and bound in Great Britain by Biddles Ltd, Guildford, Surrey

For:

Tom Peters
whose ideas and books opened the door

Anita Roddick
who gave hope that managing and caring were compatible

Gareth Morgan
whose books opened more than a few windows

and

Osho
who showed me that all things are possible.

Contents

Preface

In today's ever-changing and increasingly demanding market-places, the single most significant challenge for all of our organizations is that of how to improve performance. This challenge will not be answered by one-off exercises or special projects: it needs, demands and deserves the status of an ongoing and continuous activity if it is to catalyse both the survival and the growth of our organizations as we pass through what Tom Peters[1] calls the 'nanosecond nineties' into the second millennium. Nor is this a top-down activity which is the sole prerogative of those who manage and co-ordinate the activities of others in those organizations—it is a bottom-up, day by day activity whose success depends upon the energy, enthusiasm and creativity of all of those who, as Derek Pugh[2] reminds us, *are* those organizations.

If you are involved in or influence the process of guiding, directing or enabling that energy, enthusiasm and creativity, then this book is meant for you. It aims to answer your needs in the increasing drive to improve the effectiveness and efficiency of your business unit. This is done by providing the information, skills and knowledge which you, as an active participant in and member of an organization, can use to begin the process of improving its performance. But this is not a book for specialists or elitists.

It is deliberately written to enable readers from a variety of backgrounds, including those concerned with the provision of services, to absorb and use the concepts and tools of Performance Improvement. It is also written for the non-specialist and aims to guide the reader from a review of the need for Performance Improvement, through the basic concepts of strategy and the conversion process through to the planning, design, implementation and control aspects of Performance Improvement. In doing so it draws heavily on the concepts and experience of both the Total Quality Management (TQM) process and those areas viewed in the past as being specifically focused on technical or people aspects. Problem-solving, quality control, productivity, team building and management and project management are examples of areas explored and descriptions and examples of several analytical tools are also provided. The book deliberately makes limited use of the complex quantitative tools of operations management and research and focuses on the people aspects of Performance Improvement in a text strongly based on useful examples, pointers to appropriate methods and tools.

In addition to those who practise the 'art' of guiding, directing or enabling the activities of others, this book will also be of value and interest to undergraduate, postgraduate and post-experience students on Business or Management programmes including :

- Certificate In Management
- Diploma In Management
- BA/BSc Business Studies
- MBA

The book has three major sections. The first (Part 1) provides an introduction to those ideas and images that we need to take on board if we are to navigate our way through the maze of management 'jargonese' which has occluded itself around this subject. Chapter 1 takes a look at issues such as Efficiency, Effectiveness and Adaptability while the goals and targets of organizations are examined in Chapter 2. All organizations, whatever their nature or goals, are mechanisms for resource conversion or transformation and Chapter 3 examines this universal process. The increasingly important issue of Quality and its association to the process of performance improvement is examined in Chapter 4. Chapter 5 examines the issues of the layout and capacity of the conversion process and their influence upon the process of performance improvement.

While Part 1 is concerned with the ideas and images associated with the process of performance improvement, Part 2 is concerned with the practicalities of that process. Chapter 6 examines how it has been successfully undertaken elsewhere and identifies the key steps in its successful achievement. Improving organizational performance requires organizations and people to change and the ways in which that change can be successfully managed are examined in Chapter 7. Two of the key issues in that process are the quality of organizational communication and the effective use of teams. These are examined in Chapters 8 and 9 respectively while Chapter 10 looks at several practical and powerful problem-solving techniques which can be used on the route to improved organizational performance. Several valuable but simple techniques to help with the process of identifying and monitoring organizational health factors are described in Chapter 11, and Chapter 12 describes the contribution that projects can make to the performance improvement process and how those projects can be managed successfully.

Part 3 summarizes the key points and issues of the process of performance improvement and is followed by a list of recommended further reading.

If you wish to begin to acquire a knowledge and understanding of the Performance Improvement process then, whatever the size or purpose of your organization and whatever your prior exposure to formal management education, this book will begin that process for you. For those who hesitate to embark on this journey, let me remind you of what Dr W. Edwards Deming[3], the American Quality guru, has said: 'You do not have to do this; survival is not compulsory'. Thanks are due to all of those people with and for whom I have managed, consulted, lectured and tutored: in one way or another they have all contributed to this book. Acknowledgement is also due for the help and support given by Lavinia Porter and Fiona Sperry at McGraw-Hill, Paul Newberry without whom this book would never have happened, and Linda Baguley whose counsel and support were again given so generously during the creation of the text.

Philip Baguley
Brighton

References
[1] Peters, T. (1992) *Liberation Management*, Macmillan, London.
[2] Pugh, D.S. and Hickson, D.J. (1989) *Writers on Organizations*, Penguin, London.
[3] Deming, W.E. (1982) *Quality, Productivity and Competitive Position*, MIT Center for Advanced Engineering Study, Cambridge, Massachusetts.

PART 1
Reasons and Concepts

Every why hath a wherefore.
William Shakespeare

1. What is performance and why do we want to improve it?

The real art for the manager lies in creating challenging but achievable targets.

Tom Peters

Introduction

Performance is something that interests and concerns us all. We expect our children to perform well in their school tests and examinations; we expect our favourite soccer teams to score goals and win cups; and we buy our motor cars on the basis of some aspect of their performance, such as acceleration or fuel economy. For some of us, the salary we are paid is related to our individual work performance or that of the work unit for which we are responsible. The typical dictionary defines performance as the act of carrying out an action, which is something that we all undertake in our working lives, all of the time.

We all possess the ability to carry out these actions, and to do so well or badly. We often define 'well' or 'badly' in relation to some standard or expectation. A runner who performs well in a race is one who beats the other runners or even one whose time for the race is better than the record time, or his or her previous best time. A manager who performs well is seen as one who achieves good results and these might be better than last year's results or better than the budgeted figures.

So why is this act of performance, which is a common and familiar activity, the subject of this book? The answer lies in the fact that many of the myriad actions that are carried out every day in the organizations in which we work and play are carried out in ways which do not achieve the desired results or outcomes. Indeed, as customers of some of these organizations we all, at some time, feel justified in commenting that these actions appear to be carried out without any anticipation or thought of the consequent results! These multiple small actions can accumulate to form a downward drift in performance which, once started, is difficult to halt. And yet, if we wish to improve the ways in which the organization performs we can also achieve this by changing these individual actions. When we choose to reverse the 'polarity' of these actions, from negative to positive, then they also will accumulate to create a larger and more significant improvement in performance. In its turn, this improved performance will provide the

3

opportunity for those who work in these organizations to have choices about bigger and more significant, or even radical, changes in the ways in which their work is carried out.

Put simply, performance improvement is:

- An act of empowerment on the part of those who carry it out;
- An opportunity for personal growth, development and change;
- An opportunity for organizational change and growth.

As such, improved performance is rather like the Holy Grail: much sought after and the subject of many legends. However, unlike the Holy Grail, improved performance is not a legend or a myth. It is, whatever the size, nature or purpose of the organization, both achievable and sustainable, and can be made so by the efforts of people who work within or for those organizations rather than the efforts or dictates of outsiders.

This book is intended as a guide for managers who need and want to improve the performance of the organizations in which they work. Indeed, it is worth stating at this point that unless you have a real need and desire to change the world in which you work and to do so by improving the performance of both yourself and those around you, then there is little value in your reading any further. That need to improve, to grow, to do it better, is not an optional ingredient in the heady brew that we will create together in the pages of this book: it is a *must*, a basic requirement, a building block of the process of performance improvement. Without it you (or I) can do little; with it we can begin and continue to achieve much.

This initial chapter is about beginning that process of aiming for improved performance and later chapters in Part 1 will increase the accuracy of that aim. But, as the Italian proverb says: 'It is not enough to aim, you must hit', and Part 2 will tell us how to do just that.

How is it done?

The structure and nature of the performance improvement process have excited a tremendous range of views and comment. These have been generated by writers from a wide variety of backgrounds and with a wide range of experiences of the actual process of improving performance in an organization or a company. They include the analytic, the academic, the pragmatic and even the dogmatic! Many of them exhibit a dependence upon three-letter acronyms or initializations such as MBO, MRP, JIT, OPT or CIM. These are often described by their originators and supporters as new, unique and all encompassing answers to all of your problems. Unfortunately, as Tom Peters[1] says 'Most acronyms stink'. That is not, however, to

4

dismiss these techniques as rubbish. It is undoubtedly true that many of them represent proven and valuable techniques for improvement. However, what is *not* true is that these techniques are universally applicable. As Sir John Harvey-Jones[2] comments: '...there can never be any single correct solution for any management problem,' and as Professor Colin New[3] observes: 'If there was a single simple solution we would have found it by now.'

So any claims that these techniques can be successfully used in any organization, whatever its output, product, culture or history, should be treated with suspicion. Other views about performance improvement will insist that you need to invest in new technology to improve your performance. At this time the new technology will almost certainly involve the use of microprocessors in one form or another and Table 1.1 shows some examples of 'befores' and 'afters' for microprocessor-based and other technological changes.

Table 1.1 Technological changes

Before	*After*
Typewriters to generate mono-colour documents	Word processors driving colour printers
Information exchange by printing on paper	Networked computers with electronic data interchange
Scissors or guillotines to cut material	Lasers
People-driven trolleys to move material or parts	Automatic guided vehicles
Paper, pencil and drawing equipment to generate technical drawings	Computers with draughting software and plotters
Pigeons to send messages	Telephones, pagers and faxes

As with the MBOs, MRPs and the other three-letter acronym techniques, these technological changes can have value and relevance. However, they do need to be applied in the right circumstances and at the right time as illustrated in 'Help or hinder?' below. However good the new technology, it will not, on its own, enhance or improve the performance of any organization. What is needed is the application of relevant technology at the right time. The term 'relevant technology' embodies, at the very least, the idea that the technology employed can be used, understood and supported by the people within that organization.

5

Help or hinder?

A Western Aid agency had commissioned a study of the food crop farming patterns and techniques in a Third World country. The study had indicated that output was limited by the lack of water and the use of small plots. The proposals for change, which were linked to the provision of financial aid, recommended collectivization of the small plots into a large single farm unit, the creation of bore-holes to provide year-round water and use of modern irrigation and transport equipment. The linkage to substantial foreign hard currency aid and the desire to be 'modern' carried the project forward to the installation of new equipment and the organization of collectives. However, within a year the bore-holes had silted up, the irrigation equipment lay unused through lack of expensive foreign sourced spares and the collectives teetered on the edge of collapse through conflict about falling outputs and with the old traditional father–son inheritance patterns. Modern sophisticated Western farming technology had not been relevant to the social culture of these farmers.

Even if it is relevant, the use of new technology will often only give you a short-term advantage. That this advantage is of a short-term nature reflects the fact that if you can buy or even invent the new technology then so can your competitor. That competitor may learn to use it with more speed and urgency and also to better effect than you do!

That is not to say, however, that technology such as microprocessors or innovations such as JIT, MRP etc. should be ignored. They all have made and will continue to make contributions to the process of improving performance *but* only when used in a relevant and timely manner.

Nor is the process of improving performance a 'one-off' or a 'once and for ever' exercise. The decline of IBM from an almost six billion dollar profit in 1983 to a loss approaching five billion dollars in 1992, with a corresponding fall in market share of world-wide computer industry revenues from 30 per cent to under 20 per cent, illustrates graphically how what was right yesterday can become today's or tomorrow's epitaph.

To be effective the process of improving performance must be a continuous process which is integral to the culture of the organization. The 'once every two years' type of 'housekeeping' exercise generally fails to ensure any more than a return to the standards of two years ago while the major 'new broom' or new concept project often involves considerable cost and is usually top-down driven. Increasingly the evidence suggests that effective improvement in performance in all organizations is created and sustained by continuous incremental change: by building on success and by taking one step at a time.

Optional or compulsory?

It is also evident that the process of improving performance is no longer an optional extra. In order to survive, all organizations, whatever their size, nature, history or purpose, need to be able to respond to the social, economic, political and technical changes which pull and buffet them from all sides in today's constantly changing world. These changes have already meant or will mean, for example, that many of us work for increasingly global organizations whose hierarchical structures are flatter with fewer 'head office' staff. These and other organizations need people who are 'knowledge workers' and who are multiskilled. Falling birth rates and longer life spans in the Western nations mean that there are fewer young people and more older people. As a consequence, the ways in which people are employed are changing with both part-time working and the employment of women increasing. Advances in telecommunications and computer technology have enabled more people to work at home while those who work in the centres of production are increasingly expected to display task and skill flexibility over and beyond the traditional craft boundaries. In both global and national markets, the customer's expectations about the quality and durability of the services and products he or she buys have risen to heights which were unheard of 10 years ago, and will continue to rise.

These and other changes mean that organizations will need:

- To accept that predictability and stability are things of the past;
- To develop the capability to anticipate and embrace change; and
- To believe that change presents opportunities and challenges for growth and improvement.

Your organizations may be large or small and, as a result of a variety of internal or external factors, might be shrinking or growing. These organizations will be diverse in terms of history, size, structure, culture, technology, geographical location and stage of growth or decline. They might be concerned with the provision of tangible goods or products or with the provision of less tangible outcomes such as services. Some of these organizations will be dedicated to profit generation and others will be more concerned with break-even costing on the way to providing a service or product which is needed by the community as a whole. Many of you will command a salary which reflects the level or scarcity of your expertise while

7

others of you will volunteer your services to support an agency with whose aims you agree.

Whatever the nature of both the organization and your relationship to it, these organizations will all, as the doyen of management strategy writers Igor Ansoff[4] describes, behave in ways which are directed towards the achievement of 'identifiable end purposes or objectives'. While the nature of these objectives may differ from organization to organization, their use of and dependence upon the skills and abilities of people in the achievement of those objectives will not. In reality, this dependence upon human beings is more deeply rooted than the organization's dependence upon money or raw material or other resources. As Derek Pugh[5] points out: 'they not only work for the organization—they *are* that organization'.

As a consequence the ability of any organization to improve and enhance its performance in an environment, in which change is the norm, will depend upon the abilities, skills and capabilities of its people. It is these people who are or will become the agents for performance improvement and it is in the management of this human resource that those organizations who survive and grow by virtue of improved performance will differ from those who do not.

Measurement and monitoring

The process of homeostasis is a description of our body's automatic attempts to maintain the blood-stream in a condition which is constant and able to provide the organs, limbs and bones of the body with the material and nutrients for:

- Effective operations,
- Growth,
- Repair.

When the body is damaged or reacts to the presence of a virus this homeostatic process tells us that it is working harder or differently by a change in or feedback from one of the body's variable conditions such as temperature or pulse rate. In order to know that something has changed and to make a judgement about the significance of that change we have to measure that pulse rate or temperature and compare it to a standard or norm. For example, the parents of a child with a raised temperature may be concerned enough to consult a medical practitioner about the cause of that rise.

We can also view our organizations as organic systems or organisms. When seen as such, they also have homeostatic systems which are designed to protect the 'health' of the organization. As we saw with human bodies, this homeostatic system is triggered by feedback. For the organization, this feedback takes the form of information which tells us about changes in the interactions between the organization and its environment. This information might, for example, tells us about a fall in sales volume or an increase in customer complaints. It might also be about the success of a new sales campaign or the reaction of clients to a new reception area layout. If we listen to or take notice of this information then not only do we learn about changes in the organization's health and performance but we might also learn to identify those changes earlier. This early notice of change will enable us to limit damage or to reinforce and encourage growth. In order to do this we need to observe and measure factors which are key to or symptomatic of the organization's health. These factors should be such that they provide information which enables us to take early decisions about resource allocation and usage. The objectives of these decisions should be, at least, the maintenance of a given level of organizational health and, at best, the improvement of the health and vigour of the organization.

However, unlike the body, the organization's homeostatic process is not an automatic one. We do need to make decisions and choices about the actions that we will take. The feedback mechanism and the information it provides is essential to not only those conscious decisions which are con-cerned with maintaining organizational health but also those decisions which are intended to improve or enhance the health or performance of the organization. Indeed, it can be argued that without measurement we have no basis or platform from which to launch or start our performance improvement.

Whatever its purposes this process of measurement will involve the identification and measurement of a number of organizational health factors. The factors should be:

- *Timely* Concerned with now, not six or even two months ago;
- *Cost effective* In that the cost of their generation reflects or is compatible with their potential benefits;
- *Credible* Seen by both those who use them and those whose outputs is measured by them, as being realistic and relevant;
- *Understandable* Not 'jargonized' or requiring special knowledge for their comprehension;
- *Focused* on the key issues or pulse points of the organization.

The last factor is of greatest importance.

However, the process of measurement on its own is not enough: we need to monitor and observe this feedback—not just once or twice a year or when it suits us—but *all of the time.*

The scope of this action of monitoring can vary. It can be limited to only examining or reacting to factors when they exceed or are less than certain values or it can consist of a detailed and ongoing analysis which identifies trends and patterns. The former has limited anticipation of change—it is reactive—while the latter can be used to anticipate change and thus facilitate an effective response. Monitoring will involve:

- Systematic and regular collection of data;
- The regular conversion of that data into a variable which reflects actual performance;
- The comparison of that variable to some target, standard or unit of planned performance.

To be effective monitoring requires data and information which are both quantitative and suitable. Table 1.2 provides some examples of common forms of measurement.

Table 1.2   Common forms of measurement

Productivity indicators	Work done per person per hour
Utilization rates	Per cent utilization of swimming pool
Time targets	Average time taken to process a planning application
Volume of service	Number of repairs undertaken
Service provision indicators	Hectares of open parkland per 1000 of population
Cost indicators	Energy cost per square metre of floorspace

Whatever the variables used, the process of measuring and monitoring these organizational health factors should enable us to:

- Assess, in broad terms, the current overall health or performance of the organization;
- Identify the key factors in that performance;
- Compare that performance with that of other organizations or our own historic performance;
- Set goals or targets for improvement.

However, as we noted earlier, this process of measurement and monitoring cannot be applied indiscriminately to all the information which is generated by the organization. It must only be applied to a few limited factors which are critical to the operation or the organization. These factors can be used to express or reflect a number of basic organizational characteristics which we will now look at.

Efficiency, effectiveness and adaptability

As we have seen in the preceding section the factors which are used to measure and monitor both the health and the improvement capability of an organization are important. In the past they have arisen from or been created from the financial systems of the organization and have, not surprisingly, been concerned with money measures. Some of the simpler examples which most managers are familiar with include:

- Return on Investment (ROI)
- Liquidity
- Payback period
- Discounted cash flow (DCF)
- Indirect costs and others.

While there can be little argument about the importance of money in any organization, these financial measures are increasingly seen to be inward looking, and concerned with resource utilization rather than customer needs. Management's traditional fixation with financial measures has meant that they have overlooked and even ignored other measures such as those related to product or service quality and customer satisfaction. Other examples of these other non-financial measures might include the time taken to launch a new product or the organization's ability to respond to unusual or non-standard service or product requests.

We also saw that the measures which are used to monitor the health of an organization should be available in time to make the manager's response effective, understandable and seen by all to be reasonable, valid, relevant and realistic. It is also necessary that, if these measures are to support and help the management decision-taking process, they are focused on the key issues or pulse points of the organization.

Adopting the above criteria may mean that a hotel chain finds that while its traditional primary focus of monitoring was dominated by a financial view of the organization using factors such as cash flow or the level of return on invested capital, a performance improvement oriented view is concerned with the customer viewpoint and might include such parameters as:

- time taken to answer telephone in reservation centre;
- response time on room service;
- price performance in comparison with competitors;
- consistency of service level within chain.

Of course, it is important to be able to count the money accurately and to control the cash flow but it is more important to get people in your hotel rooms and to get them to return. If you fail to do this then you won't just have a cash flow problem, you won't have a hotel!

The factors which are commonly used to measure and monitor both the health and potential for performance improvement of an organization can be classified as follows.

EFFICIENCY

Efficiency is concerned with the way in which resources are used. It will be typically expressed as a ratio of the output from a process to the input to that process. One example of an efficiency ratio would be the miles per gallon (mpg) or kilometres per litre (kpl) ratio often used to indicate the efficiency of the car as a transport system. The input (gallons or litres of petrol or gasoline) is compared to the output which, in this case, is the miles or kilometres driven in using that fuel. This mpg or kpl ratio reflects the efficiency of the car as a transport system and not just the efficiency of the engine. The achieved value of the ratio will change with different styles of driving and for different journeys. Thus monitoring the mpg or kpl ratio will tell us a number of things which might include:

- effect of driving style,
- condition of the engine,
- effect of route or journey.

Thus as we evaluate the influence of different styles and routes we can begin to choose how and where we drive the car in order to minimize our use of fuel. In its simplest form efficiency is expressed as the following ratio:

$$\text{Efficiency} = \frac{\text{Output}}{\text{Input}}$$

When applied to conversion processes which have people's labour as one of the major inputs this ratio is often termed 'productivity' or 'labour productivity' (see Table 1.2). Other examples of efficiency ratios for a number of different tasks and roles are shown in Table 1.3. When we look closely at these efficiency ratios we can see that they are:

- only concerned with resource utilization;
- not concerned with whether the service or product generated is relevant and available when and where required.

These factors of relevance, availability and timeliness are implicit in the next concept that we shall consider.

Table 1.3   Efficiency ratios

Role/task	Ratio
Newspaper reporter	Reporter hours/story
College lecturer	Number of hours taught
	Students/class
	Number of publications
Shop assistant	Customers served/hour
Hotel reservations clerk	Minutes/call
Lathe operator	Parts completed/hour
Secretary	Letters typed per hour
Purchasing manager	Cost/purchased unit
Machine shop supervisor	% machines in use
	Machine hours used/
	machine hours available

EFFECTIVENESS

While efficiency is important, it is as important, if not more so, to ensure that the product or service generated is available for the customer when and where required. For example, the shop assistant who serves a high number of customers per hour is efficient but may not be effective in terms of both short- and long-term revenue generation. Higher levels of effectiveness, customer service and revenue would result from the assistant who is prepared to spend more time satisfying a customer's needs and hence achieve higher levels of customer repeat and referral business. That is, the customer will come back to buy again and will tell his or her friends about their satisfaction with service given. Equally an efficient hotel reservations clerk may well achieve a low minutes/call ratio but may have a low booking ratio, i.e. may not translate many of those calls into actual bookings.

The examples of effectiveness ratios shown in Table 1.4 indicate that the needs of the customer can sometimes override the short-term needs of the operating unit concerned. For example, the purchasing agent, whose efficiency is measured by how cheaply the required goods are brought, will achieve this objective by buying large lots at high discount. These large lots

13

Table 1.4   Effectiveness ratios

Task/role	Ratio
Newspaper reporter	% stories printed in paper
College lecturer	% student pass rate
	% students with job offers at end of course
Shop assistant	Average sale/customer
Hotel reservations clerk	% calls leading to booking
Lathe operator	% accepted parts/hour
Secretary	% correct letters sent out per day
Purchasing manager	% stock-outs/stock-turn
Machine shop supervisor	% orders completed on time

will, however, lead to high storage and high carrying costs. It is also possible that in the drive to get the lowest cost the purchasing agent may have rejected a supplier with a better delivery track record and a better product quality. An effective purchasing manager will balance his or her needs with those of the organization. This will involve ensuring that the benefits and costs of large lots are balanced against the risks and costs associated with low levels of stock and small lot size. This balancing act will also need to take into account such factors as the level and reliability of the quality of the goods supplied and the cost of stock-outs, i.e. not having the goods when needed.

In overall terms, effectiveness is concerned with providing the right service at the right place and time, i.e a service target, whereas efficiency is concerned with resource utilization. The relationship between these is illustrated by Figures 1.1 and 1.2.

ADAPTABILITY
It has been observed that some natural systems possess the ability to arrive at specific end-points or outcomes from different starting points and by the use of different resources in different ways. If you apply this concept, which is called equifinality and originates from the study of living systems, to organizations then it means that they must be:

- capable of adapting their products and services to meet *any* customer need;
- capable of creating, operating and refining an adaptable process for transformation of *any* resource.

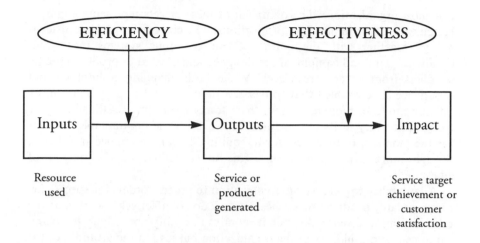

Figure 1.1 Efficiency and effectiveness

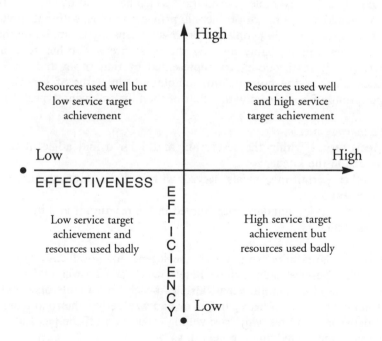

Figure 1.2 Dimensions of efficiency and effectiveness

For most organizations the attainment of these targets represents a task of Herculean, if not impossible, proportions. The current limitations of technology together with the norms of our economic systems mean that buildings, plant and equipment are designed and created to produce specific products from specific resources. While both changing technology and experience have enabled that conversion process to take place faster, more reliably and to be more responsive to customer needs, we are still a long way from equifinality in its purest form. However, while unattainable, at least for the moment, in its purest form, equifinality can be applied in a lesser, though more attainable, form. This is contained in the notion of adaptability.

Adaptability will enable an organization to process orders for special, i.e. non-standard, products or services and to do so effectively—that is at the relevant time and place. As such it requires flexibility not only in the plant, equipment and buildings of the organization but also in the attitudes of the people who work for or, as we noted earlier, are that organization. While the nature, size and technology of the capital assets of the organization may represent the boundaries of that adaptability, its presence and strength within those boundaries is dependent upon the attitudes and capabilities of those people. For example, a restaurant which has a seating capacity for 20 people would have a major problem in providing meals, within its premises, for a group of 40 or 50 people. Its processing capacity is limited by the size of its room and probably also by the local fire and other regulations. However, within the boundary represented by that room and associated kitchen, there is the potential for adaptability in terms of servicing that larger group of customers with either of the four following types of meals:

- Take-away meals;
- Meals served within the restaurant and a hired and adjacent tent but cooked in the kitchen;
- Weather permitting, meals served within the restaurant and on the pavement area;
- A quick service standard meal served in the restaurant and in batches of 20 at a time.

It is this adaptability from which the legends of good customer service originate. These legends include hotels which can answer and remember your special idiosyncratic needs, airlines which hold flights open until the last minute because of heavy traffic or bad weather on the road from town and department stores which are willing to alter an off-the-peg suit in time for a customer's wedding the next day.

The organizations who display this characteristic do so by:

- empowering their employees;
- creating and refining flexible systems;
- placing customer needs ahead of their own needs.

This adaptability is, however, the most elusive of the factors to measure and monitor. It is also, incidentally, the factor whose absence will cause the majority of your customer complaints. If your customer doesn't want onions on her hamburger, why should she have to have them just because you find it easier to make standard hamburgers with onions? Interestingly, at least one of the major fast food chains has become aware of the value of adaptability and now enables you to order a hamburger with or without whatever you want. It is the connection between the lack of adaptability and the level of customer complaints which provides the first of the adaptability or limited equifinality measures shown in Table 1.5.

Table 1.5 Adaptability or limited equifinality ratios

- Number of customer complaints about lack of adaptability of standard service or product.
- Comparison between average response time or processing time for standard and special service or products.
- % of special requests referred upwards in organization.
- % Special requests.

Learning: loops and curves

There is an old German proverb that says: 'Could everything be done twice, everything would be done better.' The modern management version of this proverb is implicit within the idea of the learning curve.[6] This view of the way in which we learn was first identified in the 1920s and has been successfully applied to a wide variety of tasks and circumstances since that time. The learning curve, when applied to people tasks, says that the time taken to perform a task will diminish the more often the task is performed. That is we learn each and every time that we do a task.

Of course, the amount we learn diminishes the more often that we do the task and is larger in the early stages when the task is relatively unfamiliar to us. This process is illustrated by Figure 1.3. and is generally said to indicate that a 20 per cent reduction in time results from each doubling of output or number of repetitions. While this curve was initially identified as a result of observation of manual tasks, evidence has accumulated to support its

17

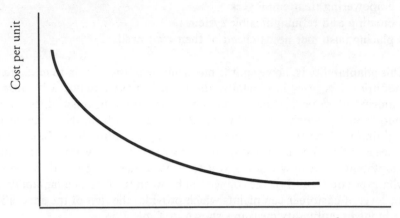

Figure 1.3   The learning curve

application to organizations as well as individuals. This organizational version of the curve is generally called the experience curve rather than the learning curve. Both of these curves, when plotted on a log–log scale, generally show a straight line with a negative slope.

Another view of the learning process was developed by Chris Argyris and Donald Schon[7] in the late 1970s. This view was focused on the ways in which organizations learn and suggested that this occurs through feedback and the consequent detection and correction of errors. Argyris and Schon say that many organizations exhibit this learning process in relation to their operations and call it 'single loop' learning. An example would be the measurement and monitoring of the scrap rates for a manufacturing process. The detection of the numbers of components that emerge from the manufacturing process in an unacceptable condition and the identification and correction of the causes of this condition and its parallels in service industries represent a process with which many of you will be familiar. This single loop learning has the focus of ensuring that current objectives and targets are met, often with minimum use of resources. As such it can be argued that single loop learning is concerned with the efficiency of the organization. It is also applied to the relationship between an organization and the environment in which it functions with the organization scanning that environment and measuring and monitoring its performance against the norms or standards it has selected. However, 'double loop' learning takes place when that detection and correction process is applied to those norms and standards. These norms and standards are subject to a process of measurement, monitoring, comparison and correction in order to establish

18

if they are still relevant and appropriate. If they are not, they are changed.

This 'double loop' learning can be seen as being concerned with the effectiveness of the organization. That is to say that it is concerned with whether the service or product which the organization generates and monitors via single loop learning is, in the context of the changing environment, still seen as relevant and timely to the needs of a changing market-place. 'Double loop' learning is also applied to the relationship between the organization and the environment in which it functions and can be seen as challenging the fundamental aims, norms and values of the organization. Single and double loop learning are illustrated in Figure 1.4.

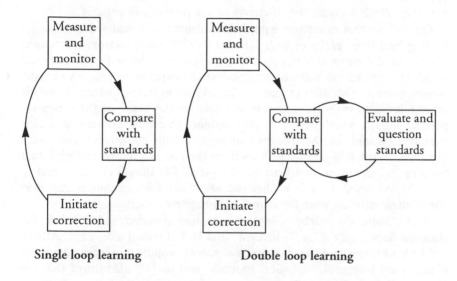

Single loop learning   Double loop learning

Figure 1.4   Single and double loop learning

The relevance of both the learning and experience curve and single and double loop learning to the performance improvement process is considerable. The learning curve says that we continue to learn and improve even when we are undertaking a repetitive task. Hence, performance improvement is not a one-off event but a continuous process. The concept of single and double loop learning tells us that while increased efficiency is a credible and worthwhile goal, it needs to be undertaken in concert with an ongoing review of the effectiveness and relevance of the overall conversion process. These views of how we learn are illustrated further in the following example.

The Fred Bloggs Plastic Road Cone Emporium

The Fred Bloggs Plastic Road Cone Emporium had been in profitable and expanding operation for some years. Mr Bloggs had, from the humble beginnings of a single injection moulding machine operating in a spare shed on his cousin's farm, created an organization which had rapidly grown to answer the plastic road cone needs of the UK from a 10-acre site with 20 Japanese high-speed automated injection moulding machines housed in modern production buildings with large associated warehouses. He had achieved this by constant attention to the detection and elimination of anything which reduced the efficiency of the production process.

Quality control inspectors sampled, measured and scanned ceaselessly, feeding back the results of their labours to machine operators who tuned and adjusted their machines, ever striving to produce the perfect plastic road cone. This perfection was not achieved at the expense of excessive plastic consumption for Mr Bloggs, being a frugal man at heart, had employed his niece Gladys to measure, monitor and control the usage of the expensive plastic granules which went into the machines to produce these cones. Nor should it be said that Mr Bloggs had neglected his customers: cones were available ex-stock in a range of hues from the familiar fluorescent pink to a tasteful and environmentally acceptable green. Mr Bloggs could be said to be a happy man: he felt he had achieved his life's ambition and was considering handing over the reins to his nephew Albert.

Now Albert was bright young lad who had attended, in his youth, the Business School of the local university and had obtained a diploma. Albert, unlike Mr Bloggs, had heard rumours of recent proposals to legislate against plastic road cones, on ecological grounds, and he had also heard that the Korean equivalent of Mr Bloggs was planning to enter the UK market with an automated, self-destructing, biodegradable road cone made from discarded washing-up liquid containers and lemonade bottles.

Albert was concerned and went to talk to his wise and old professor at the Business School. The professor told Albert that he and Mr Bloggs had learned how to make plastic road cones very well and, indeed, were the best in the land. But they were about to experience a 'negative step change perturbation' in their business fortunes because the 'goal posts had been moved'. What was needed, said the professor, was a review and evaluation of their organization's targets and goals—and one done now, not next week!

Albert hastened off to tell Mr Bloggs who said he didn't understand about the goal posts because he was a pigeon racing man himself but that he did trust Albert and anyway Fred Jones, the postman, had been saying the same sort of thing last night in the saloon bar. So Albert set about the task which later proved to be the foundation of the Bloggs empire as we know it now and in the quiet of his office, he challenged, tested and disputed all of the standards which Mr Bloggs had built over the years of making plastic road cones. When he had finished he went to see Mr Bloggs who regarded him gravely and asked what he had found. Albert, who was shaking in his boots, then told Mr Bloggs that they were really not good at making plastic road cones. What they were actually good at was the quality and stock control of the volume production from high speed plastic injection moulding machines and that they ought to apply those skills to making other products, such as, for example, babies' rattles and dummies. At first, Albert thought that Mr Bloggs was going to explode but to his delight and surprise he saw a beam of pleasure spreading across Mr Bloggs's face. His surprise rose to amazement when Mr Bloggs told him that he was going to retire, as he was really a plastic road cone man at heart, and let Albert run the business. 'Well done, lad' said Mr Bloggs as he shuffled off to his pigeon loft.

In later years Albert applied this lesson again and again, always challenging the standards and targets of the managers who ran his ever-growing empire. But when asked what the secret of his success was he would always smile enigmatically and tell the questioner to 'just watch the bleedin' goal posts'.

Mr Bloggs retired and built up a reputation as the man with the biggest, cleanest and most productive pigeon loft in Burnley.

The organization which learns from its interaction with its environment is, of course, an organization which is continually adapting and improving its performance. Tom Peters and Robert Waterman[1] describe such an organization as one which evolves by experimentation and Peter Senge[8] writes about its adaptability and its ability to focus on being creative rather than copying others. For our purposes the most relevant view of a learning organization comes from Mike Pedler, John Burgoyne and Tom Boydell[9] who describe it as an organization which 'continuously transforms itself'.

In order to enhance the organization's survival capability that transformation must ensure that the organization:

- Is efficient in that it makes the best possible use of its resources;
- Is effective in that it ensures that the products and services it produces are relevant and timely;
- Continually strives to answer the needs of its customers with maximum adaptability.

While these are not new or even novel needs, the level of the current pressure to achieve them and the severity of the penalties for failing to do are unprecedented. So what we must begin to look at is how we can get to the point where our organizations are efficient, effective and adaptable.

The way forward

Historians tell us that the first recorded use of writing was, some five or six thousand years ago, associated with the need to measure and monitor numbers of cattle and quantities of grain. While we now use computers instead of clay tablets to record the ever increasing mountains of data associated with our commercial and scientific activities, the increasing complexity and changeability of our world underlines and continues this need to ensure that we find better ways of operating and managing our organizations.

These organizations learn how to improve their operations and performance through the medium of, and because of, the learning capability of the individuals working in them. Indeed, as Rosemary Stewart[10] notes, these organizations: 'exist to achieve purposes that individuals cannot achieve on their own'.

However, that learned material or acquired wisdom must be allowed and encouraged to diffuse throughout the whole organization if it is to become truly effective. Unfortunately this doesn't always happen.

A 1991 survey[11] of some 300 American electronics companies indicated that while almost three-quarters of these companies had initiated Total Quality Management (TQM) programmes, two-thirds of these had failed to achieve better than 10 per cent reduction in their defects rates. This is one example of the results, or rather lack of results, which can come about from some programmes which claim to be targeted at performance improvement. These programmes which achieve little, often at considerable cost and expenditure of organizational energy, have been described as having as much impact as 'a ceremonial rain dance has on the weather'. It will not be surprising to discover that opinions differ as to why this is so.

However it is evident that many programmes which fail to achieve are:

- Focused on actions rather than results:
  - we will improve the quality of our product or service; rather than
  - we will reduce our failure rate to 5 per cent;
- Have long-term, wide-span and often diffuse goals:
  - to enhance the level of customer service in the company;
- Follow an approach or philosophy in a doctrinaire manner:
  - three-letter acronyms again!

- Involve the use of jargon and mystique:
  - 'facilitation roles', 'the Quality College';
- In need of substantial investment in terms of money and patience.

Successful programmes for change and improvement in performance generally involve low or even no investment and can often involve one or several of the following:

- short-term measurable goals:
  - to reduce the reject level to 10 per cent by end June or
  - to increase bedroom occupancy levels by 5 per cent by month end.
- the use of success to create and build further success:
  - 'our Scunthorpe branch used this method to reduce stock losses by half—why don't you?'
- looking for results *now*:
  - 'what have you done *today* to improve this shop's sales performance?'
- empowerment of people as the programme's driving force:
  - 'people are quality';
  - 'you take every opportunity to grab the imagination of your employees'.

It was commented earlier in this chapter that effective and long-lasting performance improvement is a continuous process which is integral to the culture of the organization. To be successful it must also involve those who do as well as those who manage. The presence of structure is also a prime requirement. The basic structure of this process is illustrated in Figure 1.5. We will take a more detailed look at this process and the practicalities of its implementation in Part 2. For the time being, we should recognize that the driving force for the performance improvement process comes from the diference between the current position and the position that we want to be in.

It is this difference which drives the process of performance improvement. The involvement of your staff and employees in the process of performance improvement is vital to the success of that process. One way of involving your people is by the use of teams. Teams can be used for routine tasks, for special projects or even to compete in the company tennis or softball competition. Their success comes from their ability to harness and encourage the creativity of all team members, often in ways or areas outside their functional expertise. Chapter 9 takes a more detailed look at some of the ways and means of setting up and running teams.

The process of involving people in a performance improvement programme, however it is conducted, will stand or fall on the quality and content of the communications which take place. Many managers forget

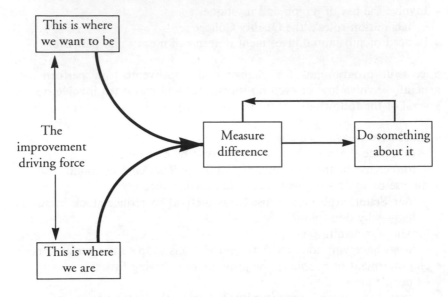

Figure 1.5 The improvement process

that communication is a two-way process and consequently fall into the trap of becoming the type of manager who talks at his or her staff without listening to them. This ability to listen well is an acquired rather than an innate skill whose absence is one of the biggest blocks to effective communication. The presence of effective listening will, however, enable the manager to acquire valuable facts, figures and opinions from others. We look at the ways in which we communicate with each other in Chapter 8.

This process of communication is also enhanced when those involved in the performance improvement programme are aware of the overall targets and objectives of the organization. It is these organizational targets and objectives which represent a view of where the organization wants to be and are often described as being concerned with strategy. We will examine these in Chapter 2.

Summary
The process of performance improvement is aimed at enhancing the ability of an organization to achieve the desired targets for and outcomes of its actions. The effective performance improvement process is:

• dependent upon the efforts of the people who are that organization;

- continuous and ongoing in nature;
- driven by the gap between the current situation and the desired future.

This driving force can be measured and monitored in terms of the organization's:

- *Efficiency* Ability to convert resources into products or services;
- *Effectiveness* Ability to ensure that those products and services are available, for the customer, at the right place and time;
- *Adaptability* Ability to respond to respond to customer demands for special products or services.

The ability of the organization to improve is limited by its ability to learn. The learning process, for both those individuals who are the organization and the organization as a whole, is described by the concepts of the learning curve and single and double loop learning. Single and double loop learning can be related to the concepts of efficiency and effectiveness.

Effective performance improvement programmes are seen to be:

- Focused on measurable results;
- Concerned with results *now* and not tomorrow;
- Using success to build further success;
- Driven by the empowerment of people.

References
[1] Peters, T.J. and R.H. Waterman, *In Search of Excellence*, Harper and Row, New York, 1982.
[2] Harvey-Jones, Sir John, *Managing to Survive*, Heinemann, London, 1993.
[3] New, Professor Colin, D.T.I Competitive Edge Manufacturing Workshop, 1991.
[4] Ansoff, H. Igor, *Corporate Strategy*, Penguin, London, 1968.
[5] Pugh, D.S. and D.J. Hickson, *Writers on Organizations*, Penguin, London, 1989.
[6] Hirschmann, W.B., *Profit from the learning curve*, in Harvard Business Review, vol. 42, Jan–Feb 1964, pages 125–139.
[7] Argyris, C. and D. Schon, *Organizational Learning: A Theory of Action Perspective*, Addison-Wesley, Reading, Massachusetts, 1978.
[8] Senge, P., *The Fifth Discipline*, Century Business, London, 1990.
[9] Pedler, M., J. Burgoyne and T. Boydell, *The Learning Company*, McGraw-Hill, Maidenhead, 1991.
[10] Stewart, R., *Managing Today and Tomorrow*, Macmillan, Basingstoke, 1991.
[11] Schaffer, R.H. and H.A. Thomson, Successful change programmes begin with results, in *Harvard Business Review*, vol. 70, Jan–Feb 1992, pages 71–79.

2. Directions, goals and strategies

First, you have to have fun.
Second, you have to put love where your labour is.
Third, you have to go in the opposite direction to everyone else.

Anita Roddick

Introduction

We saw at the end of Chapter 1 that the engine of the performance improvement programme is fuelled by the difference between:

- where we are now, and
- where we want to be.

This difference is a considerable force for change, at both work and play, for all of us. The comparison between our present condition and a future and better condition can stimulate us all to change the ways in which we work, play and live. For example, for those of us who play golf the difference between our current handicap and those of better players around us provides incentives for us to change the way in which we drive or putt. We can often be frustrated by the ways in which our work (and play) are organized. When these are compared to other models of organizational structures or ways of working, that comparison can provide us with the energy and zeal to change and enhance the formal structure and relationships of our organizations. Similarly, the difference between the profitability of our organization and the higher profit levels of others in the same market can often provide the incentive to apply increased sales or marketing effort or to seek new products or services to sell.

However it is expressed and whatever it is about, this view of 'where we want to be' or 'vision of the future' can represent a very potent and tangible expression of our desires and aspirations.

At an individual level, these desires and aspirations are often very different in their nature and objectives. For example, they can be expressed as ambitions which are related to possession of objects—'my ambition is to have a Porsche 968CS'—or wealth—'I want to be a millionaire by the time I'm thirty-five'—or even states of mind—'I want to be happy'. Each of these, and the many other ways in which we express our desires, provide the incentive for change and improvement. But these ambitions are not fixed or static. They can and do change as we mature and gain more and varied experience or as the environments in which we work and play change around us. They also can be influenced by our success or failure to achieve earlier ambitions. Nevertheless, whatever their focus or origin or the nature of their change or modification, these ambitions represent a major force in all our lives.

Organizational aims and aspirations

What we now need to look at is whether these patterns are also displayed in the targets, goals and ambitions of our organizations. In Chapter 1, we identified that these organizations, far from being the machines of bureaucracy, consist of and are the people who work in and for them. As such their goals, aims and objectives will reflect the desires and aspirations of those people or are a consensus of those desires and aspirations. We also noted that these organizations can provide a way for us to achieve what we are unable to achieve on our own.

However, the range of people who influence an organization's goals and targets is not limited to those who work within that organization. The term 'stakeholder' is often used to describe those who can exert this influence. A typical list of these stakeholders can:

- Involve many different roles and groups;
- Extend beyond the formal boundaries of the organization;
- Include anyone whose interests or 'stake' are affected by the actions of the organization.

The range and type of these stakeholders is illustrated, for a hospital, in Figure 2.1. In another example—that of a small food processing factory situated, as the major employer, in a market town—the list of stakeholders would include:

Shareholders	Employees	Suppliers
Directors	Senior managers	Customers
Local Authority	Local schools	River Authority
Employees' families and relatives		Local community

All of these groups or individuals are affected by the actions of the organization: they can gain or lose by those actions. The wide nature of this stakeholder group means that those gains and losses can be direct, as in the case of an employee, or indirect, as in the case of a local shopkeeper.

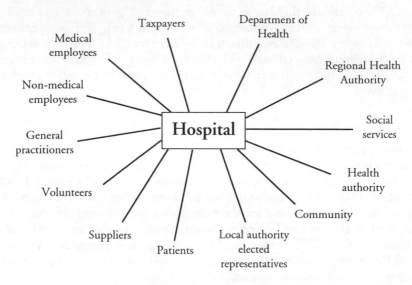

Figure 2.1 Stakeholders

Similarly, they all have needs and desires which will also, directly and indirectly, reach out to influence the goals, aims and objectives of the organization. But the variety and diversity of these stakeholders' needs and desires means that they will often be in conflict with one another and with the needs and desires of the organization. This is illustrated in the example below.

The John Mountain potato crisp factory

The John Mountain Potato Crisp factory had been operating on the outskirts of the market town of Hatlon for several years. Until recently the relationship between the factory and the local community had been good. The factory had provided secure, well-paid employment for the local people. It had also been seen as a source of future job opportunities for the young people and children of Hatlon. Ideally the community would have preferred this to take place without pollution, noise or heavy road traffic which resulted from this factory but, in the past, they had been prepared to compromise on these for the sake of jobs and security. The factory manager, Dick Lawn, was an accountant who wanted the company to grow, expand and to increase its profits. Those who knew Mr Lawn were aware that the reason for these ambitions was the anticipated expansion of his individual power and salary. However, Mr Lawn was also aware that this increased profitability and expansion was not likely to be achieved without automating the factory, with subsequent job losses. The factory owner, Mrs Mountain, was a widow who had inherited the factory when her husband John died. She needed Mr Lawn to run the factory so that it made a good profit or return on her sole capital. However, she had recently received a very tempting offer to buy the factory from the conglomerate, Megafry. If she accepted this offer she would not only reap a handsome profit but also be able to spend the rest of her days in comparative luxury. Falling sales and increasing unrest in the factory and local community, who had heard of her and Mr Lawn's plans, made an early decision imperative. Mrs Mountain had to decide—and soon—which of these conflicting stakeholder interests was to be the one which influenced her decision.

Order or chaos?

So how does order emerge from this complex web of interactions and influences or does it remain as chaotic or disordered as it seems to be? At least part of the answer seems to lie in the observation that within all organizations there exist a number of what are called systems. In its simplest form a system consists of an organized assembly or collection of components which are intended to achieve a particular outcome. Those which exist in our organizations are broadly concerned with:

- the conversion of resources (money, materials, people etc.);
- the provision and control of people skills in the form of the occupations and roles which are required by the organization (structures, organization charts, role definitions, etc.);
- the politics and politicking within the organization itself and at its interface with the larger external environment (interests, conflicts and power).

These systems can manifest themselves in the physical arrangements of objects or in ideas or ways of doing things. An example of a physical system would be an assembly line or production system while a conceptual or abstract system would be an organization chart. These systems may have gradually evolved over time or may have been deliberately designed or selected and introduced.

An organization which survives and grows can be seen to:

- consist of a complex network of interrelated systems and subsystems;
- have systems and subsystems that operate together in such a way as to

29

ensure congruence or compatibility between their differing demands and needs;
- have an open and continuous relationship with the environment in which it exists.

These systems, in order to work effectively, require standards or targets. For example, the system which is concerned with resource conversion will have targets which reflect the efficiency and effectiveness of that conversion process and might be expressed as output rates, per cent material conversion, failure rates etc. The occupational or role system will be targeted towards ensuring that the skills and abilities of the people resource are adequate to support the needs of the resource conversion system and that the interactions of those people are structured in such a way as to enhance the effectiveness of those skills and abilities. The targets of this system might include labour turnover rates, job descriptions, etc. The targets of the political system will, by their nature, be less easily identifiable or definable. However, it can be argued that the absence, in an organization, of a mechanism which allows employees to influence that organization's decisions, will affect people's choices about whether they remain with that organization, or even join it in the first place. As such, measures like the number of unfilled vacancies or number of applicants/job vacancy can be seen as measures of the efficiency or effectiveness of the political system. Similarly, the percentage of an organization's planning applications which are accepted could be said to be a reflection of the nature and quality of the interface and dialogue between that organization and the local community. Whatever their nature or complexity, it is within these systems and their mutual interaction that the mechanism for resolving the differences and contradictions of the stakeholder's ambitions lies.

However, the nature of this mechanism will depend upon the type of the organization. For example, for many bureaucratic organizations with their heavy dependence upon rules and procedures as a way of exercising top-down authority, the thought of adopting or even identifying organization-wide consensus views is an anathema. The decisions about these organizations' future aims and objectives will typically be taken by those members of its hierarchy who hold high roles and are seen to possess seniority. This type of organization will rely upon the formal power and authority of these managers to create order from the disorder and conflict of stakeholder ambitions. On the other hand, the type of organization which Tom Burns[1] described as 'organismic' will handle things in a different way. This type of organization places great reliance upon free and informal communication and the investment of authority on the basis of skill rather than role. In such an organization, consensus views about aims and objectives may well evolve spontaneously and also involve many stakeholders. This can be seen as a demonstration of the power of the political system.

We have already seen that organizations that learn are able to continually adapt to the needs of their customers and the larger environment. Organizations with this capability are seen[2] as allowing the involvement of all their stakeholders in the creation and evolution of their aims and objectives. This process assumes that:

• All stakeholders take part, by right, rather than by summons or invitation;
• The resultant rich and complex variety of views, interests and opinions will give rise to better ideas, aims and objectives;
• Striving to meet the needs of stakeholders will lead to success.

However it is conducted, the outcome of this process is significant for the future of the organization.

As Anita Roddick,[3] founder of the Body Shop chain, says: 'If you have a company with itsy-bitsy vision you have an itsy-bitsy company'.

This vision of an organization's goals and aims is often called its strategy and it is this and its value to organizations that we will now examine.

Strategy

The use of the term strategy has become an increasingly popular addition to the lexicon of business words and phrases. Originally its use was associated with the military and, as such, was concerned with the creation of large scale plans for winning battles, campaigns or even wars. However, by the early 1960s the business use of this term began to emerge. Its use in this context has grown since that time and now receives considerable attention in the literature of business. However, since its emergence it has been subject to many changes in direction, focus and even description. These changes have resulted in this view of organizational activity being variously described as corporate strategy, business policy planning, long range planning and even general management. Whatever its focus, state of growth or title, these views of the strategies of our organizations have become increasing influential to our understanding of the ways in which these organizations grow and change.

So what does strategy mean and what does it contribute to the growth and change of the organizations in which we work?

In the context of business, strategy is primarily concerned with such matters as what products or services the organization will offer and to which clients and in which markets they will be offered. In making decisions on these matters the business strategist is concerned with:

- The whole organization rather than its parts:
  - the firm rather than the division or department;
- the long term rather than the medium or short term:
  - the development of markets rather than intial sales rate;
- The broad scope of that organization's activities:
  - to manufacture cars or to manufacture furniture.

These decisions and the resultant choices will also be strongly influenced by the nature and characteristics of the larger environment in which the organization operates. We saw in Chapter 1 that this influence operates through the medium of the social, technological, political and economic aspects of that environment. All of these factors will influence the ambitions and aspirations of all organizations and the vision which they have of where they want to be in the future. The outcome of this influence—the organization's vision—will also reflect and, in its turn, influence the nature and scope of the resources used by the organization. The scope and range of this vision can be considerable. It can be, for example, about entering a new market, about investing a considerable sum of money in building a new factory to service that market or about shifting the focus of an entire organization's business activities into a new and untried technology. Other examples of the nature and scope of the decisions arising from or involved in this vision are shown in Table 2.1.

It is worth reminding ourselves that the decisions which lead to the identification of the organizational vision are concerned with:

- The scope of what the organization does;
- The organization's long-term objectives;
- The organization's responses to the external forces and influences;
- Resource issues;
- Stakeholder issues.

It is also worth while taking note of the differences and linkages between the strategic decisions and the other decisions taken in the organization. One difference is that of time-scale: strategy is about long-term objectives while many of the other decisions are about short-term manoeuvres. These other decisions are often called tactical or operational decisions.

Further refinement to our view of the differences between these is added by Igor Ansoff[4] who points out that the decisions taken within any organization are concerned with certain issues:

1. *Strategic* issues These are concerned with the organization's relationship with the larger environment and the choice of what service or product will be sold in which market.

Table 2.1 Strategic decisions

Area	Example
Technology	Investment in new computers or plant, purchase of 'next generation' vehicles, etc.
Services	Increase range of services by provision of more frequent bus service, provide walk-in counselling service in doctor's surgery, etc.
Location	Build new factory, close or move head office, reduce number of branches or outlets relocate warehouses, etc.
Products	Launch new car, washing-up liquid, soft drink, range of cakes, computer, etc.
Organization	Restructure company into autonomous divisions, merge Sales and Marketing Departments, etc.

2. *Administrative* issues These are concerned with factors such as organization, work flows, information flows and location of channels.
3. *Operating* issues These are about the efficiency with which resources are converted.

But are these equally important and are they taken by the same people ? When strategic decision-taking was examined,[5] it was found that these decisions:

- are organization-wide in their implications;
- can involve the commitment of substantial resources;
- are *not* routine, regular or frequent;
- often have few, if any, precedents.

The nature, implications and importance of these decisions also generally leads to their being taken by those who are high in the hierarchy of the organization, i.e. senior managers, directors, chief executive officers (CEOs), etc.

However, when we look at operating decisions we find that they are:

- regular, frequent and routine;
- concerned with a part, rather than the whole, of the organization
- related to a short- or medium-term time scale
- concerned with the use of medium to small resources
- taken by middle managers or below

Organizational improvement and strategy

So how can these infrequent, high level strategic decisions make a contribution to improving organizational performance? At least part of the answer to this question lies in the relationship between these types of decision, and this is illustrated in Figure 2.2.

To be effective the vision contained in the organization's strategy must be concerned with the overall task of the organization. As you would expect there have been many descriptions of this task. However, for our purposes the description generated by Igor Ansoff[4] will serve best. This states that the overall task of the organization is that of arranging, managing and controlling the 'resource conversion process in such a way as to *optimize the attainment of the objectives*' (my emphasis).

For profit-making organizations, these objectives will be concerned with a complex mixture of often conflicting issues such as profit maximization, growth, revenue increase and power. Non-profit-making organizations will be concerned with an equally complex mixture which might include service

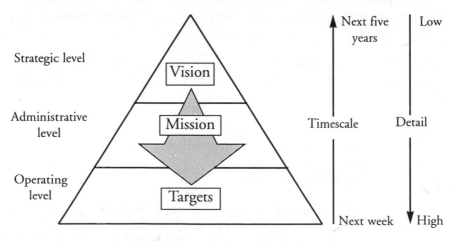

Figure 2.2 From vision to targets

provision, resource maximization, influence etc. Whatever the nature or detail of these objectives might be, one thing is evident: they are all concerned with gain. However, the gain involved may be represented in a multitude of ways which will reflect the different natures of these organizations. For example, a church may have objectives which are not concerned with profit but are concerned with the enhancement of its capability to persuade or convert people to its system of beliefs and a local authority will be primarily concerned with the scope and effectiveness of the services that it provides. Other views of this organizational gain might include factors such as increase in assets held, increasing independence or even increase in the rewards or power of the organization's managers.

The common presence of this gain in the strategies of all organizations means that we can begin to view strategy as an improvement process, or, at very least, as a required precursor to the improvement process. This is so because the strategy or vision of an organization, and the decisions taken to arrive at it, represent a deliberate and conscious attempt to improve outcomes of the actions or performance of the organization. This improvement is, however, one which is chosen or selected and, if achieved, gained for the organization as a whole rather than the individual parts or subsections of the organization.

These strategic decisions can be described as generating the framework within which performance improvement can take place or, to use another analogy from physiology, as providing the skeleton which supports the flesh and organs of a living and growing process of performance improvement. What is certainly true is that the absence of organizational strategy will mean that any efforts at performance improvement might be short-lived, in conflict with each other and even irrelevant.

However, that strategy must not only exist: it must also be communicated to all those who can positively influence its attainment. This communication must also be in a form which is unambiguous and understandable. But even when that is achieved, and the organizational strategy is seen to be clear and understandable, there may still be problems. It is vital to the implementation of the strategy to ensure that the targets and objectives identified at the different levels and in the different parts of the organization are both integrated and compatible with:

- the overarching aims and objectives of the organization's strategy, and
- each other.

Failure to achieve this integration and compatibility will lead to internal conflict and waste of resources.

One way of achieving this integration is by the generation and use of hierarchies of objectives or objective trees. These, which consist of

35

structured diagrams of linked and desired objectives, can help to identify:

- conflicts,
- measures of performance,
- pathways towards the higher level strategic objectives.

The outline of part of an objective tree associated with the introduction of a new piece of legislation for local authority child care and protection is shown in Figure 2.3. Those of you with experience of this type of organization may feel that this illustrative objective tree could be more comprehensive in both scope and detail. However you will also recognize that it highlights organizational constraints and conflicts and provides a view of the organizational objectives which possesses structure and continuity.

The importance of the compatibility and continuity of organizational objectives is also recognized by those who have taken a more theoretical view of strategy. Harvard University's Professor Michael Porter[6] recognizes this need in his description of the systems of any organization as being a chain of interlinked activities.

The links in Porter's chain are:

- *Inbound logistics* Supply, purchasing, transport and warehousing;
  ↓
- *Operations* The conversion process;
  ↓
- *Outbound logistics* Transport, warehousing, delivery;
  ↓
- *Marketing and Sales* Agents, sales, distributors, brand image;
  ↓
- *Service* After sales, product or service maintenance, warranty.

This chain is supported by activities in the areas of human resource management, technology, procurement and the general management subsystems of the organization.

In order to ensure that the chosen visions of the organization are both realistic and achievable all organizations need to make sure that they understand and have adequate information about:

- their own capabilities and skills;
- the threats and opportunities of the environment in which they are operating or intend to operate.

We will now take a look at this relationship between the organization and the environment and the results of the environment's influence upon the organization.

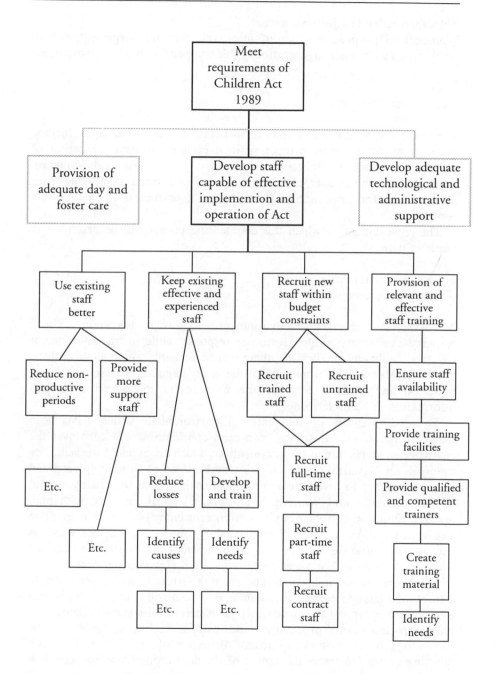

Figure 2.3 An objectives hierarchy

The organization and its environment

Whatever the purpose or vision of an organization, that organization is in competition with other organizations. This competition is about two things:

- resources,
- customers.

There are few, if any, exceptions to this state of being. Examples include government departments competing with each other over allocation of government funding, churches competing over converts and influence, charities competing over donations, commercial firms competing over market share and local authority direct work departments competing with contractors.

The environment in which this competition occurs can be described in terms of its:

- volatility or stability,
- simplicity or complexity.

A volatile and changeable environment will display uncertainty about resource availability and/or customer response while in an environment which is stable and predictable, there will be certainty about these factors. Similarly, a simple environment will be easily capable of description and understanding while a complex one will require specialized skills and information to be understood.

These dimensions of this external environment, which have been described by Henry Mintzberg,[7] can exert considerable influence over the character and structure of the organizations which are exposed to them. For example, an organization which is in the business of producing recorded music is exposed to a volatile and complex environment with many market 'niches' (Country and Western, Soul, Jazz, Classical etc.) and with high levels of change in customer buying patterns for many of those 'niches' (Top Ten etc., etc.). As such it will tend to shift towards a structure which is decentralized (in order to cope with environmental complexity) and organic (in order to cope with environmental volatility). However, an organization which is producing bulk chemicals, such as fertiliser, will be exposed to a stable and less complex environment and as such will tend to shift towards a bureaucratic type of structure which is concerned with standardization of work processes and procedures and with a high investment in the technology of its business. Luciano Benetton of the Italian Benetton clothing group illustrates the power of the environment's influence when he tells us that:[8]

'You have to know how to reinvent yourself. This is true about any industry, but it is mandatory in the fast paced world of fashion.'

As we have noted earlier, this environment also exerts influence through the mediums of its social, technological, political and economic aspects. The emerging strategy needs to be firmly rooted in a comprehensive under-standing of these aspects of the environment. Failure to achieve this understanding can easily result in strategies which are inappropriate and ineffective and as such do not contribute to the organization's gain or growth. The variety and complexity of these aspects are considerable and the influence which they exert is particular and specific to the organization. Table 2.2 illustrates this diversity and complexity for two very different kinds of organization: a local authority social services department and a bank.

Table 2.2 Aspects of environmental influence

Aspect	Social Services department	Bank
Technology	Computerization of records, portable phones and pagers	Electronic point of sale, Smart cards
Economic	Unemployment level, Benefit rates and changes Local government funding restrictions	Interest rates, Exchange rates, Credit restraints
Social	Fewer children, more old people, Race relations More single parent families	Falling birth rates Changing service expectations More working women
Political	New legislation Privatization Housing policies	Growth and planning restraints Level of business confidence

Other factors which can modify the influence which the environment has upon the organization include:

• the size of the organization,
• the complexity of its technology,

- the organization's age,
- the nature of its prior experience and its ability to learn from that experience.

All of these influence the ability of an organization to respond to the tides and climatic changes of the environment. IBM is an example of a large monolithic organization whose business is computer technology. By the early 1990s the size of this organization was considerable. Its 1992 world-wide gross revenue exceeded the gross domestic products of Ireland, Portugal and New Zealand and during the previous decade its research spend exceeded that of the UK Government by a factor of six. And yet in 1992 IBM faced a loss of almost five billion dollars! So why didn't its age (78 years), size or experience protect IBM and enable it to ride out the world-wide economic downturn of the early 1990s?

Part of the reason is simply that IBM didn't change when the environment and market-place did. Its earlier dominance of the mainframe computer market-place led to an organizational culture which was conservative, inward looking, centralized and bureaucratic. This culture failed to identify the importance of technical developments which led to the availability of silicon chips which were powerful *and* cheap. As a result the market-place changed: it grew from a $35 billion market in the early 1970s to a $400 billion market in the early 90s. But, more importantly, it also grew from a market which was supplied by around 2000 organizations to one which was supplied by some 50 000 intensely competitive organizations. IBM's structure, culture and leadership, all of which evolved during the time it was market leader, was not equipped to cope with the rate of change in the environment. IBM's intial response to these events has been to decentralize—to fragment the company into separate and smaller units each with their own Chief Executive Officer (CEO)—in an attempt to strip away the old bureaucratic systems and thus enable unit managers to be in touch with their markets. At the giant's 1993 annual shareholder conference new chairman Louis Gerstner stated that IBM's objectives for 1993 would include:

- defining the industries which IBM will pursue,
- improving customer relations,
- decentralizing.

Time alone will tell whether that strategy will be effective.

Retrospective views always have the power of 20/20 vision so it is easy to comment, but nevertheless true, that one technique which might have forestalled the collapse of the old IBM is that of Attribute Analysis. The dimensions of this analysis are shown in Figure 2.4.

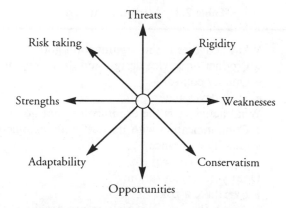

Figure 2.4   Organizational attributes

The use of this technique challenges the organization to look at itself and decide what are its:

- Strengths and weaknesses,
- Current and future opportunities and threats,
- Levels of adaptability and rigidity,
- Ability to take risks or to remain conservative.

Table 2.3 illustrates the range of this attribute analysis and shows examples of the questions to be asked during the process. This analysis can generate benefits for the organization and make a major contribution to the performance improvement process. However, it will only do so when conducted with honesty and objectivity; failure to do so will only reinforce the delusions and fantasies that many organizations have about their own standards and performance.

To be effective this process needs to be conducted in an honest and objective manner. This requires those involved to have the freedom to say what they wish, without fear or hindrance, and without regard for the prejudices, preconceptions and power of those who run the organization.

For those of you who run these organizations and feel that your fellow employees already communicate with you in an honest and objective manner, I would ask one question:

When was the last time that a key decision of yours was challenged or openly criticized by someone whose salary or promotion prospects lie within your control: and what happened to him or her when she or he did it ?

Table 2.3   Attribute analysis

Strengths	What activities is the organization good at? • Product or service design and development • Quality control • Staff development, etc.
Weaknesses	What activities is the organization not good at? • Communicating with its staff and customers • Quality assurance • Financial control etc.
Risktaking	Does your organization: • Ever take a risk? • Assess the degree of risk before deciding? • Strike out into new and unknown areas?
Conservatism	Does your organization need to be sure about all the potential results and implications before it takes decisions on key issues? Does it leave other organizations to launch new and novel products and services ?
Threats	What are those things which stop your organization getting to where you want it to be: • Activities of others inside and outside the organization? • Environmental factors? • Competition? • Lack of efficiency, effectiveness or adaptability?
Opportunities	What could you do if allowed to: • Enter a new market? • Launch a new product or service? • Overcome your weaknesses? • Exploit your strengths further?
Rigidity	Is your organization more interested in answering the needs and demands of its own systems and procedures or the needs of its customers? Does it embrace the unusual customer request *or* does it see it as a threat?
Adaptability	Does your organization change and modify its systems and procedures to meet the needs of the customer? Does it ask its customers what they want before designing its services or products?

I also have a question for those of you who work within these organizations:

> When was the last time that you told your boss that you didn't agree with a decision which she/he had made *and* offered a constructive alternative?

All of those who are involved in this review will need to be open-minded and able to accept that all who contribute have something of value to say and share, even if you don't agree with or like what they say.

In addition to honesty and objectivity, another of the essential ingredients in this review is information. This will be information about a wide range of issues, factors and elements both within and without your organization. This information will include answers to questions such as:

1. What is the potential size of our market?
2. What are the contributions and sales of our own current product mix?
3. What is the performance and product range of our competitors?
4. What do our customers *really* need?

The following and final section of this chapter will take a look at one of the many ways of focusing this search for information.

Bench-marking
The typical dictionary defines the bench-mark as a mark made by a surveyor and used as a reference for determining heights or distances. However, when we apply this, as a concept, to the ways in which our organizations operate we find that the process of bench-marking changes. The reference mark is not always one which we make ourselves: it can also be one which represents the best for the industry or sector in which our organization operates. This means that the performance of our organization is not only compared to the best which it has achieved but also to the best which has been achieved anywhere else.

The process of benchmarking is:

- Continuous,
- Measures the performance of your organization,
- Compares that performance against the best for your industry or sector.

That 'best performance' becomes, in terms of our original definition, the bench-mark against which your organization's performance improvement is measured. You will recall that it is the gap between the organization's current performance and where it wants to be which fuels the performance

43

improvement process. Bench-marking provides a way of identifying that target or goal and of ensuring that the subsequent performance improvement programme reflects the reality of the external environment.

Put simply, bench-marking is about goals and these goals can reflect the performance of:

- Your competitors,
- World class' organizations,
- The best within your own organization.

It can also be applied to any or all of the operations which go on within your organization. For example, when Xerox[9] was searching for bench-marks in the late 1980s, it identified a wide range of organizations which it felt represented the best for a number of activities which also took place within Xerox. These activities included warehouse operations, document processing, bill scanning, service parts provision, information systems and automation assembly. But the organizations who were identified to represent the best in these activity areas were not Xerox's competitors: they were organizations which were concerned with vehicle manufacture, clothing manufacture, banking and finance and other products or services which were not even indirectly related to the main thrust of Xerox's activities. This type of benchmark will enable your organization to identify and evaluate ways of doing things which are new and innovative (to you) but which have also been tried and tested.

While competitive and world-class bench-marks can require extensive research and analysis, internal bench-marks, i.e. those from within your own organization, do not. These 'home grown' bench-marks can also be transferred more easily since the learning curve is steeper due to:

- the absence of any confidentiality constraints on 'know-how' transfer;
- the ease of access to people who are experienced in the process or activity which generates the bench-mark.

However, internal bench-marks can suffer from lack of credibility and if not compared with competitor performance may also be symptomatic of organizational myopia or insularity.

Nevertheless, whatever their origin, the use of bench-marks as performance targets or goals is a powerful and important step on the road to performance improvement. An implicit element in that journey is the process by which the organization converts its resources or inputs into the products and services which it perceives are needed by its customers. It is this process—of conversion or transformation—that we shall next examine.

Summary

The ambitions of the organization arise from the ambitions and desires of its stakeholders. These stakeholders:

- Exist inside and outside the organization;
- Represent all those whose interests are affected by the actions of the organization;
- Often have divergent and conflicting interests.

The differences and contradictions of the stakeholders' ambitions are resolved by the systems of the organization. These are concerned with:

- The conversion of resources;
- The occupations and role within the organization;
- The politics of the interactions which take place between the organization and its environment and within the organization.

It is the mutual interaction of these systems which provides the mechanism for resolving these conflicts. However, the nature of this mechanism is significantly influenced by the nature of the organization.

All organizations express their goals and aims in the form of their strategy. This is about what an organization wants to be rather than how it wants to get there. Strategy is about:

- The long term;
- The whole organization;
- The scope and nature of that organization's activities in its interaction with the external environment.

Strategic decisions are different from administrative or operating decisions because of their:

- Infrequency,
- Lack of precedents,
- Considerable implications and consequences.

The strategy of an organization can be seen as the beginning of the performance improvement process or a framework upon which that process is built. That strategy should be:

- Based on a comprehensive understanding of:
  - The nature of the external environment,
  - The influences exerted by that environment,

– The attributes of the organization itself.
● Communicated to and understood by the stakeholders of the organization—particularly those who are involved in its implementation.

Both attribute analysis and bench-marking can contribute to the process of acquiring that understanding.

References
[1] Burns, T. and G.M. Stalker, *The Management of Innovation*, Tavistock, London, 1961.
[2] Pedler, M., J. Burgoyne and T. Boydell, *The Learning Company*, McGraw-Hill, Maidenhead, 1991.
[3] Roddick, A., *Body and Soul*, Random Century, London, 1991.
[4] Ansoff, H. Igor, *Corporate Strategy*, Penguin, London, 1968.
[5] Hickson, D.J, R.J. Butler, D. Cray, G.R. Mallory and D.C. Wilson, *Top Decisions: Strategic Decision-making in organizations*, Blackwell, Oxford, 1986.
[6] Porter, M.E., *Competitive Advantage: Creating and Sustaining Superior Performance*, Free Press, New York, 1985.
[7] Mintzberg, H., *Structure in Fives*, Prentice-Hall, Englewood Cliffs, New Jersey, 1983.
[8] Garfield, D., 'Benetton and the secret of youth', in *Evening Standard*, London, 9 July, 1993.
[9] Camp, R.C., *Benchmarking—The Search for Industry Best Practices that Lead to Superior Performance*, ASQC Quality Press, Milwaukee, Wisconsin, 1989.

3. The conversion process

... the organization is typically viewed as an open system in constant interaction with its context, transforming inputs into outputs as a means of creating the conditions necessary for survival

Gareth Morgan

Introduction

All organizations are mechanisms for conversion or transformation. Whatever their aims or objectives, organizations are deeply and inextricably involved in and committed to this process as though it is built in to the DNA of the organization's being. It is this process of conversion or transformation that enables organizations to take in and use a wide range of materials, energy, skills and knowledge and to convert these, with varying degrees of efficiency and effectiveness, into a variety of outputs, i.e. products or services. This process and its implications represent a core issue for those who are concerned about or wish to understand the ways in which their organizations change and develop.

We ignore it at our peril and if we wish to improve the performance of our organizations then we need to understand the what, how and why of this conversion process.

For many of us the most familiar conversion process is that which occurs when we manufacture or make something. In the factories of our manufacturing organizations, material, in forms which include metals, plastics, wood, ores, raw foodstuffs and even air and water, are taken in, processed and converted into an immensely wide range of material objects. These are then sold or used to create other products. These material outcomes of this conversion process include the products which we buy such as cars, refrigerators, radios, TVs, hi-fi units, toys, crockery, furniture. They may also be materials, such as sheet steel or paint, which are used in another manufacturing or conversion process.

In other organizations the inputs or the outputs are less substantial and might even be immaterial. For example, when we go to see our doctor we usually do so because some part of our body is causing us some concern. This concern may be a result of the presence of a pain, an ache, stiffness, high temperature, etc. The process which occurs in the doctor's surgery is designed to identify the reason for our concern and the treatment required. The identification of this treatment will then start the process of converting our bodies from that state of ill health to a state of well-being. The inputs to that process include our body, our experience and knowledge of that body and the doctor's skill, experience and knowledge. The outputs consist of our body and our enhanced knowledge of it—enhanced by the doctor's feedback to us—together with a package of information (a prescription) to enable us access to pharmaceutical chemicals or treatment elsewhere. Nothing is manufactured within the doctor's surgery but nevertheless a change does take place, albeit a change which is concerned with the level of our knowledge or information about our body and the 'cure' for what ails it.

Similarly, when we go to buy our groceries or food at the local shop or supermarket we become part of another type of conversion process. In this case the process is concerned with a change in ownership. In these locations we select the bread, soups, fish, fruit and meat which we require from a range which is owned by the supermarket and then purchase these at the checkout or till. By this process the goods are converted from the ownership of the supermarket to our ownership and, again, nothing is manufactured.

This chapter is concerned with:

- looking at this process of conversion;
- identifying how and for what reason it takes place;
- finding out how a knowledge and understanding of that process can help the process of improving organizational performance.

The first step in that journey will be concerned with the inputs and outputs of the conversion process.

Outputs and inputs
As we noted earlier, the conversion process needs access to inputs of a required or specified nature. It also needs to be able to dispose of or make use of its outputs. Given that these conditions are met then the conversion process will:

- take in resources
- consume or convert these resources and, in so doing,
- create desired outputs or outcomes.

This sequence of events is illustrated in Figure 3.1.

As we saw earlier in this book, the nature and characteristics of the outputs or outcomes from this process are the results of conscious choices or decisions which reflect the needs and ambitions, or strategy, of the organization. We also saw that these choices and decisions are influenced

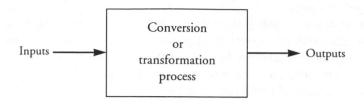

Figure 3.1 The basic conversion process

by the characteristics of the larger environment in which the organization functions.

These outputs or outcomes can be in a form which is either tangible or intangible. The tangible or material outputs from the conversion process are very familiar to us: they are present in or represented by the food we eat, the cars we drive, the clothes we wear, the houses we live in and the furniture that we use in our everyday lives. While we are, perhaps, less aware of the intangible or immaterial outputs of the conversion process, they are, nevertheless, just as important to our lives. We make use of or consume these non-material outputs when we take a ride on a train or a flight on a plane. We consume them when we attend college or school or when we visit our hospitals for health care. All of these and many other conversion process outputs are not evident in physical form and as such are not touchable but nevertheless we value and need their presence since they can make us well or transport us from place to place or enable us to become better informed or educated.

The inputs to this conversion process are also the children of both the strategic decisions and the influences of that environment. These inputs are generally described as resources. In the view of managerial economists, these resources can be divided into three groups:

- *Natural* resources Examples of these are mineral deposits, land for building, land for raising crops and even air and water.
- *Capital* resources These include all of those objects which have been made in order to enhance or enable the conversion process. They are the physical form of the organization and include its buildings, machinery, equipment, etc.
- *Human* resources These consist of the skills, physical labour, creativity and abilities of the people who are involved in this conversion process.

However, our experience of organizations and the ways in which they work might lead us to challenge this limited view, particularly with respect to the 'natural' resources. For example, we might observe that while some organizations are only concerned with the direct conversion of these natural resources into a variety of products, other organizations use these natural resource based products as inputs and convert them into other products or outcomes. Examples of organizations which consume the economist's 'natural resources' would be those concerned with oil, coal or mineral ore mining. Other organizations convert these extracted materials into iron, steel, coal or oil-based products and, in their turn, these products are used by other organizations to generate the products that we buy in the shops and market-places of our cities. A simplified version of this sequence is shown in Figure 3.2.

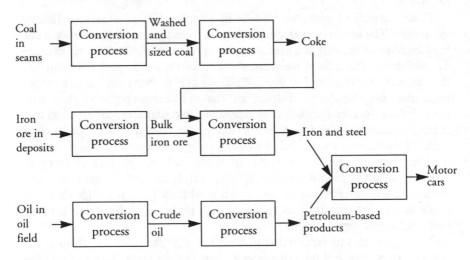

Figure 3.2   Linked conversion processes

As we examine these inputs or resources further it will also become evident that they, too, are present in both tangible and intangible forms. The organizations in the examples above are primarily concerned with the conversion of tangible inputs while others, i.e. firms of accountants, colleges, etc., are concerned with inputs which are intangible such as information, data, concepts, knowledge and ideas. These challenges and our other observations will lead us to an extended and more detailed model of the conversion or transformation process. This model, which is illustrated in Figure 3.3, can be seen to show that:

- inputs and outputs can be in a tangible or non-tangible form;
- a resource can be both an input and an output.

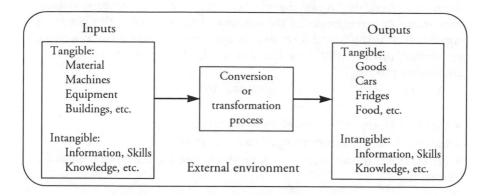

Figure 3.3 The extended conversion process

However, the nature of the conversion process is such that input will be changed as it passes through the process. Some of the inputs shown in Figure 3.3, i.e. information, skills and knowledge, are present as inputs and outputs but are added to and increased by the act of conversion. This, in its simplest form, is another demonstration of the learning curve, which as we noted in Chapter 1, says that we learn each and every time that we do a task.

The next step is for us to probe further into the box labelled the 'Conversion or transformation process' in Figures 3.1, 3.2 and 3.3. We will do that in order to try to find the answers to such questions as:

1. For what reason and in what way does this conversion process take place?
2. Does its nature change with the nature of its outcomes?

The conversion or transformation process
The most effective way of examining this process is to do so from the point of view of the customer. When we do that we will find that:

- there are several types of conversion process;
- most of the differences between these types arise from the different nature of their aims or objectives;
- the customer's relationship to the conversion process also reflects these differences in aims or objectives.

The first step in identifying the types of conversion process is to establish if the physical form of the outcome is different from the physical form of the

51

input. By 'form' we mean the physical shape, outline, texture, colour, appearance or arrangement of the outcome. The presence of this change is significant. If this physical form has changed then we have a *manufacturing* conversion process. But if it has not changed then we have a service conversion process.

A service process can also be identified by:

- the often intangible nature of its outcomes,
- the high level of customer/organization contact,
- the fact that the outcome is often produced and consumed or used at the same time.

These and other characteristics of manufacturing and service organizations are compared in Figure 3.4 and Table 3.1.

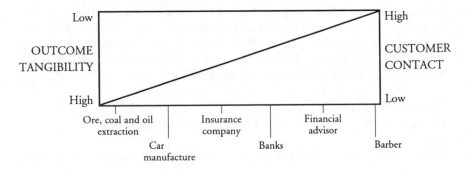

Figure 3.4 The manufacturing–service spectrum

There are, however, a number of types of service process. One way of describing[1] all conversion processes is by identifying their functions or purposes. This enables us to identify service conversion processes which:

Table 3.1 Manufacturing and service conversion processes

	Manufacturing	*Service*
Outcome tangibility	High	Low
Direct customer contact	Low	High
Variation in output nature	Low	High
Level of labour involvement in process	Low	High

- Transport customers or their possessions,
- Supply customers,
- Treat customers or their possessions.

So how do these differ from one another and from the manufacturing conversion process?

Manufacturing or service?
As we noted earlier, a manufacturing conversion process is primarily concerned with:

- Creating a change in physical form,
- Converting tangible inputs into tangible outputs.

As such, it takes in materials, such as steel and other metals, chemicals, plastics and even food, and using plant and equipment and people, converts these into tangible products. This basic process takes place in the factories or workshops of our organizations which are concerned with manufacturing and is used to create all of the tangible goods that we buy in the places where we work and play. The primary function of the process is to achieve a *change in physical form* and the customer's contact with the conversion process is limited to that of buying the outcome from it. However, this purchase often takes place away from the manufacturing location and these outcomes often need to be transported to the customer or held in storage until needed by that customer. The typically distant nature of this customer relationship means that the manufacturing process can:

- Be located:
  - away from the customer,
  - near to its resources or inputs;
- Make products to be held in store until the customer wants them;
- Be operated in a manner which is independent of the variations and changes in customer demand.

Exceptions which need to overcome this 'distance rule' occur in those situations concerned with the manufacture of goods which deteriorate in storage. One example of this is the hot food which we go to a restaurant to buy—as we know from experience this will cool and deteriorate if left waiting for too long. However, even this is changing with technology, in the form of microwave cookers, being used to quickly heat up precooked and frozen meals.

This remoteness from the customer can cause problems. Henry Ford's oft quoted comment that his customers could purchase any car 'as long as it was black' was an extreme example of the insularity that this separation can encourage in the manufacturing systems of our organizations. We look at the implications of this remoteness from the customer and other characteristics later and in more detail in Chapter 5.

The purchase of these outcomes by the customer is also undertaken through the medium of a conversion process—the first of the service conversion processes—and one which is primarily concerned with a *change in ownership or possession*. This type of conversion system is very common and is found in our shops, stores, hypermarkets and malls. The first difference, between this type of conversion process and that of manufacture, is that the customer:

- Initiates the process by choosing the inputs that he or she wishes to purchase;
- Is essential to the conduct of the process, i.e. no customer, no sale.

The second difference is one that we noted earlier. It is that the outcome, i.e. change of ownership, is intangible. You can own, possess or acquire a tangible object, such as a house, or intangible commodity, such as knowledge about the sun, but you cannot own or possess ownership itself. That state of ownership or possession is one which is applied to objects or commodities. However, the ownership conversion process can also be applied to inputs which are both tangible and intangible. You can buy material objects (for example, a TV set) and you can buy immaterial products (for example, financial advice).

The second type of service conversion process requires the customer to not only start the process but also:

- Be an input to the process;
- To be involved in the process itself.

This conversion process is concerned with a *change in location* and as such it involves the transportation of the customer or something belonging to the customer from location to location. This process takes place when we get on a train or plane, and when we drive to work. It also takes place when the products of our factories are transported to the locations at which they are sold. While generally applied to tangible inputs, it can also be applied to intangible inputs. As such, it also takes place when we fax information or when we use the telephone to provide or ask for information. It is a customer driven process: it needs the presence of the customer, as an input, to take place.

The third and last type of service conversion process is that in which there is what Ray Wild describes[1] as a *change in state*. In this type of process the customer, or something belonging to the customer, is treated or accommodated in some way. Examples of this type of service conversion process can be seen in barbers, dentists, laundries, hotels and hospitals. Again, the customer is needed to start and continue the process and also to be treated or accommodated. It cannot take place without the customer or something belonging to the customer and as such it is customer driven. During this process nothing is manufactured, relocated, or changes ownership. However, the state of the outputs will differ from that of the inputs—hair will be cut, clothes washed or illnesses treated—and these changes occur because of other inputs such as skill, knowledge and experience. Other descriptions[2] of this type of service conversion process suggest, in more general terms, that it is characterized by the nature of its customer/organization interaction. These and other features of conversion processes are examined in more detail in Chapter 5.

As we noted earlier in this chapter, the range and variety of the inputs and outputs for all of these conversion processes is considerable and this is illustrated, for a typical service organization and a typical manufacturing organization in Figure 3.5. Despite the complexity and variety of these inputs and outputs, all of these contribute to and reflect the nature and structure of the conversion process and we shall take a look at that later in this chapter. In the meantime a sequence for the identification of the conversion processes present in your organization is shown in Figure 3.6.

The dominant conversion process

By now, it will be evident to many of you that the organizations in which you work are involved in many, if not all, of these types of conversion process and often at the same time! However, this does not mean that these organizations are confused or ineffective or that the typology that we have used is wrong.

Most organizations, when viewed as a whole rather than a set of parts or components, may well be using all or several of these conversion processes. However, when we examine their sections, departments, subsystems or parts we will find that fewer conversion processes can be seen. We may even find that these departments or sections are concerned with a single conversion process. Generally, we will observe that each of these subsections or departments has a primary interest in or commitment to a single conversion process. As such this process is, or should be, the main target for that department's efforts to improve its efficiency and effectiveness.

For example, a typical computer manufacturing organization:

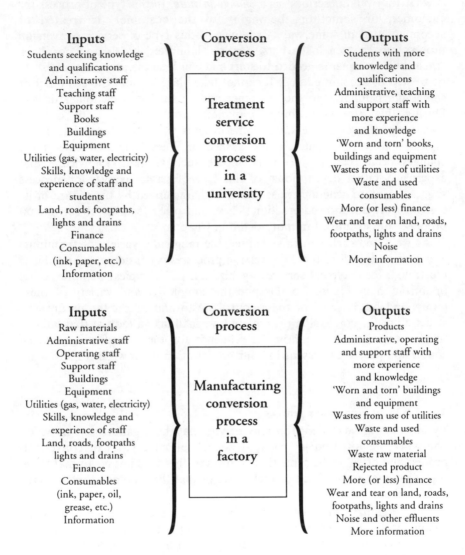

Inputs

Students seeking knowledge
and qualifications
Administrative staff
Teaching staff
Support staff
Books
Buildings
Equipment
Utilities (gas, water, electricity)
Skills, knowledge and
experience of staff and
students
Land, roads, footpaths,
lights and drains
Finance
Consumables
(ink, paper, etc.)
Information

**Conversion
process**

Treatment
service
conversion
process
in a
university

Outputs

Students with more
knowledge and
qualifications
Administrative, teaching
and support staff with
more experience
and knowledge
'Worn and torn' books,
buildings and equipment
Wastes from use of utilities
Waste and used
consumables
More (or less) finance
Wear and tear on land, roads,
footpaths, lights and drains
Noise
More information

Inputs

Raw materials
Administrative staff
Operating staff
Support staff
Buildings
Equipment
Utilities (gas, water, electricity)
Skills, knowledge and
experience of staff
Land, roads, footpaths
lights and drains
Finance
Consumables
(ink, paper, oil,
grease, etc.)
Information

**Conversion
process**

Manufacturing
conversion
process
in a
factory

Outputs

Products
Administrative, operating
and support staff with
more experience
and knowledge
'Worn and torn' buildings
and equipment
Wastes from use of utilities
Waste and used
consumables
Waste raw material
Rejected product
More (or less) finance
Wear and tear on land, roads,
footpaths, lights and drains
Noise and other effluents
More information

Figure 3.5 Typical inputs and outputs

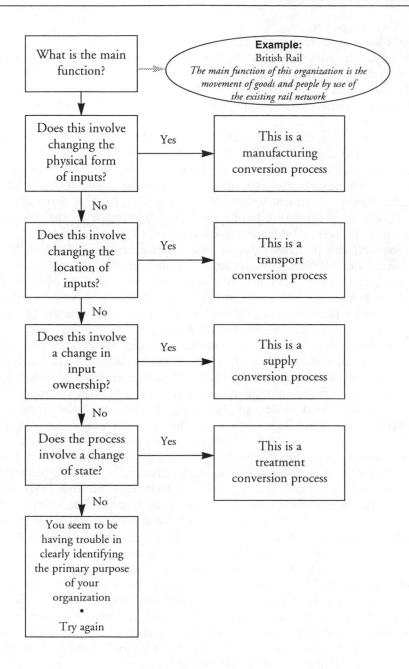

Figure 3.6 Identify your process

- Makes computers,
- Sells these to its dealers and resellers,
- Arranges for the transport of these computers to these dealers and resellers,
- Provides technical support for its products to both dealers and customers;
- Advertises these products to the general public and other organizations.

We can see that the whole organization is involved in most of the conversion processes that we identified earlier. However, the subsections or departments of the organization will have functions which are concerned with or responsible for one of these processes, for example, the manufacturing department or the sales department. In these departments the efforts for performance improvement will be focused on the primary conversion process: manufacturing or supply.

However, one of these types of conversion process will be dominant within the organization. It is the aims and ambitions of the organization, discussed in Chapter 2, that exert the most significant influence over which of the conversion processes is dominant. For example, a railway company might have a strategic objective of becoming the dominant surface passenger transport system on the Eastern American seaboard. As such, its operations will be dominated by the transport conversion process. However, it may well also manufacture and sell, in large numbers, the meals and drinks which its customers require during their journeys. It will generally only undertake these conversion processes of manufacture and supply in order to support its dominant conversion process of transport. This feature of the dominant conversion process is illustrated below, for the McDonald's hamburger chain.

The significance of this dominant conversion process is considerable. Not only does it act as a channel or enabling mechanism for the organization's strategic decisions, but also it exerts considerable influence over the administrative and operational decisions of the organization. It will also influence the careers and career choices of managers who work within the organization and the interactions between the systems and subsystems of the organization. Its most pervasive form of influence will be within the political systems of the organization. Within this system it will act in such a way as to colour or bias the compromises made between the conflicting aims and ambitions of all the organization's stakeholders. When this influence is exerted effectively it can act to ensure that organizations keep in touch with their core skills. But it can also act in such a way as to limit or blinker the view of and decisions taken about the organization's future goals and targets. The blinkered view might be said to reflect the organization's preoccupation with the efficiency of its existing activities (single loop learning) whilst the unconstrained and unblinkered view might be seen to be concerned with the relevance or effectiveness of these activities (double loop learning). Again, Figure 3.6 can be used in a sequential process to aid your identification of the dominant conversion process for your organization.

McDonald's hamburger restaurants

The chain of McDonald's hamburger restaurants exists for the purpose of selling quality hamburgers, and similar foods, to customers. This is undertaken in warm, pleasant and clean surroundings with excellent service. As such the primary conversion process of a McDonald's restaurant is concerned with the change of ownership of hamburgers and similar foods. This means that the strategic and administrative decisions of McDonald's management are dominated by the need to make this supply conversion process as efficient and as effective as possible. In support of this dominant objective, McDonald's products are made in the restaurant by McDonald's staff. This means that McDonald's make, i.e. manufacture, their food products and do so by means of a manufacturing conversion process. This process takes, as inputs, potatoes, buns, meat, milk, coffee, orange concentrate, etc., and converts these into the hamburgers, french fries and other tangible products which its customers purchase. In so doing McDonald's management can exert direct control over the quality, quantity and timeliness of the outputs from the manufacturing process. In order to achieve fast service and value for money these products and their method of manufacture are standardized and subject to exacting portion control standards.

These different conversion processes coexist within the McDonald's organization but the supply conversion process is dominant.

Batches, bulk and customers

Earlier in this chapter we found that two of the significant differences between manufacturing and service conversion systems were:

- The level of direct customer contact involved,
- Whether the outcome was consumed as it was produced.

If we look at these systems in more detail we will find these differences exert an influence upon the structure and sequence of the events which together make up the conversion process. The key to that influence lies within the contrasting needs of the customer and the conversion process.

For example, the manufacturing conversion process needs a customer:

- who has demands which are stable and predictable;
- who is loyal and is prepared to wait for the product;
- who will accept that sometimes things go wrong.

As a consequence many manufacturing systems find themselves attracted towards a position which means that they:

1. Make their products in large batches or long runs.
2. Distance themselves from customer demands by carrying large stocks of finished goods.
3. Schedule what is made on the basis of stock policy rather than customer demand.
4. View quality control as an 'add-on' extra.

This can often mean that those who manage these organizations become overly concerned with issues about the technology and the control of production such as:

1. Reducing processing time by using faster machines.
2. Using automatic machines which run for longer.
3. Setting up dedicated, i.e. one product, factories.
4. Processing families of products together (group technology).
5. Making product batches whose size is related to the costs of storage and production.

All of these and other production technology issues are concerned with the efficiency, and *only* the efficiency, of the production conversion process. As a result of this 'tunnel vision', manufacturing conversion systems were often set up to make a narrow range of standard products on production line or continuous systems. Even when this is not possible the economies of scale mean that the preferable size of the batches of products is large rather than small.

However, the customer needs a manufacturing system which is:

- Responsive and flexible;
- Consistent: in terms of product performance and reliability;
- Competitive: in terms of price and quality;
- Provides the product when it is needed.

This means that in order to break out of the confines of large batches of standard products, organizations begin to look at 'niche' or specialist markets or to widen or 'de-standardize' their product ranges. It also means that the manufacturing process needs to integrate all quality issues at a very early stage in the process rather than limiting quality to a feedback control issue and an 'end of the line' add-on extra.

In contrast, service type conversion processes have a very close relationship with their customers. Indeed, for some of these service conversion processes, such as transport or treatment, the customer is an integral part of the conversion process itself. However, for others and particularly the supply conversion process, the customer relationship still contains echoes or traces of the distance that we noted in the manufacturing conversion systems. Supply systems are concerned with the transfer of ownership to the customer from:

- Stock, e.g. supermarket shelves, or
- Source, e.g. pick your own fruit outlets.

In both these situations customers are often serviced in large numbers. For example, supermarket customers will often judge the quality of the service provided by the range of goods held, their prices relative to other supermarkets and the queuing time at the check-out point or till. It is at this till that the actual conversion of ownership takes place and its importance is reflected not only in the large number of tills present in most supermarkets but also in the large number of queuing or waiting line studies which have been conducted. A simple example of the issues involved is shown below and looks at the number of tills required in a small supermarket. The same techniques could also be applied to queuing at bank counters, toll booths, etc.

The Supermarket

The small branch of the large supermarket chain in the market town of Munchester had steadily increased its turnover since its opening in May 1989. However, the manager had recently noticed that some of his regular customers were beginning to desert him for the larger supermarkets situated on the edge of the large town of Dinster, some 10 miles away. His staff told him that these ex-customers had said that the till queues were so long at his supermarket that it was quicker and easier to drive the extra 10 miles there and back. So the manager set out to find out how he could justify an additional and fourth till. He knew from previous studies that his customers arrived at the average rate of 40 per hour and that each of his tills could handle an average of 15 customers per hour. So with three tills working he shouldn't have any queues! But as he watched he saw that customers arrived in a random and irregular way and that some customers took more time to serve than others. He knew from his records that the average customer spent £36 and that each till clerk cost him a wage of £2 per hour.

His experience told him that if a customer had to queue for more than 5 minutes then they became restless and unhappy. Using his son's operations management textbooks he worked out that with the existing three tills he would have an average of one customer queuing most of the time. But he also knew that the customers arrived irregularly and that at peak times the queues were much longer than that. So he then worked out the average queue size for four tills and found that it fell to one customer for about one fifth of the time. The manager then calculated that the increased revenue from the fourth till would pay for the new till and the clerk's wages very quickly and keep his customers happy. So the new till was installed and his customers came back. However, being a wise man the manager was not happy to leave matters there. He decided that after Christmas he would see if he could increase his revenue further by matching the till service to customer demand. This he thought he might do by only opening the fourth till when he had a rush on as he did on Saturday mornings and Friday evenings.

The service conversion processes of transport and treatment can also be concerned with queues or waiting lines. Bus schedules and airline timetables both reflect a compromise between the need of the customer to get on a bus or an aeroplane when she/he wants to and the cost of providing capacity (buses and planes) which may not be fully utilized. One way of coping with this problem is to run larger capacity buses and planes, but to run them less often. This means that customers will have to queue until the scheduled 'big bus' arrives. It also means that they will get on a competitor's bus which comes along in the meantime. The short-haul shuttle services between big cities in the USA and the UK have developed a further variant: they provide medium-size new technology planes with low operating and staffing costs, run them on a schedule which reflects customer demand and promise (and deliver) a service which says, in effect, 'turn up at these times and we'll fly you'. We will explore, in more detail, the implications of these and other factors in other chapters which will look at the issues of quality and the influence of the form and structure of the conversion process.

At this point, however, it is vital to underline that, however the organization's dominant conversion process is organized and whatever its outcomes are, it is its 'closeness' to its customers and their needs which will lead to efficient *and* effective operation. Tom Peters[3] observes that we need to go 'beyond listening to customers to intertwining with them' and 'beyond satisfied customers to committed customers'. Our knowledge and understanding of our organization's conversion processes play a vital role in that process, but so will our ability to control those processes.

Dynamics and control

So far we have portrayed organizations in static terms by looking at the inputs and outputs which they use or create. The illustrations of this process (Figures 3.1–3.4) have been static and frozen. But organizations are not static and frozen. They are, or should be if they wish to survive, reactive and active, energetic, and changeable. In short, they are dynamic entities which grow, change and mutate and in so doing reflect and respond to the demands of and changes in the environment in which they exist.

What we need to do is to take a look at how the behaviour and direction of these dynamic entities can be controlled and how this can be done in such a way as to ensure that the efficiency and effectiveness of the organization are enhanced. Not surprisingly, the systems which help us to do that are called control systems. The first and most common of these control systems is called the feedback control system and is illustrated in Figure 3. 7.

This system operates in a simple sequence which is started by the measurement of the outcome of the conversion process. The information

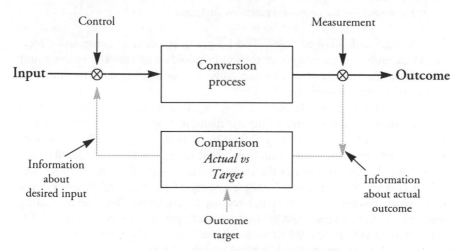

Figure 3.7 Feedback control system

obtained is sent back to the comparison unit in which its value is compared to the value of the outcome target. The difference between these two is used to generate a signal to the unit which controls input and the input is adjusted.

The level and direction of the adjustment to the conversion process input will depend upon:

- The difference between the value of the actual outcome and the target value for that outcome;
- Whether the target or the actual value is the larger.

For example, if we are driving a car at 35 mph but want to go at 40 mph, then the small difference between the actual (35 mph) and target (40 mph) speed will mean that we only move the accelerator pedal down (increase the fuel input) by a small distance. If however, we suddenly realise that we are driving at 100 mph in a 70 mph zone, then our reaction will probably be to reduce the fuel input by a large amount by taking our foot off the accelerator pedal. In general, when the target value exceeds the actual or achieved value, the result will be an increase in input, and when the target is less then the actual or achieved, the result will be a reduction in input. How often we measure the value of the outcome will depend upon the time taken for two things to happen:

1. The consequences of a change in input to travel through the conversion process: *for the car to slow down after we took our foot off the pedal.*
2. The measurement of the consequences of that change: *for the speedometer to show and for us to see a reduction in speed.*

This is often called lag or delay. Too long a time between cause and effect, i.e. an extended or high lag, can cause undesired outcomes to continue and increase while too short a time can cause the control system to 'hunt' or cycle rather than to operate steadily.

The second and less familiar control system is called the feedforward system and is illustrated, in its simplest form, in Figure 3.8. This system acts in a way which is significantly different to that of the feedback system. Instead of measuring the outcomes and acting upon the inputs, the feedforward system measures the input and acts upon that input. However, it is necessary to have a good understanding of the conversion process for this control system to produce the required outcomes. This understanding must be at a level which is able to accurately predict the consequences for the outcome when the level or value of the input is changed.

As we saw for the feedback control system, the level and direction of the adjustment made, by the feedforward system, to the conversion process

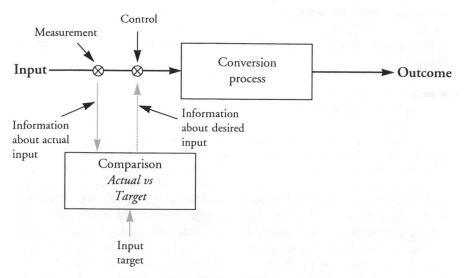

Figure 3.8   Feedforward control system

input will depend upon the difference between the values of the actual input and the target value for that outcome and the relative size of these values. So a measured value of input which exceeds the target value by a large amount will result in a large reduction in input while an input target value which exceeds the actual input value by a small amount will result in a small increase in input.

Everyday examples of the use of these control systems are shown in Table 3.2. So how do we apply or use these systems in our organizations and what is their contribution to the process of improving organizational performance? It is these organizational control systems that we will now take a look at.

Organizational control systems

Both the feedforward and the feedback control systems achieve the required control by using the difference between an actual value and a target value. When applied to the organizations in which we work, these control systems can enable us to ensure that resources are used efficiently and effectively. However, this will only be achieved if these systems are applied to features or characteristics of the organization which:

- are understandable and meaningful;
- can be measured, and measured accurately;

• provide timely feedback.

If these characteristics are present then the use of control systems can enable managers to:

• monitor performance,
• focus on continuous improvement.

Table 3.2 Example of feedback/feedforward control systems

Feedback control system	Feedforward control system
The thermostatic control valve on a central heating system radiator is a simple feedback control system. It measures the air temperature and then adjusts the flow of hot water into the radiator. When the temperature is low, relative to the target which you have set, then the valve opens to allow more hot water flow through the radiator and vice versa.	The weighing of the ingredients in preparation for the baking of a cake is a simple example of a feedforward control system. The recipe for the cake represents the model for the conversion process. This model specifies the nature and quantity of the inputs, and the cook, acting as the control system measurement, comparison and control unit, adds each ingredient until the specified target has been achieved.

These control systems can be applied to a wide range of outcomes and inputs and can also be applied at the strategic, administrative and operational levels of the organization.

A familiar example of the use of a feedback control system occurs in the quality control systems which have been applied for some time in the manufacturing conversion processes of our organizations and are beginning to be applied increasingly in our service conversion processes. In order to be effective the quality control system needs a target, that is, a clear definition of the desired condition of the product or service. This definition must be expressed in terms which are understandable and measurable. For example, when applied to the production of dolls, the inspector will check the doll's size and colour and that its hair is stuck on or that its eyes are straight. If any of these are not correct then the inspector will reject the doll and tell (feedback to) the operator. The operator should then change the way in which she or he is assembling the doll. The use of the feedback control system is not restricted to the tangible products that are generated by the manufacturing conversion systems of our factories. Feedback control takes place when any output is sampled, tested and compared to a specification or desired state and the resulting difference used to adjust the input to the conversion system. Other examples of feedback control include the maintenance of equipment when wear or falling performance indicates that it is needed, the control of expenditure by the use of budgetary targets and the control of operator outputs by the targets based on works measurement or work study data.

Staying with our doll example, we can see that feedforward control takes place when, in choosing a supplier of dolls' eyes, the past performance of all potential suppliers is assessed and their quality control systems reviewed. The supplier chosen will have the best record and the best quality control system, thus giving the buyer confidence that this input to the manufacturing process will be correct. Other examples of feedforward systems exist in the ways we decide what sort of people (qualifications, skills, personalities, etc.) and how many of them we will recruit to join our organizations.

All of these and many other applications of the control process take place because it is necessary to control and regulate the activities that occur within our organizations. For the static or shrinking organization, that control and regulation can be concerned with such issues as power, domination and the limited horizon of efficiency on its own. For the growing and learning organization, control and regulation are enabling mechanisms which can be used to empower employees and focus their efforts towards the improvement of efficiency, effectiveness and adaptability.

Organizational conversion processes and performance improvement

Earlier we identified that the effective performance improvement process or programme is driven by the gap between the current situation and the desired future. We noted that 'winning' programmes are also associated with measurable results gained and used in a 'real time' situation.

The brief look that we have taken at the conversion processes that take place in all of our organizations has shown us that the understanding of these processes provides a rich and fertile field for the performance improvement process. The dominant nature of some of these means that they lie deep within the cores of our organizations and are often the outcomes of history and technology of these organizations. As such they represent both a major opportunity and a major challenge for the performance improvement programme. However, despite the dominance of one type of conversion process, other conversion processes will exist within the organization and contribute to its growth and development.

The outputs of these conversion processes are increasingly assessed, by both customers and creators, in terms of their quality. It is the nature and sources of this attribute that we shall explore in the next chapter.

Summary
All organizations are conversion mechanisms. As such they are concerned with the transformation of inputs into desired outputs or outcomes. These are described as resources (inputs) and as products or services (outputs). They can also exist in a tangible or intangible form and be any one of a very large number of the features of our organizations and the environment in which they operate.

The types of the conversion process are:

1. *Manufacturing conversion process* This transforms the physical form of its outputs from that of the inputs. It generally has a low level of customer contact. Its extreme forms are often concerned with generating large volumes of a limited range of standard products. Examples of the manufacturing conversion process exist in our coal mines, our factories and in the kitchens of our restaurants.
2. *Service conversion processes* These are concerned with the generation of outcomes which:
   (i)   are often intangible;
   (ii) involve high levels of customer contact;
   (iii) can be produced and consumed at the same time.

Examples of service conversion processes include those which transport people or their possessions (taxis, bus services, trains, etc.), involve an change of ownership (shops, supermarkets, etc.) or are concerned with the treatment of people or their possessions (barbers, accountants, dentists, etc.).

The presence and involvement of the customer is essential for all of these service conversion processes; for those involving transport and treatment the customer is one of the inputs.

Many organizations will use several, if not all, of these conversion processes. However, one of these will be dominant within the organization and as such will exert considerable influence over a number of aspects of that organization. One of the areas of influence of this dominant conversion process can be the structure and sequence of events which together make up that and other conversion processes. These are also influenced by both the nature and the degree of the compromise between the often conflicting needs of the organization and the customer.

Organizations are dynamic and changeable and as such require control and direction. This is undertaken by the use of feedback and feedforward control systems which can be applied to any of the wide range of inputs and outputs of the conversion processes.

The effective performance improvement process is driven by the gap between the current situation and the desired future and uses measurable results gained and used in 'real time' situations. A knowledge and understanding of the conversion process provides a rich and fertile field for that performance improvement process.

References
[1] Wild, R., *Production and Operations Management*, Cassell, London, 1989.
[2] Voss, C., C. Armistead, B. Johnston and B. Morris, *Operations Management in Service Industries and the Public Sector*, Wiley, Chichester, 1985.
[3] Peters, T., *Liberation Management*, Macmillan, London, 1992.

4. Quality and performance improvement

*Quality is not a **thing**. It is an **event**.*

Robert M. Pirsig

Introduction

Quality is no longer an optional extra: it has become an essential component of any organization's armoury in the battle for survival and dominance which rages in the early 1990s.

We are all a part of that change and as consumers of goods and services we are expecting and demanding more. We expect our mail to be delivered quickly, we expect the meals that we buy in restaurants to be cooked and served in a manner which reflects the price we pay and we react badly if the video games that we buy for our children are not reliable, entertaining and value for money.

In our workplaces we see that the customers of our organizations are increasingly placing quality high on the list of their expectations about the goods and services which we sell to them. They also have rising expectations about the reliability, value for money and durability of these goods and services. So why has this interest in quality come about and where has it come from?

The roots of this quality 'revolution' which swept into America and Europe in the late 1970s and early 1980s, go back to the manufacturing industries of Japan in the early 1950s. At that time Japanese car manufacturers were beginning the introduction of the 'just-in-time' (JIT) concept for the manufacture and assembly of the cars and trucks which they were making for their growing home market. This concept, which later spread across America and Europe (see Chapter 5), placed an increased emphasis on the need for operators to make fewer mistakes and to 'get it right first time'. But this was not the first time that the Japanese had shown an interest in quality. As early as 1943 the development of the now classic 'Cause-and-Effect' or 'Fishbone' diagram (see Chapter 10) by Dr Kaoru Ishikawa had been an early and formidable sign of a growing interest. This interest was further encouraged by Dr Edwards Deming's courses and lectures on statistical quality control during the period 1947–50. These and other factors led to the development of the quality approach which we now call Total Quality Management (TQM).

By the mid 1980s it was evident that the tidal wave of this quality revolution was sweeping the issue of quality well beyond its historic boundaries. This new approach to quality was spreading out beyond that traditional home of quality concepts, manufacturing, and penetrating deep into the service areas of our economy. Tom Peters in his 1982 best-selling review of America's best-run companies *In Search of Excellence*,[1] reported that many of these companies were obsessed with service and quality and cited, as examples, such diverse organizations as Caterpillar Tractor, Digital Computers, McDonald's Restaurants and Holiday Inn hotels. By the early to mid 1980s the concept of TQM had arrived in Europe and was being explored, adapted and adopted by a number of major service and manufacturing organizations. These organizations spanned a wide variety of industry sectors from telecommunications to food and from glass manufacture to building societies.

This considerable interest and attention indicated that the concept of quality had:

- become an issue of major importance
- radically changed in its nature.

There can be little doubt that this is still true! As we approach the end of the 20th century the increasingly competitive marketplace for both goods and services means that it is no longer good enough to just concentrate on quantity. 'Never mind the quality—just feel the width' is a dead and even dangerous attitude when faced with a rising tide of quality goods from all points to the west and east and a hurricane of increased customer expectations. In many of our organizations, quality has, in the past, been managed as an afterthought, and often an inconvenient one at that! However, an increasing awareness of the limited effectiveness and rising costs of the inspector-driven quality control has gained many converts to the quality revolution. Philip Crosby, one of the American quality gurus, summed up[2] one of the benefits, and a major driving force of this change, by stating that:

'If you concentrate on making quality certain, you can probably increase your profit by an amount equal to 5 to 10 per cent of your sales.'

All of these and other factors have created a situation where quality is a major weapon or tool for all organizations to use in the drive to improve their performance.

This chapter will take a look at that weapon and explore how it can be used to improve organizational performance.

We will start that exploration by defining what we mean by the word 'quality'.

What is quality?

A typical dictionary might define quality as 'degree of goodness or value' and a thesaurus identify synonyms of 'worth, grade or condition'. Yet for our purposes neither of these are correct. Quality is not an attribute or a characteristic that has an absolute meaning or a separate existence since you cannot buy 'quality'.

However, what you can do is to make or buy things that have or display quality. For example, as customers we expect to be able to purchase goods which we find acceptable and meet our requirements. The shop from which we might purchase these goods expects, in its turn, its supplier to supply goods or items which are acceptable and do not deteriorate in transit or storage. When we buy a service in the form of a meal in a restaurant we expect it to be as described in the menu and of reasonable quality. Similarly, when we get on a bus and purchase transport we expect it to go to the destination shown on the indicator and to do so without undue delay.

In all of these situations we have expectations of the goods or services and we often describe these expectations in terms of their 'quality'. We also describe the goods or services which do not meet these expectations as being 'lacking in quality'.

So what is quality? The British Standard[3] for quality vocabulary describes it as: 'the totality of features and characteristics of a product or service that bear on its ability to satisfy stated or implied needs', while Philip Crosby[2] identifies it as: 'conformance to requirements'. A simpler definition, and one which we shall use, is that given by another American quality guru, Joseph Juran. He suggests[4] that the presence of quality, in a product or service, is demonstrated by its 'fitness for purpose or use' This concise definition means that anything and everything can be described as possessing quality providing:

- its purpose is adequately and clearly defined,
- its performance meets that definition.

This view of quality is quite different to the dictionary definition that we started with. That definition related the presence of quality to an object's worth or value, while Juran relates quality to the object's ability to carry out its purpose. This shift in definition is significant. It means that a paper handkerchief is as much a quality product as a silk handkerchief and a Citroen 2CV as a Rolls-Royce car. The purposes of these products are different but they all are able to demonstrate 'fitness for purpose' and, hence, quality. That purpose or list of performance requirements is often called its specification. It can be used to identify:

- the characteristics of what the product or service does, i.e. its functionality;
- how it is styled or appears, i.e. its non-functional characteristics.

Both of these are important to us, in our roles as either providers or users.

Functional or non-functional?

We often buy goods or services for reasons other than their functionality. One example of this is given by the choices that we face when we buy a box of paper clips. These can be plain or coloured, large or small. For most of the uses that we have for these paper clips, the correct choice, in terms of the function of the clips, would be to buy clips which are medium sized and plain. However, because we like the colours or perhaps because of the unusual appearance of the 'jumbo' clips, we might decide to buy clips which are coloured and much larger in size than those needed to hold a limited number of papers together. Any of these clips are able to carry out the purpose of holding papers together but some possess other non-functional characteristics.

This means that the specification for a product or service can be used to identify its:

- Functional features:
  - utility of purpose: will it do the job I want it to do?
  - reliability: will it keep on doing that job?
  - people aspects: comfort, safety and convenience.
- Non-functional features:
  - style, appearance: how does it look/feel?
  - user/purchaser aspects: price (can I afford it or does it show that I am wealthy?) and prestige (does it give me social status?)

For example, the specification for a paper handkerchief would include definitions of functional factors such as:

- wet strength: so that it doesn't fall to bits when wet;
- dry strength: so that it doesn't come to pieces when you handle it;
- weight: so that it appears light;
- softness: so that it doesn't feel coarse or rough.

The specification would also recognize the probable 'one-off' nature of the paper handkerchief's use.

The non-functional features of the specification for this handkerchief would include:

73

- colour,
- packaging,
- the image portrayed by associated advertising.

You will recognize a low quality paper handkerchief as being one which, for example, does not feel smooth or soft, or tears when you blow your nose into it or is made in unfashionable colours.

Similarly the non-functional characteristics of a Rolls-Royce car might include:

- high grade internal and external finish and fittings;
- very low internal noise levels: 'you can hear the clock ticking';
- a recognizable Rolls-Royce radiator/emblem.

The choices and decisions that the consumer takes when purchasing goods and services are often influenced by a combination of these functional and non-functional aspects. This is clearly illustrated by Table 4.1 which gives a fuller, though by no means exhaustive, list of the features which might influence your choice when buying a motor car. All of these features reflect or contribute to the 'fitness for use or purpose' of the car, for you as the consumer.

Before we take a look at where quality comes from, let's take a brief look at some of the common fallacies and misunderstandings about quality and check these out against the 'fitness for purpose' definition.

Table 4.1   How do you define the quality of a motor car?

Safety	Acceleration
Air conditioning	Purchase cost
Braking	Radio
CD player	Fuel economy
Maintenance cost	Ride comfort
Seat adjustment	Noise level
Power steering	Rear seating space
Load capacity, space and accessibility	Corrosion resistance
Cold starting	Fuel injection
Ease of body repair	Choice of colours
Unleaded fuel	Steering column adjustment
Automatic transmission	Cruising range
Ease of parking	Body style
Advertising	Insurance cost
Proximity of dealer and service garage	

Fallacies about quality

The following are five common fallacies about quality:

FALLACY 1: QUALITY CAN'T BE EXPRESSED IN NUMBERS

This view of quality tries to tell us that it is an intangible characteristic, often related to taste, and as such cannot be measured. But quality can be measured by measuring how much it costs to meet the specification identified, agreed or even understood for the product/service—even if some parts of the customer requirement/specification are aesthetic! (See later section on quality costs.)

FALLACY 2: QUALITY = HIGH COST OR VALUE

We often assume that things with high cost or value possess quality. Examples are designer dresses or fur coats which are seen, because of their cost, to be 'quality' garments, and cars of the Ferrari or Cadillac genre which are seen, again because of their cost, as 'quality' vehicles. This use of the word 'quality' is incorrect as it reflects only the value or price of the goods—rather than their functionality. However, a Cadillac can, in the true sense, be a quality car—but only if it satisfies the needs of the customer. For a Cadillac these will be not only to do with functionality, i.e. transport, but also social prestige and status. However, the expectations of another customer may be more modest and fulfilled by a smaller and less expensive vehicle. But this also is a quality car—because it satisfies customer needs.

FALLACY 3: ORGANIZATIONS WITH QUALITY CONTROL DEPARTMENTS ARE QUALITY ORGANIZATIONS

Almost all quality control departments are concerned with trying to measure the degree to which the outcomes of the conversion process conform to the specification. They may also be concerned with applying that same process to inputs to the conversion process. This is called quality control. It does not create quality: it is only concerned with its measurement or identification of quality. It takes a lot more than the presence of a quality department to create a quality organization (see section on TQM later).

FALLACY 4: QUALITY IMPROVEMENT COSTS MONEY RATHER THAN MAKING PROFIT

The Japanese were the first to prove that quality improvement generates benefits in terms of productivity, market share etc. and is a benefit generator rather than a 'cost sink'. The sequence of events which leads to increased profits is illustrated in Figure 4.1.

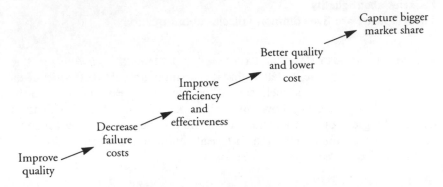

Figure 4.1 Quality and profit

FALLACY 5: QUALITY PROBLEMS BEGIN WITH PEOPLE AT THE 'SHARP END'
This fallacy originates from the fact that most quality problems are identified or surface at the 'sharp end', e.g. over the counter or at the reception desk, etc. In fact, this is only where they surface and their roots and origins are often in other parts of the organization such as design, accounting, purchasing or marketing.

Sources of quality

We noted earlier that quality was primarily concerned with fitness for use or purpose and that this purpose or required performance is often embodied in what is called a specification. However, that specification will only lead to a product or service which is fit for use if it is firmly rooted in the customer's needs. The steps which lead to that condition of 'fitness for use' start and end with the customer and his or her needs.

These steps are:

- *Step 1* Identify the customer need.
- *Step 2* Make decisions about which part of that need will be answered by the product or service.
- *Step 3* Detail key characteristics or performance of the service or product to answer that part of the need.
- *Step 4* Design that product or service taking into account both the customer need and the capabilities of the organization.
- *Step 5* Create that product or service in a manner that ensures that it meets customer needs and in response to an evident or anticipated customer demand.

QUALITY

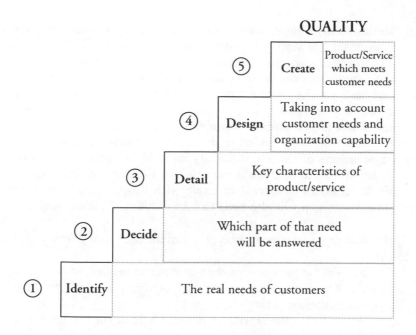

Figure 4.2 The five steps to quality

The use of these steps in the generation of a new course or programme at a university would, or should, involve the following activities.

STEPS 1 AND 2

These two steps should involve discussions with student employers, past and potential students and external bodies, such as BTEC, or professional bodies, such as the Institution of Chemical Engineers. The outcomes would result from decisions about who the course is for—accountants or midwives or managers—and what are its aims and objectives.

STEP 3

This step would involve decisions about course level (certificate, diploma, degree, postgraduate or post experience), its duration (1 year, 3 years) and its delivery mode (part-time, full time, block release, distance learning). In general terms the resultant specification would, for a service, focus on issues which will include customer contact level, service delivery method, service speed and consistency while the specification for products will identify factors like performance, appearance, cost, demand and delivery/launch date.

STEP 4

For our university course, step 4 will involve the generation of detailed course proposals for vetting by internal committees—faculty development review committee, academic standards committee, etc.—and the costing of the programme. This design stage *must*, at all times keep customer needs identified earlier as its guiding light. The course must also be designed so that the current staff and other resources are able to produce the required outcome. There is little point in planning to teach philosophy if you do not have the staff who are qualified to do so or the rooms in which to do it. These assessments of existing capability must be conducted with honesty and objectivity. Ambition is not enough and the organizational attribute analysis described in Chapter 2 can help with this step. In more general terms this design step will also need to take account of factors such as:

1. *Maintainability* Can you service or maintain the product easily and at low cost?
2. *Reliability* Will the service or product continue to perform without failure?
3. *Durability* Will the service or product continue to perform without failure from excessive wear?
4. *Reproducibility* Can the service or product be consistently produced or provided?

The importance of getting the quality of design right should not be underestimated as all subsequent attempts to produce a product or service at the desired quality level will fail if there are deficiencies in the design of the product or service.

STEP 5

This final step is concerned with the operations end of an organization. During this step the specifications generated in the design stage will be converted into the service or product by:

- *The purchase of material* A major concern for physical product manufacture and retail services but often limited to minor items, i.e. office materials, in other service areas.
- *The use of facilities and equipment* An important area involving equipment, furniture, layout of reception areas and queuing zones, etc.
- *The actions of people* Selection and training are important issues as well as the ability to cope with the high levels of uncertainty contained in service customer transactions.

Any or all of these can introduce a deviation from the design specifications.

In our university example, it is at this point that the product (course) and the students or customers meet. This step includes those activities associated with the creation of the product or service in response to an evident or anticipated customer need and subsequent demand. The capability of the creation process will also have a significant influence upon the resultant quality. For example, an ante-natal clinic without the equipment needed to measure blood pressure or sufficient consulting rooms will be limited in terms of process equipment (blood pressure measurement equipment) and capacity (rooms). As such, it will be seen by its customers as not providing a service which meets their requirements, and as being of inadequate quality. Similarly, students will perceive that low levels of quality are present in a course which is conducted in rooms that are too small or too hot or with inadequate equipment such as overhead projectors or with lecturers who don't communicate well or don't know their subject.

We mentioned the value of the control systems to the organizational improvement process in an earlier chapter. Feedback questionnaires or course assessment sheets are one example of a feedback control system in the educational sector as are customer surveys in the manufacturing and service sectors. Other examples of feedback might include the use of prototypes or pre-production or pre-launch pilots.

All of these will provide feedback on whether the product or service has:

- Met its objectives, and/or
- Met the needs of its customers.

In a badly designed service or product these two criteria are not congruent. For example, the objectives of a course may have been met in that it ran and produced revenue but the student needs may not have been met because the course didn't provide the knowledge or information that they needed. If this happens it is not only short-sighted but also inaccurate to suggest that the fault lies in a lack of effective discretion or knowledge on the part of the customer. A quality product is one which has the objective of answering the customer's needs, rather than the producer's. But as Dr Edwards Deming says[5]: 'You do not have to do this; survival is not compulsory'.

It will be evident by now that the management of quality is not a straightforward or simple task but one that requires considerable skill, ability and commitment from all within the organization if it is to be effective. The ways and styles in which that process of quality management have been carried out have changed as the quality revolution has made its influence and presence felt in all of our organizations. However, what is common to all of these is the fact that the presence or absence of quality is reflected in the costs of the organization.

Quality costs

Most people assume that quality costs are limited to those involved in running a quality control department. In fact, the quality costs of an organization are often considerably larger than those associated with the salaries and equipment of quality control inspectors and are associated with many, many other areas. However, we can group these under the following three headings:

PREVENTION COSTS

These include the costs of quality planning, quality investigation, supplier approval, training, specification of testing equipment and new product review.

APPRAISAL COSTS

Costs of inspection and inspection equipment maintenance are included in this group. This inspection can be applied to incoming materials and resources, goods, products and service during production and final products or goods.

FAILURE COSTS

These include costs associated with internal failure (scrap, rectification, downgrading and retest) and external failure (return of goods, replacement, customer liaison, warranty).

The above cost sources are not comprehensive but do provide an indication of the cost areas which are affected by quality. These costs are not small in magnitude. Professor John Oakland[6] states that for many organizations they can exceed 15 per cent of sales revenue and are typically split:

- failure costs: 65 per cent,
- appraisal: 25 per cent,
- prevention: 10 per cent.

The benefits of the effective management of quality and the subsequent reduction of these costs can be considerable. For example, one comparison[7] of room air conditioner manufacturers in the USA and Japan found that the quality costs of the American manufacturers were at least three to four times higher than their Japanese counterparts. Reduction of those costs to the Japanese level would have generated an increase in profit of around 5 per cent! The benefits of measuring, managing and reducing quality costs are illustrated in Figure 4.3. This indicates that when quality is effectively managed not only do total costs fall but also:

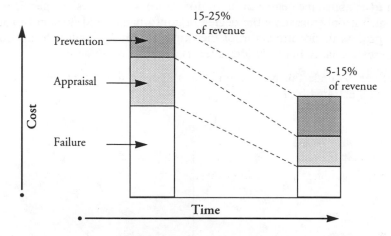

Figure 4.3   Quality costs

- appraisal costs and failure costs fall as percentages of total costs, and
- prevention costs rise as percentage of total costs.

These changes occur because of a significant and important shift from the 'after the event' focus of quality control to the 'before the event' focus of quality assurance and total quality management. The next section will take a look at that shift.

Quality management
The ways in which our organizations manage quality have shown considerable change over the past 10 years. These changes have enabled quality to become an active and major contributor to the performance of these organizations. This has happened because of:

- a radical shift in the focal point of quality management, and
- the empowerment of the people involved in the generation of the goods and services.

The starting point for this change process was the use of quality control systems in our manufacturing organizations.

QUALITY CONTROL
Quality control is the process which is used to check the product or service

81

and to establish the degree of its conformance with the design specification. As such it only measures the degree of conformance and does not provide any process for identification of the cause of failure. Quality control does not create quality but only identifies its presence or absence.

It can be undertaken in several ways and the differences between these can be illustrated by Figure 4.4.

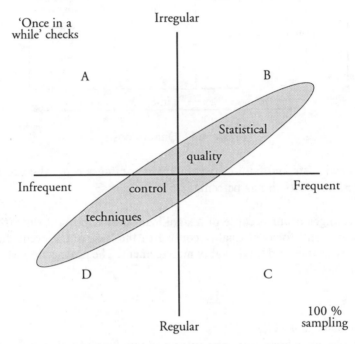

Figure 4.4 Quality control

The quality control systems which are used irregularly and infrequently lie in sector A of Figure 4.4. Their use is usually influenced by factors external to the organization such as a customer complaint or when an order lost through poor quality draws the attention of management to the value of consistent and better quality. However, in the absence of any formal support system or structure, they usually fade away particularly when faced with the need to complete orders against deadlines. The limited degree of checking involved provides no real confidence or data about the product's conformance to specification. In the short term it has a low cost but the costs of product return and failure often outweigh this limited advantage.

At the other extreme, sector C type quality control systems involve regular and frequent quality checks. They often involve systematic regular inspection, which can be at levels as high as 100 per cent, at specified points in the production process. These high levels of sampling do provide considerable data which is about the degree of product conformance. However, the level of sampling is not related to the actual performance of the process and operatives but it remains the same whether this performance is good or bad. These high and costly levels of sampling and conformance data can lead some managers to believe that they are managing the quality of their products. In reality, they are doing nothing more than measuring the quality of those products.

The core issues of the management of quality control involve:

1. The identification and elimination of those cause and effect chains which lead to product non-conformance: finding and getting rid of the causes of low quality levels rather than just measuring those levels.
2. The adjustment of levels of sampling and measurement so that they reflect the performance of the conversion process: sampling infrequently when quality level is high and frequently when it is low.

These not only make sound economic sense but also reflect the common sense of applying corrective action only when that process is not performing well. These needs are answered by the quality control systems which are based on the use of statistical methods. These methods, which span across sectors B and D in Figure 4.4, can be applied both frequently and infrequently and at regular or irregular intervals. They all provide a degree of control which is objective and responsive. In order to do this Statistical Quality Control (SQC) draws heavily on probability theory and involves, at its core, the selection and testing of a random representative sample. This can be taken from the outcomes of a continuous process, in order to assess whether that process is performing as it should, or from a batch of process inputs or outputs in order to establish whether the whole of that batch can be reasonably expected to be satisfactory. It uses sampling plans and other techniques such as Statistical Process Control (SPC) which facilitate the assessment of data. In a manufacturing environment these techniques will be used to predict whether a batch of product will be of acceptable quality or to enable the control of a continuous process. In a service environment quality control is often based on subjective criteria such as 'good' or 'bad' which are applied to service attributes which might include supplier staff attitude, service accessibility, timing and availability and will use monitoring/ measurement systems such as complaint logging and customer feedback.

However and whenever these SQC methods are applied, they focus on the process of measuring the absence or presence of quality. Later quality management methods broadened this focus and began to look at the assurance, rather than the control of quality.

QUALITY ASSURANCE
While quality control systems are focused on measuring the presence or absence of quality, Quality Assurance (QA) systems are designed to give 'adequate confidence that a product or service will satisfy given requirements for quality'[8]. The presence, commitment to and use of such a system by a company is intended to demonstrate to its customers that their quality needs are of prime importance As such, many organizations see quality assurance as a way to achieve a competitive edge in an increasingly hostile economic environment. They argue that QA is a way to keep your existing customers and grow with your new ones. In the UK, most QA systems conform to the relevant British Standard (BS 5750) and aim to provide an environment in which management has confidence that the product or service is fit for its specified purpose. In order to achieve this it is necessary to ensure that all of the inputs to every stage of the process conform to specification. These inputs will include material, equipment, training, performance of personnel, data (i.e. drawings, customer records, etc.), storage of physical products and information and inspection.

Table 4.2 BS 5750 and ISO 9000 series

BS 5750	Part number	ISO number	Title
Part 0:	Section 0.1	9000	Guide to selection and use
Part 0:	Section 0.2	9004	Guide to quality management and quality system elements
Part 1		9001	Specification for design/development, production, installation and servicing
Part 2		9002	Specification for production and installation
Part 3		9003	Specification for final inspection and test
Part 4		No equivalent	Guide to the use of: BS 5750 Part 1 BS 5750 Part 2 BS 5750 Part 3

The development of BS 5750 reflected concern, in the late 1970s, about the lack of competitive edge of UK products. This led, in 1977, to the creation of BS 5750 Parts 1, 2 and 3. These standards, which had their roots in MoD standards DEF STAN 05-21 to 05-29, were extended by the addition of Parts 4, 5, and 6 in 1981. The adoption of these standards was

84

encouraged by the National Quality Campaign and the British Standards System for Registration of Firms of Assessed Capability. In the late 1980s the BS 5750 series was revised in order to conform with the international ISO series of standards (Table 4.2).This series is now accepted in almost 50 countries to date, being adopted, for example, in West Germany as DIN ISO 9002, in the USA as ANSI/ASQC Q92-1987 and in France as NF 50-132. Like BS 5750, this series of standards provides the 'bare bones' requirements for a QA system.

However, what this standard does *not* lay down are specifications for the product created by that company. However, it does identify the requirements for a QA system which, if properly set up and operated, will ensure that:

• raw materials and services conform to specified requirements;
• satisfactory sampling procedures are created, used and maintained;
• the process stage is controlled;
• adequate storage and packaging are used;
• personnel are trained;
• statistical techniques are used to verify product conformance;
• off-spec or non-conforming material is identified and segregated.

By early 1993 some 25 000 organizations had applied for and been granted the BS 5750 accreditation. The diversity of these organizations is considerable, with representatives from manufacturing, telecommunications, building societies, the legal system, education, house building, and the nursing professions. They range in size from the chemical giant ICI to much smaller family-run companies and even include the Notting Hill police station in London.

Despite the power and value of these quality assurance systems it has become evident that they are not enough. In the final analysis, it is the degree to which the customer's needs and expectations are met which defines the quality of a product. This, together with evidence that successful organizations are those who 'delight' their customers, led to the development of a much larger and powerful view of the management of quality. It is this view that we shall now explore.

TOTAL QUALITY MANAGEMENT

Total Quality Management (TQM) is not just a way of managing quality. It is, in fact, a way of managing organizations. As such, it is targeted towards the situation where every job and every process are carried out correctly, first time and every time. It is also a way of improving the effectiveness, flexibility and competitiveness of the business as a whole. For an organization to be effective all its parts, systems and subsystems must work well and work together. If, as we saw earlier, quality can be defined as meeting customer requirements then the TQM concept states that the customer–supplier relationships which are internal to the organization are as important as the external and more conventional customer–supplier relationship. These internal customer–supplier relationships exist throughout all of our organizations. They include, for example:

- The supervisor and his/her staff.
  - are they receiving the right instructions and information?
- The sales department and the manufacturing department.
  - are the sales people receiving the product when promised and in the desired condition?

These relationships or 'quality chains' permeate all organizations and the failure of any link in these chains leads to failures in other parts of the organization. TQM focuses on making sure that these 'chains' are effective and that the outcomes are those which 'delight' the organization's customers.

In order to do that the TQM approach ensures that organizations:

- Focus on the needs of their market;
- Achieve top quality performance in all areas;
- Remove non-productive activities and waste;
- Develop a team approach to quality;
- Review performance continually.

Its application is as relevant and valuable to service industries as it is for manufacturing and this is reflected in the contents of BS 7850—Total Quality Management—which recognizes that the objectives of the business and customer satisfaction are mutually dependent.

The introduction of TQM is a company-wide and management-led process. It is based on the involvement of all employees with the following typical steps:

1. *Information gathering*:
   (i) What are current costs of quality?
   (ii) What are customers', managers' and employees' views of current quality performance?
2. *Management commitment and focus*:
   (i) Review findings of information gathering.
   (ii) Agree and commit to next steps.
3. *Planned involvement*
   (i) Training in TQM.

(ii) Identify and prioritize problems.

(iii) Set up and run problem-solving teams.

4. *Review, reinforce and restart*:

(i) Feedback on successes.

(ii) Identify further goals.

Experience indicates that the initial cycle of these events can take up to 18 months but since TQM is a continuous process, rather than a one-off event, this cycle will be repeated with further problems being identified and solved.

The TQM approach acts by changing the culture of an organization and empowering those who work within that organization to be responsible for the quality of their own work. As such it can be viewed as a 'radical' approach. However, the rewards of this process can be high with quality costs falling by as much as 60 per cent! Some of the attributes of the TQM approach are illustrated in the example below and a comparison of the characteristics of TQM with those of QA and QC is given in Table 4.3.

The Ron Dunning Pizza Chain

Despite several successful years in the restaurant business and a chain of three profitable restaurants to prove it, Ron Dunning felt uncomfortable. He had just had to sack one of his best and longest serving waitresses: not only had she got an order wrong but she had also dropped salad dressing down a customer's best suit. To crown it all she'd forgotten to offer the standard compensation of free drinks. Ron knew that this wasn't the first time that customers had left unhappy but this time he was determined to do something about it. After some days of thought he called his employees together and told them that the old way of doing things was out. From now on everyone was responsible for ensuring that every customer left his restaurants totally satisfied with the service and meal that they had. To help this change Ron had created these four simple rules.

1. Our motto is 'your delight is our delight'.
2. The customer is always right.
3. The customer is in your care.
4. All employees are problem-solvers.

He also set up a new training programme aimed at eliminating the old sources of error such as order miskeying and poor service. Employees were encouraged to use their initiative in solving customer problems and were

87

also given bonuses based on customer questionnaire results.

Initially, operating costs went up but when employees became used to the new authority he had given them and the word of mouth got round about the new service policy, then revenue went up. As wastage and spoilage went down so did the customer complaints and as the advance bookings rose, profits rose with them.

Ron's employees knew that he meant what he said—he did want to delight the customer—so if he took it seriously, so did they. Ron, however, knew that while success bred success, perfection was another thing all together.

Table 4.3 The three approaches

	Quality control	*Quality assurance*	*Total quality management*
Acronym	QC or SQC	QA	TQM
Approach	Detection of non-conformance	Co-ordination of management efforts	Integration of everyone's efforts
Tools	Inspectors, sampling plans and outcome specifications	Quality manuals and procedures	Multi disciplinary teams
Objective	Feedback control	Prevention	Customer delight

It is worth noting that, however radical or revolutionary it may appear, TQM uses, builds upon and integrates a number of proven quality management components such as:

- quality assurance systems based on BS 5750;
- quality tools and techniques such as SPC and SQC;
- problem-solving teams.

One of the ways in which these teams can be focused and managed has been widely used outside the TQM process and will be examined in the next section.

Quality circles

The concept of Quality Circles (QC) originated in Japan in the early 1970s and has been used very widely in both Europe and North America. It involves the use of small groups (5 to 15 people) of employees usually drawn from one area of the organization. The objective of the group or 'circle' is the identification and solution of quality-related problems. Each group operates under the chairmanship of a leader and meets typically once a week at an appropriate on-site location. The group uses a systematic approach involving the typical steps of:

• problem identification,
• fact finding,
• problem definition,
• cause and effect analysis,
• data collection and analysis,
• solution identification,
• implementation planning.

The group will use a variety of techniques including Ishikawa diagrams, Brainstorming, Pareto analysis etc. (see Chapters 10 and 11).

However, Quality Circles on their own are not always successful—even in Japan! Factors which do contribute to their success include:

• voluntary membership,
• power to implement their proposals,
• operation as a part of a larger quality movement or company initiative,
• management support,
• good commissioning and organization,
• provision of adequate resources and training,
• modest initial targets.

Quality Circles are just one of a number of ways of tapping into the people who, as we said earlier, are the organization. It is these people who create and run the processes, systems and procedures which can result in the fulfilment of the needs and expectations of the customer. Other ways of tapping into this human resource of creativity and energy are examined in Part 2.

TQM and performance improvement

We saw in Chapter 1 that effective performance improvement programmes are seen to be:

• results driven,
• continuous and on-going in nature,

- focused on key and measurable issues,
- dependent upon the efforts of those people who are the organization.

The process of TQM is also a continuous and ongoing process which, though management led, ultimately depends upon the empowerment of people for its driving force. Just as the performance improvement programme requires the continuous monitoring of information about the interaction between the organization and its environment, so also does the TQM process tie itself to a continuous assessment of customer needs and wants.

As you can see these processes have much in common: both are targeted at the enhancement of the organization's performance. However, there are differences. The broader and more generic performance improvement process is concerned with a wide range of key organizational issues, while TQM focuses on ensuring that the organizational outcomes answer the needs of the customer. As such it might be argued that while performance improvement is concerned with the means, the TQM process is only concerned with the end. It could also be argued that the performance improvement process could be applied before, during and after the TQM process. However, such debates are, in the ultimate analysis, divisive and unhelpful.

TQM is a way of improving the performance of the organization. It is not, however, the only way nor is it the easiest and shortest way. But as the proverb says: 'There is more than one way to skin a cat'.

The next and final section of this chapter will take a brief look at some of the great names in what we have called the quality revolution.

The quality gurus

A number of individuals, including the seven described below, have developed concepts and approaches to quality which have made a major impact in both the manufacturing and service sectors.

These have included:

- Technical tools to control design and manufacturing;
- Management tools to achieve quality;
- Organization-wide concepts.

W. EDWARDS DEMING

Dr Deming worked for many years in US government service but his rise to fame started in Japan. He first visited Japan in 1947 to help prepare for the first post-war census and was particularly associated with the application of statistical control. He returned to lecture several times in the early 1950s and his methods of statistical quality control were taken up with enthusiasm by Japanese engineers and managers. The success of these led to the establishment, in 1951, of the Deming prize for contributions to quality and the award, to Deming, in 1960 of Japan's premier Imperial honour, the Second Order of the Sacred Treasure. Subsequent work by Deming and his followers moved away from the statistically based approach taught to the Japanese towards a more management based approach. This approach has fourteen key points and a seven-point action plan.

JOSEPH M. JURAN

Juran is a Balkan-born American engineer who was invited to lecture in Japan in the early 1950s and conducted training courses on the management of quality. He is often credited with converting the influence, upon the Japanese, of the technology and statistical control-led Deming approach into a broader, more overall concern with the management of quality. He has published twelve books which have been translated into some thirteen languages and has received more than thirty medals and awards in various countries. His 'Quality Planning Road Map' has nine steps and believes that the majority of quality problems originate in poor management.

SHIGEO SHINGO

A Japanese engineer who became involved in management training and consultancy after the Second World War. He applied and extended the ideas of quality control to develop the 'Poka-Yoke', mistake proofing or 'Defects = 0' concept in the early 1960s. This concept was applied with great success resulting in plants with several years of totally defect-free operation. He first visited Europe in the early 1970s and subsequently provided training and consultancy in Europe, North America and Australia. He has written over fourteen books which have been translated into English and other European languages.

PHILIP B. CROSBY

An American who now runs the very successful Philip Crosby Associates and Quality College in Florida, Crosby has held a variety of quality jobs from line inspector to Quality Director for ITT. He is best known for the concepts of 'Do It Right First Time' and 'Zero Defects' and states that companies can spend 20 to 35 per cent of revenue 'doing things wrong and doing them over again'. He puts forward four absolutes of quality:

- Quality = conformance to requirements;
- Quality systems are about prevention and 'right first time';
- Cost is the measure of quality;
- Zero defects is the standard of performance.

These are used as the basis of a 14-point quality improvement plan which is illustrated in Crosby's four best-selling books.

ARMAND V. FEIGENBAUM

Feigenbaum was discovered by the Japanese in the early 1950s via his role as Head of Quality at GEC and his books. He argued for a move away from a focus on the technology of quality control towards the use of quality control as a business method. Other major themes were the cost of quality, the need for a 'right first time' attitude and the need for everyone to be responsible for quality.

KAORU ISHIKAWA

A leader in Japan's quality movement since the early 1950s, Ishikawa has paid particular attention to both techniques (Pareto, cause and effect diagrams, scatter diagrams, Shewart control charts etc.) and organizational approaches (Quality Circles, Company Wide Quality Control).

GENICHI TAGUCHI

By the late 1970s Taguchi had won Deming awards in application and quality literature and had developed the 'Quality Loss Function' concept. Following a visit to the United States in 1980, more and more American manufacturers began to adopt his ideas which are based on the routine optimization of the product and plant prior to manufacture. Quality and reliability are moved back to the design phase instead of being reliant upon quality through inspection.

The generation and maintenance of the presence of quality in the outcomes of the conversion processes present in all our organizations can be influenced by:

- The nature and structure of those processes;
- The arrangement and layout of the capital resources involved.

These factors and some of the issues raised by the need to balance the capacity of the conversion process with the demand for its outcomes will be examined in the next chapter.

Summary

The quality revolution has created a situation where quality is:

- a key issue for all organizations,
- a source of competitive advantage,
- a source of profit and growth

Quality is best defined as 'Fitness for purpose' and that purpose:

- Reflects the customer's needs,
- Can be functional or non-functional.

The five-step pathway to quality is:

1. Identify: the customer's needs.
2. Decide: which parts of those needs will be answered.
3. Detail: the key characteristics of the product.
4. Design: taking into account those needs and the organization's capability.
5. Create: a reliable, durable product or service which answers the customer's needs.

Quality costs are concerned with:

- prevention,
- appraisal,
- failure.

Effective management of quality will start from the baseline of quality control and grow through quality assurance to total quality management. TQM builds upon and integrates the basic components of:

- quality assurance systems based on BS 5750;
- quality tools and techniques such as SPC;
- problem solving teams.

It is targeted towards the situation where every job and every process are carried out correctly, first time and every time. It is also a way of improving the effectiveness, flexibility and competitiveness of the business as a whole.

References

[1] Peters, T.J. and R.H. Waterman, *In Search of Excellence*, Harper and Row, New York, 1982.

[2] Crosby, P.B., *Quality is Free: The Art of Making Quality Certain*, Mentor, New York, 1979.

[3] BS 4778, *Quality Vocabulary: Part 1 International Terms*, British Standards Institution, London, 1987.

[4] Juran, J.M. and F.M. Gryna, *Quality Planning and Analysis*, McGraw-Hill, New York, 1980.

[5] Deming, W.E., *Quality, Productivity and Competitive Position*, MIT Center for Advanced Engineering Study, Cambridge, Massachusetts, 1982.

[6] Oakland, J.S., *Total Quality Management*, Heinemann, London, 1989.

[7] Garvin, D.A., 'Quality on the line' reprinted in *Unconditional Quality*, Harvard Business Press, Boston, Massachusetts, 1983.

[8] *B.S. 5750, Part 0 Section 0.1 Guide to selection and use*, British Standards Institution, London, 1987.

5. Process and plan

Let all things be done decently and in order.

2 Corinthians, 14:40

Introduction

If our organizations, as mechanisms for the conversion of resources, are to be successful then they must to be able to answer the needs of the customer in a dynamic and interactive manner. To do so, they must be able, in an efficient, effective and adaptable way, to convert resources or inputs into outputs or products and services which are desired by the customer.

The nature of the conversion process, together with its layout, arrangement and capacity, are all factors which can significantly influence the organization's potential and actual efficiency, effectiveness and adaptability. For example, as we saw earlier, because of the large costs involved, many manufacturing conversion processes need to be efficient in the ways that they use to convert expensive resources. This drive to be efficient is strong and can result in organizations that are distant from their customer and preoccupied with the technology of the conversion process. These organizations will also often generate their products in large batches or long runs and distance themselves from the customer by both geography and large stocks of finished goods. However, as we also saw earlier, service conversion process organizations need to have close customer relationships. The extent and nature of this contact will vary with the nature of the service provided.

The high levels of interaction between patient and doctor represent an example of one extreme in the range of service conversion process interactions while the lesser levels present in an automobile service station represent another. However, whatever the level of contact or interaction, the customer is often directly involved in that service conversion process. One result of this involvement is that those who operate and manage these service conversion processes have *less* freedom to structure and arrange that process in such a way as to ensure its efficiency. Above all, that process will need to be adaptable and effective if it is to 'delight the customer.'

This chapter will take a look at the different forms of the conversion process together with the ways in which we can lay out, arrange and manage those forms in order to identify their potential contribution to the process of performance improvement.

Which process?

The conversion processes of our organizations are configured, arranged and structured in a variety of ways. This variety has, not surprisingly, given rise to a number of descriptions and names for the structures or configurations of that conversion process.

Many of these descriptions have their roots in the ways which we use to manufacture goods and products. For example, the term 'mass production' has become a familiar part of all our vocabularies since it was first used, in 1915, to describe the continuous assembly lines which Henry Ford used to produce automobiles. On these lines the automobiles were moved past operators who added wheels or headlights or body parts to a stream of gradually growing but identical vehicles which finally came off the assembly line complete and ready to be used. Similarly the term 'jobbing shop' is often used to describe those places in which piece-work, i.e. work that is paid for work done rather than time taken, was undertaken on large groups or batches of identical products.

These descriptions are just as applicable to the conversion processes of our service organizations as they are to those organizations concerned with manufacture. For example, the self-service counters of our eating places have much in common with our manufacturing assembly lines. In both of these a component in the process moves past locations dedicated to specific activities. For the automobile assembly line, the body is the component and the locations are the work stations dedicated to adding wheels, seats, engine or windows. For the self-service counter the customer is the component and the locations are those self-selection display areas containing sandwiches, drinks, etc. For both of these situations, the key to smooth and efficient operation is the design of the line so that the activities conducted at each of the locations takes the same time, otherwise the 'line' will 'hiccup' or flow erratically. Similarly, the lecture halls of our universities are the locations of a batch conversion process in which groups of students are simultaneously exposed to an identical process of information transfer or lecturing. This batch process is also used in transport where the size of buses or aeroplanes and the frequency of their journeys are designed in order to provide an economical service for customers. The manufacture of products in groups or batches is also a common feature of those of our organizations concerned with changing the physical forms of their inputs.

Batch, project or line?

The commonest descriptions of the forms of these conversion processes are as follows:

- a project process: concerned with the production of one or a limited number of specialized products;
- a batch process: concerned with the production of a small or medium sized group of standard identical products;
- an assembly line process: concerned with the continuous production of standard products.

Further characteristics of these structures are shown in Table 5.1.

Table 5.1 Typical characteristics of conversion processes

	Project	*Batch*	*Assembly line*
Outcome volume	low	medium–high	high
Outcome variety	high	medium–low	low
Outcome group size	small	medium	large–very large
Outcome inventory or stock	very low	medium	high
Adaptability	high	medium	low
Customer contact	high	low	very low

If we look at these descriptions we will find that, for example, a project is usually concerned with a single unique outcome while an assembly line is concerned with the continuous production of large numbers of identical outcomes. It is also evident that while both the assembly line and the batch process are repetitive in nature, in that they are used to generate numbers of identical outcomes, the project process is non-repetitive. From these and earlier observations we can take our understanding of these forms further when we perceive that they can be represented by the following dimensions:

- standardized–customized outcome dimension;
- low–high direct customer contact dimension.

Using these dimensions we can see that many manufacturing conversion processes are concerned with standardized outcomes or products and have low levels of direct customer contact while many service conversion processes show the characteristics of high levels of direct customer contact and a range of outcomes that reflects the variety and diversity of those customers' needs. However, despite their widespread presence, conversion processes with these characteristics do not represent all manufacturing or all service conversion processes. There are, for example, manufacturing

97

processes which create unique one-off products for individual customers such as custom-made furniture or clothes or painted portraits, and there are also service conversion processes with low levels of direct customer contact such as cash point or ATM machines or catalogue mail order systems. An example of the application of a process concept, which evolved in manufacturing, to a service conversion process is given below.

Conveyor belt surgery

Professor Syvatoslav Fyodorov's Moscow Institute of Eye Surgery operates on up to 100 people per day using an ergonomically designed operating theatre. This theatre has eight beds which are arranged in a daisy-wheel and rotate past work stations at which the tasks of local anaesthetic, incision, operation, suturing, dressing and recovery take place. Each of these work stations is manned by a doctor or nurse and the most popular procedure is that of radial keratotomy in which incisions are made, altering the shape of the cornea of the eye, and thus correcting short-sightedness.

Processes and performance improvement
So how does our understanding of the types and characteristics of these processes contribute to the process of performance improvement? Part of the answer to this vital question lies in the ways in which the organization makes use of the skills, abilities and capabilities of its people. Unfortunately some organizations are structured in such a way as to limit, rather than encourage, that contribution. For example, organizations that are concerned with the provision of large volumes of standardized products or services will also be concerned with ensuring that these services or products are generated:

- in a manner which ensures conformity to standards;
- with minimum use of resources.

As a result these organizations will tend to be centralized, i.e. controlled from a central location, and tend to implement that control by use of documented procedures, standards and specifications. As a consequence the freedom for individuals to deviate from the norm or standard way of doing things is limited. Indeed, in some of these organizations such deviance is seen to be threatening and disruptive and as such is frowned upon.

However, in organizations that are concerned with the provision of unique or custom-made products or services, i.e. project-type organizations, the presence of the freedom to be creative and to be responsive to customers' needs is a vital, indeed essential, component. Without it the outcome of the customer–organization relationship would not be a customer who is satisfied, even delighted and willing, indeed keen, to return.

Surprisingly, technology can contribute to the enhancement of this relationship, but as an enabling rather than a driving mechanism. One example of this contribution lies in the changes in manufacturing technology which have enabled equipment to become automated and thus perform complex tasks with minimum human intervention or supervision. This technology, on its own, enables the cheaper production of large volumes of standard products. However, when allied with a flexible and skilled work-force it can be used to break out of the confines of the large batch process form and break into the production of goods which are customized to a much higher degree and whose range and variety can be changed quickly. Reviews of American 'best practice' organizations[1] indicate that even those concerned with high volume manufacture are learning to combine the economies of scale with this 'flexible specialization' approach and thus have:

- shorter product runs
- faster new product introduction
- greater sensitivity to customer needs.

Another example is the use, by mail order supply organizations, of CD ROM databases of postal codes which enable the customer's address to be located quickly, thus enhancing the responsiveness of the organization.

Whether this sophisticated technology is used or not, it is evident that the form of the conversion process and the ways in which its human inputs are managed can have a significant effect upon the performance improvement process. The presence of 'user-friendly' or 'people-centred' factories and offices is an increasingly important factor in the process of improving organizational performance. Descriptions[2] of modern versions of car assembly lines reflect this shift with the presence of adjustable height lines and robots to carry out tasks involving welding and heavy lifting. This shift is further illustrated by the change from the traditional single line to several mini lines each manned by teams operating under a group leader.

It is also increasingly evident that the more that we study the ways in which these different processes operate the more we become able to change and improve the ways in which they operate, providing, of course, we are prepared to take the risk of allowing that process of innovation to take place. One of the clearest examples of how this can take place is present in the development and application of the 'Just In Time' approach.

Just in time

As we saw in Chapter 4, the roots of the Just In Time (JIT) concept go back to the manufacturing industries of Japan in the late 1940s and early 1950s. At that time Japanese automobile manufacturers were beginning to respond to the growing demand, from their home market, for cars and trucks. Many of these manufacturers decided to develop relationships with American or European manufacturers and to copy the 'best practice' techniques developed by those high volume manufacturers. These best practices involved, at that time, the following:

- high levels of equipment and operator specialization;
- long production runs on high capacity machines with long set-up times;
- high buffer stock levels so that equipment and operators were never idle;
- scheduling systems that were concerned with keeping machines running;
- quality systems that used the concepts of 'acceptable quality levels' and thus accepted the presence of defectives.

However, Toyota and later Nissan decided, initially as a reaction to the much lower demand levels of the Japanese market, that the best approach was to increase the flexibility of:

- equipment,
- operators,
- suppliers.

This approach demanded and resulted in faster set-up times for equipment, operators who could be shifted from job to job or machine to machine and tighter linkages between parts deliveries and assembly needs. The introduction of these changes and the development of a number of other innovations meant that Toyota productivity levels had passed those of the major American producers by 1965. Inventory or stock levels also fell, partly as a result of the Kanban 'pull' scheduling system. This system required the operator to go back to the previous work station to retrieve the parts and assemblies required. This is done when, but not before, these are required and only for the amount required. Hence the material arrived at the assembly point 'just in time' for its use. Stocks were also reduced by closer relationship with suppliers who were expected to deliver, often directly to the assembly line, several times a day. As a result of these falling stock levels there were fewer spare parts to use if the items were defective—so quality levels had to rise. This, in its turn, led to the practice of operators conducting their own quality control inspections.

There can be little doubt that JIT is a very powerful and effective concept which has enabled the Japanese automobile manufacturers to make massive gains in the world automobile market. It is also a concept that is not limited, in its application, to the assembly of automobiles. The Center for Technology, Policy and Industrial Development at MIT reports[3] that this concept will

'supplant mass production and the remaining outposts of craft production in all areas of industrial endeavour to become the standard global production system of the twenty-first century.'

The JIT concept came about because of a number of radical and innovative changes which challenged and almost turned upside down the contemporary conventional production management wisdom about assembly line manufacture. However, as we saw earlier, these 'manufacturing' techniques are just as easily applied to service conversion processes as shown in the example, below.

Kanban hospital

Leeds's St James Hospital is reported[5] to be applying the principles of JIT to the control of its stocks of disposable goods at ward level. Two boxes or containers are held and when the first box is empty, the second is opened and an order for a replacement box initiated. Plans include the use of bar codes to trigger orders and the reduction, by multidisciplinary teams, of the range of items stocked and suppliers used. Admission procedures were also examined and the number of 'processing stages' reduced, leading to fewer operation cancellations.

The seven wastes

It can be argued that JIT is more than just a new way of manufacturing products and as such is applicable to more than just manufacturing conversion processes. At its core, JIT is concerned with waste reduction and Shigeo Shingo[4] in writing about the Toyota production system identifies seven sources of waste. These sources of waste (shown in Table 5.2) are present in all of our organizations, whether they manufacture products or provide services, and the reduction or elimination of their causes and sources can make a major contribution to the performance improvement process.

101

Table 5.2   The seven wastes

Wastes of over-production
Waste of waiting
Waste of transportation
Waste of processing itself
Wastes of stocks
Waste of motion
Waste of making defective products.

Examples of these wastes include:

1. *Wastes of over-production* This is reduced or eliminated when products or services are made or provided in small lots and when the arrival of the resources required is synchronized to be 'just in time'.
2. *Waste of waiting* This is reduced when the change-over or set-up times, involved in switching from one product or service to another, are reduced and when a balance between load and capacity is achieved.
3. *Waste of transportation* This is reduced by improvement of the layout and location of the conversion facilities.
4. *Waste of processing itself* The disciplines of value engineering (VE) and value analysis (VA) demand answers to such questions as:

   (i) Why are we generating this service or product?
   (ii) Why are we generating it in this particular way?
   (iii) Why are we using these inputs to do so?

   Answers to these questions can produce a longer lasting and more effective improvement in the conversion process than those associated with improving the technology of the process itself.
5. *Waste of stocks* Stocks cost money and take up space, so reducing stocks reduces waste.
6. *Waste of motion* Shingo wrote that 'time is only the shadow of motion' and argued that the positioning of the tools and equipment used so as to reduce the motion needed in their use was, in fact, reducing the waste of money.
7. *Waste of making defective products* Shingo argued that the inspection process should be focused towards *preventing* rather than *finding* defective outputs.

It will be a very unusual organization, whatever the nature of its conversion process, that does not display at least two or even three of these wastes in the way in which it operates and reacts to its customers.

The remainder of this chapter will be concerned with identifying some of the ways in which these wastes can be reduced and we will start that process by taking a brief look at the role and contribution of those inputs to the conversion process that are called 'capital resources' by the management economists.

Machinery, equipment, tools, computers and other artefacts

Among the considerable variety of organizational inputs there are those which are described as capital resources. These generally consist of the physical assets of the organization and will include the buildings, machinery, equipment, tools, computers and other artefacts which have been made or acquired in order to enhance or enable the conversion process. These represent the physical form of an organization and as such are often what the customer sees or uses during transactions with that organization.

These physical assets are crucial to the conversion process. It is, for example, difficult to conceive of a bus company that does not own and use buses, garages, maintenance facilities and bus stops or depots. Even those service organizations in which the conversion process involves non-tangible inputs and outputs require physical assets to facilitate that process such as offices for people to work in with desks, chairs, computers, telephones, fax machines, etc. The surgeries and consulting rooms of our doctors require patient waiting spaces with chairs, consulting rooms with desks, tables, chairs and examination couches as well as the equipment that the doctor uses. In the fast food restaurants these assets include kitchen equipment, tills, counters, chairs, tables and waste disposal bins, all of which are needed in order that the product can be made cooked, sold and consumed. Table 5.3 shows more examples of these capital resources or physical assets.

Not only are these assets crucial to the conversion process but they also exert a considerable influence upon the efficiency, effectiveness and adaptability of that process. They do so by virtue of their:

- layout or arrangement,
- capacity.

Layout

The word layout is used in this context to mean the arrangement and relative positions of the capital resources which, as we saw earlier, are so vital and integral to the conversion process. Layout can be concerned with the arrangement of all or any of these resources such as equipment, desks, computers, work stations etc., in, for example, any of the following situations:

Table 5.3 Organizational capital resources

Organization	Capital resources
Car manufacturer	*Equipment*: presses, lathes, assembly lines, robots, computers, etc. *Buildings*: for assembly, storage of parts and finished cars, office blocks for support staff, etc. *Work stations*: desks, benches, chairs, etc.
Building society branch	*Equipment*: computers, tills, security systems, UV signature check devices, printers, etc. *Building*: for customer cash transactions and for mortgage transactions. *Work stations*: desks, benches, chairs, etc.

- a factory,
- a department,
- a room,
- on a desk top.

If we get this layout right, then we can reduce the waste created by transportation of resources and outcomes and, at an individual level, we can reduce the waste of unnecessary motion.

Most of these layouts or arrangements are based upon:

- the process or function being carried out;
- the product or outcome being generated.

PROCESS OR FUNCTION-BASED LAYOUT

In this type of layout the input to the conversion process, which can also be the customer, passes through the conversion process steps or stages by moving from stage to stage as required. At each of these stages the capital resources required for the function carried out are grouped together. This type of layout is present in many manufacturing and service conversion processes and examples include:

1. A hotel in which the customer is an input to a change of state service conversion process (see Chapter 3) and in which he or she will visit and use, as required, the bar, bedroom, sauna, gymnasium, cashier and restaurant. All customers need not or will not use all of these facilities which are located in different parts of the hotel.

2. A supermarket in which a change in ownership takes place (see Chapter 3). The customer will visit different areas of the market to pick up the particular foodstuffs or goods required. These areas are dedicated to the display of different items such as cereals, dairy products, meat, fish.

This type of layout can be illustrated as shown in Figure 5.1 in which the different routes for products 1 and 2 are shown for a small batch manufacturing unit.

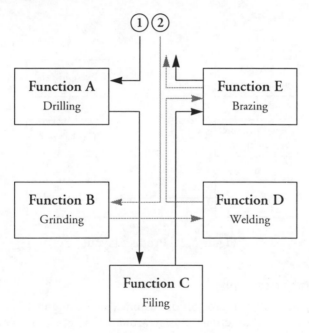

Figure 5.1 Process layout

PRODUCT OR OUTCOME-BASED LAYOUT

In this type of layout the sequence of actions or stages in the conversion process are defined by the needs of the product or outcome. This means that the activities or stages are arranged in a set order and the input (product or customer) moves through these in a defined sequence. Motor vehicle assembly lines, automatic car washes and self-service restaurants are all examples of this type of layout. Our experience will tell us that it is possible for the customer to not interact with all of the stages, as when we only buy a cup of tea at a motorway service station restaurant. Nevertheless, all of the stages have to be passed through in order to complete the process.

Figure 5.2 illustrates this type of layout for a health check/screening clinic with client 1 experiencing the full checking process while client 2 is exposed to a 'quick check' to monitor the patient's weight and blood pressure levels. Both the process-based and the product-based layout require the inputs to the conversion process to be mobile. In a limited number of conversion processes this is not possible either because the size or nature of the product or because of that movement would limit or put at risk the efficiency of the process.

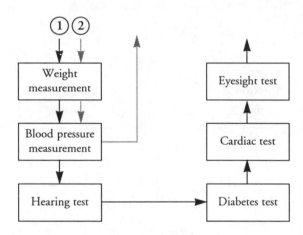

Figure 5.2   Product layout

FIXED POSITION LAYOUTS

These take place with the product or customer remaining in a fixed position and the activities or functions cluster around that position. This type of layout, illustrated in Figure 5.3, is used in shipbuilding, civil engineering projects, hospital operating theatres and aircraft assembly. So when do we use these different types of layout and how do they contribute to the Performance Improvement process?

MAKING THE LAYOUT DECISION

Our own experience will tell us that ways in which we arrange or position the computer screen, keyboard, printer, chair and telephone on or around

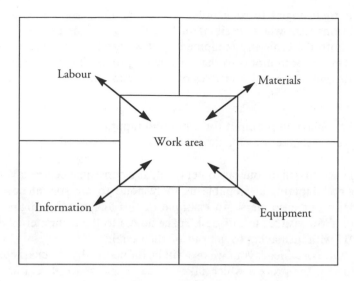

Figure 5.3   Fixed layout

our desks make a considerable difference to the ease, effectiveness and even the duration of our use of these tools. A layout which helps us to use these tools will need to be flexible and accessible since we may wish to use or access these tools at different times and in different ways. Since we also only have a limited amount of desk or office space available and we want to be able to access these tools from a comfortable working position that we can sustain for long periods of time, that layout will also involve the maximum use of area or volume and the minimum of movement. The science of making a task fit the natural body movements of the operator, i.e. ergonomics, would also help us to design a layout that limited our bodily fatigue and maximized our comfort levels. The benefits of a good layout are not restricted to those which result in our physical comfort: they also include our social interactions with those who share our work spaces. Allen[6] examined, in research and engineering laboratories, the effect of separation upon communication. His results indicate that if work positions are more than 10 metres apart the probability of communicating once per week was between 8 and 9 per cent. When work stations were 5 or less metres apart this figure rose to 25 per cent. Hall[7] writes about our use of space and notes the existence of several zones of physical proximity. These include the *personal zone* which extends from 18 inches to 4 ft and is usually used for most of our two or three person conversations and the social zone, from 4 to 12 ft, in which the majority of business interactions, such as meetings, interviews and presentations take place. Other research[8] reports that when we sit at right angles to each other we are far more spontaneous in our conversations than when we sit either face to face or side by side.

Since both the tools and equipment that we use in these spaces and our own energy are both inputs to the conversion process it can be argued that the best layout is one which enables our conversion of those resources to be both:

- efficient—maximum output for minimum input;
- effective—resource is available when and where required.

We also need to delight our customers and, as a consequence, the layout will need to be adaptable and enable us to respond to the special needs and demands of our customers. An example of this adaptability might be the ability to allow visitors to our desk space access to the computer keyboard and VDU without having to get out of their chair.

The choice of which layout we use will be influenced by the characteristics and nature of the process which takes place in that space. Facilities which provide or manufacture large quantities of a limited number of services or products are generally best served by a product type of layout. This type of layout enables the product or service to be generated in a consistent and controlled manner and is less demanding in terms of the skills or abilities of its operators. However, since the product type of layout is designed with specific products or services in mind, it is inherently inflexible. This type of layout will not be able to delight the customer by responding to his or her special needs and demands. We have already seen that examples of the product type of layout are found in car assembly lines, self-service counters, snack bars, cafés and health screening clinics.

As we noted in Chapter 4 the ability to be able to respond to customer needs is important. This adaptability is provided by the process type of layout. This layout is generally very flexible and responsive but requires higher operator skill and ability levels to be so. Its inherent adaptability extends not only to the nature of the service or product provided but also to the ability to respond to varying demand levels for those products and services.

DESIGNING A LAYOUT

The design of a layout is often a complex task with a strong creative element. Computers can be used to speed up the planning process and the range of computer layout programs is wide. However, Ray Wild[9], while providing a comprehensive list of some 26 different programs, also comments that the results generated are 'only marginally better' than those of manual methods.

Whatever method is used the process of designing a layout can only begin once the basic information has been gathered together. This information (Table 5.4) must be accurate and comprehensive enough to provide a strong foundation for the options we shall review during the layout design process. There is little purpose in attempting a layout design unless you have this information and have confidence in its accuracy.

Table 5.4   Layout information

Dimensions and layout of space to be used
Known current and future product or service demand
Operations to be undertaken
Sequence of operations
Storage needs
Access needs including fire exits
Labour needs including washrooms, changing rooms.

The sequence generally followed for planning a layout is as follows:

1. Identify key objective for layout. This might be to minimize handling, to minimize congestion or queuing, or to maximize equipment usage.
2. Identify the key operations. These are the operations which account for the majority of movements or revenue or workload.
3. Establish flow patterns for the key operations using a flow chart (Figure 5. 4) and or a from/to diagram (Figure 5.5).
4. Establish an interdependence chart for these key operations (Figure 5.6).
5. Sketch out (Figure 5.7) the relative positions using established interdependencies.
6. Convert this sketch into a layout using known or estimated area needs (Figure 5.8).

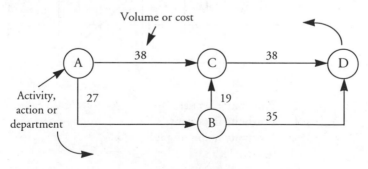

Figure 5.4   Flow chart

109

From ＼ To	A	B	C	D	Total
A		27	38		65
B			19	35	54
C				38	38
D					
Total		27	57	73	157

Figure 5.5   From/to diagram

	A	B	C	D
A		E	U	I
B	E		U	E
C	U	U		I
D	I	E	I	

Key

E: Proximity essential
I: Proximity important
U: Proximity unimportant

Figure 5.6   Interdependence chart

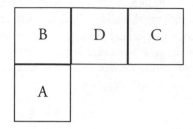

Figure 5.7 Relative position sketch

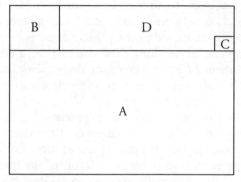

Figure 5.8 Actual layout

This layout will now need to be examined in detail to ensure that:

• access pathways are adequate;
• design floor loadings are not exceeded;
• safety requirements regarding fire escape, fume removal, etc. can be met.

This process can be applied to the capital resources of all the conversion processes which we identified in Chapter 3.

Bad layouts often make themselves evident by the presence of congestion, queues of people or high work-in-progress stocks, damage to goods in transit, frustration and even unsafe conditions of work. Good layouts suffer few of these problems and can also be adapted to meet changes in demand and service or product content. As such a good layout can make a real and positive contribution to the performance of any part of an organization. It enables people to work efficiently and effectively. In those service conversion processes where the client is an input to the process, the layout of the facilities at the point of initial client physical contact can have a considerable effect upon the subjective image that the client has of the organization. Examples of both good and bad layouts are evident in the

111

reception areas of our banks, hotels, universities and hospitals. Good layouts welcome and inform the client: bad layouts confuse and repel.

So far we have looked at where these capital resources are located and how they are arranged; now we must look at how the capacity of these resources can be related to the demands for product or service and the ever-present need for improved performance.

Capacity

The capacity of a conversion process is a measure of its ability to convert inputs into products or services. This capacity can be measured in a variety of ways but is usually expressed as the volume of output or throughput that the process is capable of handling. The capacity of a conversion process represents a statement of its maximum or designed output or throughput whereas the load of that process represents the current or intended output or throughput. For example, the capacity of an aeroplane may be 109 passengers but its load may only be 75 passengers. The ways in which capacity is expressed for different systems will often reflect the nature of the conversion process or the major capital resource used. For example, a gas or petrol station may express its capacity in terms of the number of petrol or gas pumps it has while a power station will express its capacity in terms of its potential output (megawatts). Similarly a hospital will be seen as a 200-bed hospital and a telephone system as a 20-line system. All of these are direct or indirect expressions of the potential throughput or output of the conversion system.

The size of that capacity and the ways in which it is managed in relation to the ups and downs of demand can have a considerable effect upon the efficiency and effectiveness of the conversion system. Our ability as managers to match the capacity of our conversion systems with the demands that our customers make upon those systems is crucial, both to our customers and to our organizations. Failure to balance capacity with demand can, for example, lead to dissatisfied and frustrated customers or overstocking of unwanted products. This failure will also mean that we are wasting organizational inputs (see Table 5.2)

However, demand will vary and can often be difficult to predict. For example the demand for soft drinks and ice cream rises as temperature and hours of sunshine rise, but neither of these are easy to predict, in the long or medium term, with any accuracy. Consequently, ice cream and soft drink manufacturers have developed products with extended shelf lives or capable of cold storage to buffer against the vagaries of the weather. The capacity of their plant is such that the annual demand can be met by operating at a steady and constant rate throughout the whole year and freezing or storing the product until needed, as well as encouraging non-summer consumption.

The balance between capacity and demand can be achieved in one of two separate ways:

- adjusting the capacity to meet the demand;
- manipulating the demand to meet the capacity.

These options are illustrated in Figure 5.9.

The 'easy' way to compensate for the ups and downs of demand is to hold outcome stock. However, these stocks are:

- not feasible for all conversion processes;
- expensive to both finance and store;
- used to mask or hide the problems present in the conversion process.

Shigeo Shingo[4] draws an analogy between stock levels and the depth of water in a pond. As you reduce the water level (stock), the obstructions and rocks (problems) emerge and can be removed, thus creating an 'entire levelled bottom'. This 'level bottomed pond' does not tie up or waste the water (resources) which flow into it and is also more responsive to changes in demand. Stocks can also cause problems by taking up valuable and expensive floor space which could be used to increase the capacity of the conversion process. They can also put at risk or diminish the quality of the product or service.

As we saw in Table 5.2 stocks are one of the sources of organizational waste and the act of reducing stock levels or inventory *can* be a major step towards improving organizational performance. I say 'can be' because as an act on its own, stock reduction may not increase customer service levels. Lesser stock levels can easily lead to less satisfied customers and longer queues. However, when allied with a continuous effort to improve the conversion process, then stock reduction can enable problems to be identified; and that is the first step towards finding solutions. Schonberger[10] describes how, on the Toyota car production line, the response of Japanese managers to the solution of a production problem was to remove still more stock in order to expose the next problem.

However, exposing the problem is not enough: you have to be able to solve it by identifying and implementing a solution. Part 2 will focus on that issue: the actions and techniques that you will need in order to improve the performance of your organization.

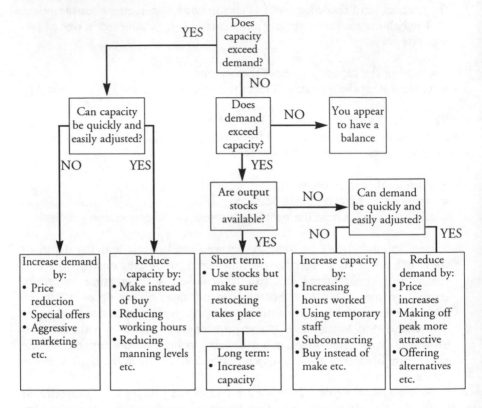

Figure 5.9 Balancing capacity and demand

Summary

The form or structure of the conversion process, together with its layout, arrangement and capacity, are all factors which can significantly influence the organization's potential and actual efficiency, effectiveness and adaptability. These conversion processes are configured, arranged and structured in a variety of ways which are just as applicable to service organizations as they are to those which manufacture our goods and products. These are:

- a project process: concerned with the production of one or a limited number of specialized products;
- a batch process: concerned with the production of a small or medium sized group of standard identical products;

114

- an assembly line process: concerned with the continuous production of standard products.

These forms can also be seen to coexist on the dimensions of:

- standardized–customized outcome dimension;
- low–high direct customer contact dimension.

The ability of these forms to contribute to the performance improvement process reflects their ability to:

- allow and encourage the creativity of those who work within them;
- provide an environment for innovation and change.

There are seven sources of organizational waste which exist in many if not all of our organizations. Some of the ways in which these wastes can be reduced are concerned with:

- the layout or arrangement of capital resources;
- the size and management of the conversion process's output and its relationship to the demand patterns of the customers.

References

[1] Dertouzous, M.L., R.K. Lester, and R.M. Solow, *Made in America: Regaining the Productive Edge*, MIT Press, Massachusetts, 1989.

[2] Rafferty, K., Car plants where the robots sing while assembly lines hum, in *The Guardian*, 21 August 1993.

[3] Womack, J.P, D.T. Jones and D. Roos, *The Machine That Changed The World*, Rawson Associates, New York, 1990.

[4] Shingo, S., *Study of Toyota Production System*, Japanese Management Association, Tokyo, 1981.

[5] Bowen, D., Trading places, in *Independent On Sunday*, 4 July 1993.

[6] Allen, T.J., Communications in the research and development laboratory, in *Technology Review*, Oct–Nov 1967.

[7] Hall, E.T., *The Hidden Dimension*, Doubleday, New York.

[8] Sommer, R., Studies in personal space, in *Sociometry*, vol. 22, 1959, pages 247–260.

[9] Wild, R., *Production and Operations Management*, Cassell, London, 1989.

[10] Schonberger, J. *Japanese Manufacturing Techniques*, The Free Press, New York, 1982.

Part 2
Planning and Implementation

Great cultural changes begin in affectation and end in routine.
Jacques Barzun

The journey of a thousand miles begins with the first step.
Mao Tse-Tung

6. Making it happen

Effective executives do first things first and they do one thing at a time.

Peter Drucker

Introduction

In the first part of this book we looked at the whys and wherefores of the ways in which our organizations can:

- Measure and monitor their performance in terms of efficiency, effectiveness or adaptability;
- Decide their long-term goals and targets;
- Convert or transform the resources they use;
- Describe, control and assure the quality of their products and services;
- Choose and arrange their conversion processes.

All of these concepts and ideas are vital to our understanding of the ways in which our organizations work and interact with the environment. However, despite their importance they are, nevertheless, only concepts and ideas. These concepts and ideas, or 'mindsets', are, by their very nature, abstract, idealized and sometimes simplified models of a portion of the world and the ways in which it works.

The focus of this second part of the book is on that process which enables these ideas and models to be translated into the 'real' world and in so doing enable us to design and undertake the actions which will result in the improvement of the performance of our organizations. As such, it contains chapters about a number of issues and processes which are vital to the construction of the bridge between those concepts and ideas and the reality of achieved performance improvement; chapters about managing change, communication, teams, problem-solving, ways of analysing information and, finally, ways of managing projects, all of which are key issues in the process of improving performance. However, as we noted at the start of the book, it is *your* need to improve, to grow, to do it better, which is a key ingredient in the process which will move these words off the pages to become a concrete reality. That need is still a *must*, a mandatory factor, if we are to make these words leap off the pages and into the 'real' world.

The other vital ingredient in that translation process is the enthusiasm, commitment and creativity of those people who work with you in those organizations. Without their creativity and energy, these models—as powerful and sophisticated as they are—will fail to produce the tangible bottom-line results that we desire. That enthusiasm and creativity will enable our organizations to cope with and exploit the volatile and ever-shifting nature of the environment in which they function. In short, these two vital ingredients will enable the translation of these models from the neat and tidy cloisters and spires of academia into the hard, messy and often harsh reality of our organization's interactions with the 'real' world.

This chapter begins that bridge-building process by:

- Looking at how other people have achieved improved performance;
- Providing a framework from within which we can view this process of performance improvement in later chapters.

However, before we start that journey, it is worth reminding ourselves of the key characteristics of the performance improvement process. As we saw in Chapter 1, a process which is:

- Continuous and ongoing in nature;
- Focused on measurable results;
- Concerned with results *now*, rather than tomorrow;
- About using success to build further success.

Also, if it is to provide sustained and continuing results for our organizations, it is not a top-down, enforced process but one which relies upon and grows from the efforts and creativity of those people who are those organizations. We have also seen that successful performance improvement programmes are fuelled by the gap between:

- Where we want to be,
- Where we are now.

and we also noted that these programmes start by measuring and monitoring key factors in the relationship between the organization and its environment. So, let's first take a look at how it has been done.

Democracy and the workplace
Ricardo Semler took over the management of Semco, in São Paulo, Brazil, in 1980 when most of its business was in marine products such as pumps, water/oil separators, etc. By 1993[1] Semco had diversified its product range into dishwashers, mixers, cooling units and even biscuit factories. In the

same period it had increased its productivity sevenfold, its profits fivefold and achieved exports equivalent to almost a quarter of its turnover. All of this was achieved despite the chaos and hyperinflation prevalent in Brazil's national economy at that time. But it is not these achievements which draw managers from Ford, GM, Bayer, Goodyear, Pirelli, Mercedes-Benz and many, many other multinationals to visit this small company. What does draw them is Semler's bold and successful experiment in industrial democracy which is embodied in a simple truth: 'A company should trust its destiny to its employees.'

In Semco this trust means, for example, that employees can[2]:

• Paint the walls whatever colour they like
• Co-ordinate their own work hours with their co-workers
• Wear whatever clothing makes them comfortable.

They also interview all potential employees, publicly grade the performance of their managers every 6 months and have a target of extending the 25 per cent of employees who set their own pay rate to 100 per cent. Each of these employees has a vote on important decisions such as take-overs, major new contracts or plant relocation.

This process of democratization has involved cutting nine levels out the corporate organization chart and creating a 'circular' structure which, for example, involves the rotation of the CEO role between six 'counsellors'. Role titles have been reduced to those of:

• Counsellors who co-ordinate policy and strategy;
• Partners who run business units;
• Co-ordinators who are first level management;
• Associates who are everybody else.

Production equipment is arranged so that multiskilled teams can assemble a complete product—rather than add an item or part of that product as on an assembly line. Offices are free from the usual status symbols, and perks and the division of profit sharing remuneration (usually about 25 per cent of profits) are decided by employees.

There can be little doubt about the success of this unique experiment which, as Semler writes[1], succeeds because of its answer to the 'most difficult of all challenges': that of how to get people to 'look forward to coming to work in the morning'. There can also be little doubt that this success is based upon Semler's vision of Semco as a team with shared values and responsibility; he writes of 'our company' and decisions that 'we share', despite the fact that he is still the majority shareholder. It is also evident that the change process involved a great deal of hard work, discussion, mistakes and false starts. Its results spring from the willingness of Semler and his fellow managers to let go of their power and to share this with their fellow employees: a heady and ambitious step which is not without its risks. For those who work at Semco, however, that risk has paid off.

Work-outs

The current CEO of General Electric, Jack Welch, is said[3] to have an ambition to increase his company's productivity, each and every year, by 6 per cent. One of the ways which Welch aims to do that is to tap into and use the creativity of his employees. He does this by means of the 'work-out' session. These sessions, which aim to encourage the voluntary involvement of employees, are gradually penetrating down through the company hierarchy. Their objectives are:

- The systematic identification of factors which have limited efficiency and effectiveness in the past;
- The identification of ways of overcoming these factors.

They have been applied to a wide variety of these factors ranging from general issues through to specific detailed problems.

Richard Pascale[3] describes the stages of the 'work-out' process as follows:

1. Describing the vision for the future for the company or business unit. This is done in order to remind people:
   (i)   Where they are now going.
   (ii) That solving 'problems' will help them to get there.
2. Work-out team members are then asked to estimate what the result, in terms of increased efficiency, would be if the 'problems' were removed. This is said to usually generate a consensus view of the order of 40 per cent!
3. The 'problems' are then identified. This involves:
   (i)   Generating lists of all wasteful work practices.
   (ii) Grouping like with like.
4. These 'problems' or groups of 'problems' are reviewed. This involves making decisions about:
   (i)   What are we trying to accomplish?
   (ii) Who needs to be involved to do that?
   (iii) What resources are needed to do that?
5. Members then split into functional groups and review their own work. This also involves decisions about:
   (i)   What could be done better?

(ii) By how much?

(iii) Who needs to be involved to do that?

(iv) What resources are needed to do that?

6. Mixed cross-functional groups are now generated in order to review their co-operative efforts. This involves identifying activities or procedures which either:

(i) hinder teamwork, or

(ii) help teamwork.

7. Contracts and action plans are then generated. These involve specific targets and commitments made by functional areas to the whole of the work-out group.

8. Feedback to the whole group takes place within 8 weeks. This involves each function making specific proposals for the elimination of identified 'problems'. These proposals are accepted or rejected by the business unit senior manager who chairs this session.

The 'work-out' session is seen as a way of:

- Clearing out the old accumulated bad habits and practices which have built up over the years;
- Establishing a regular and frequent dialogue between managers and their people.

Welch is reported[4] to have said that he wants to get to the point where employees challenge their bosses 'every day' about wasteful and inefficient practices.

Sausage or banana skins?

Another powerful story of employee empowerment comes from Johnsonville Foods, a sausage manufacturer in Wisconsin, USA. Starting in 1980, Ralph Stayer, CEO of this family-owned company, transformed the organization from a top-down family-managed hierarchy with a $7 million annual revenue to an organization in which the self-managed team is king with an annual revenue of around $130 million in 1991.

So how did this happen? Stayer's remarkably honest description[5] of the process tells us that the transformation was not without its mistakes. This started from a vision of an organization in which: 'people took responsibility for their own work, for the product, for the company as a whole', and Stayer's intial attempts to achieve this, by delegation of power, failed. The change, from authoritarian control to what Stayer himself described as 'authoritarian abdication' was too demanding a change.

123

However, from this initial failure, which cost him all three of his top managers, Stayer recognized:

- His own need to control;
- That you cannot give responsibility to people: they have to want, need, even demand it.

As a result, Stayer began to change the 'environment' of his organization by changing two of its key aspects. These were:

- Systems,
- Structures.

Stayer gives an example of his attack upon the systems of his organization by his approach to quality control. In the past, quality had not been managed but had been measured by a traditional quality control function. Top management had, several times a week, aided and abetted this measurement process by checking the product for colour, flavour, taste and appearance. Stayer broke away from this by telling line workers that it was now their responsibility to ensure that only top quality product got to the customers. One of the changes that this led to was that the people who made the sausage *started* tasting it and the top management *stopped* tasting it. This also led to the formation of teams aimed at solving quality problems. These teams gathered data, identified problems, talked to suppliers and even visited customers. These were not management led or driven teams but teams consisting of people who manned machines, drove fork-lift trucks and made sausages. In short, teams of people who were not biased or influenced by management education but people who were paid for working with their hands, not their brains. The success of these quality teams led to reject levels falling from 5 to 0.5 per cent and to the spread of the team concept into areas which had previously been the sole prerogative of management. These included efficiency, costs and performance. With Stayer's support and encouragement, these teams expanded their influence until they were, astonishingly, responsible for:

- Recruiting, hiring and firing,
- Cost control and budgeting,
- Quality assurance,
- Capital investment proposals,
- Training,
- Setting and monitoring performance standards.

One of the astonishing aspects of this list of worker team activities is that it exceeds the responsibilities of many middle manager roles. Given the magnitude of these changes, it is perhaps not surprising to find that, in parallel with these team developments, the structure of the organization began to change. Stayer introduced a number of changes which meant that teams took over a number of the functions previously undertaken by managers and, as a result, the number of organizational levels fell from six to three. Departments which radically changed their function or disappeared were:

- Quality control, which took on a technical support role;
- Personnel, which was replaced by a learning and personal development team.

These changes mean that Johnsonville Foods has broken away from the old traditional top-down management controlled system and made major strides along the road to what others[6,7] have called a 'learning organization'. This change is even evident in the job titles used:

Old title	New title
Employee or subordinate	Member
Manager	Co-ordinator or coach.

Stayer identifies the three major lessons of this change process as:

1. Don't wait until you have all the answers: just start.
2. Start at the most visible system: it signals your intent to all.
3. Change will occur in fits and starts, and you can't control it.

The Johnsonville teams now also make major contributions to strategic decisions about the company's future! Stayer himself recognizes that getting improved performance from any group of people, however big or small, means changing the way in which you relate to and with that group.

Body or Buddy Shop?
In 1976, Anita Roddick opened a small shop in the English coastal resort town of Brighton. This shop sold a limited range of cosmetics made from natural ingredients and packaged in five different sizes of cheap plastic containers. By the early 1990s, this humble beginning had grown to a chain of over 1000 shops trading in 42 countries. This Body Shop chain, unusually for a cosmetics business, also:

125

- Employs its own anthropologist;
- Recycles its own plastic waste;
- Employs very few people with formal business training.

So how and why did all of this happen? At least a part of the answer to that question lies with Anita Roddick's personal vision which is expressed,[8] with undoubted passion and commitment, in statements such as:

'Business can be fun, it can be conducted with love and a powerful force for good.'

'I think all business practices would improve immeasurably if they were guided by 'feminine' principles—qualities like love and care and intuition.'

This vision also extends beyond the boundaries of the Body Shop chain embracing environmental and social issues such the destruction of the Amazonian rain forest and orphanages in Romania. Exciting and stimulating as this very different approach to the role of business is, to do it full justice is beyond the scope of this book. Those of you who share my excitement about this caring view of business should read Anita's own version[8] of how the chain developed.

Of interest to us at this point in our journey is a glimpse of how the people of the Body Shop organization are involved in that process of growth. It is evident that the founder's enthusiasm about the business also extends to and includes the people who are that business. They are described as 'family'—despite the size of the chain—and communication within this family is seen as a major contributor to the success of the chain. This communication is not just one way as staff are expected to question and challenge the standards and assumptions of the management and to generate new ideas about how to do it. The DODGI—Department of Damned Good Ideas—is one example of the mechanisms used to encourage this challenging feedback as is the view that those who question are those who will also push the organization ahead.

The language of the Body Shop is the language of passion, commitment, and above all, of people. This 'people' language is about partnership and empowerment, a state of being which is described[9] as: 'taking responsibility into your own hands, deciding upon the quality of your own experience'.

Nor is the expression of this vision limited to rhetoric with the creation of a factory in Glasgow with 25 per cent of its profits donated to a charitable trust and international job swaps among shops in different countries being current organizational outcomes. Despite the fact that many Body Shop staff are, or work for, franchise holders, there can be little doubt about an impressively high level of commitment to the ideas or vision of the organization. What is also impressive is the power and intensity of Anita Roddick's personal belief that empowered people can 'move mountains' and the very real and tangible results of that belief. Her visits to these outlets are reported[9] to be surprise visits with the aim of 'keeping close to staff'. She shares this characteristic with Ingvar Kamprad, founder of the 111-store IKEA furniture chain, and during these visits, like Kamprad, she talks and listens to her staff.

Keys to success?

What we have seen in these, all-too-brief, glimpses of very different organizations are four different ways of making it happen. However, despite their differences in size, geography, history and product or service, the approaches adopted by these organizations have a number of features in common.

1. An overarching vision of where or what they want to be which is communicated to all in the organization.
2. A leader who wants to work in partnership with the people of that organization.
3. The commitment and enthusiasm of those people.
4. The use of teams to focus that commitment and enthusiasm.
5. A track record of very real success and achievement.

In every case, these successes and achievements are not, as the theorists would say, 'a transitory phenomenon': they are the real and tangible results of years of hard work. Whether these achievements will continue to persist and to grow will depend, as we saw in Chapters 2 and 4, upon the continuing ability of these organizations to stay close to and in touch with the real needs of their customers. The next step in our journey is to see if we can build on those features and create a model or pattern of 'a way of doing it' that can and will enable our organizations to start and continue the process of enhancing their performance.

Building blocks to success

As we have seen in earlier chapters, there is an enormous range of views and comment about how to make performance improvement happen. These views range from the generalized to the specific and from the abstract to the pragmatic. This section of this chapter will harvest the best features of these views and collate them in an understandable form that will provide the steps to lead you towards improved performance. The criteria used in choosing this harvest were:

- Practicality,
- Realism,
- Demonstrated success.

That is not, however, to claim that these are the *only* steps that lead to improved performance but merely that these are the steps which are common to several views about what constitutes a successful programme of performance improvement. However, these building blocks which together form the bridge which spans from theory to effective practice have all been tempered in the furnace of experience. One way of viewing these 'building bricks' is to group them under the headings of:

- Preparing,
- Measuring and monitoring,
- Identifying and choosing,
- Implementing actions.

and this is what we shall do.

Preparing

STEP 1: IDENTIFY YOUR TARGET
When we prepare ourselves for the process of improving organizational performance our first step is that of choosing our goals or targets. As we saw in Chapter 2, these often arise from a vision of where we want to be in the long term and can be the result of a consensus of stakeholder views. We also saw earlier in this chapter that these targets can arise from a personal and individual vision or set of values. Whatever their origins, source or nature, they are the starting point of the performance improvement process.

As such these goals or targets may be, initially at least, expressed in general and diffuse terms. For example:

'To be the dominant supplier of health and fitness care in the South West.'

That, however, is not sufficient for our purposes. These goals and targets must be:

- Specific,
- Attainable,
- Quantified.

These general goals and targets can also generate or lead to subgoals/targets. For example, the overall goal of a fitness clinic might be:

'To increase revenue by 20 per cent within 6 months.'

Its subgoals/targets might include:

'To increase the proportion of clients who successfully complete weight reduction programmes from 60 to 80 per cent within 6 months.'

or

'To increase the proportion of clients who use fitness training facilities more than twice per month from 25 to 35 within 6 months.'

We met these hierarchies of objectives in Chapter 2 (Figure 2.3) and the key to their use, at this stage of the performance improvement process, is that they should:

- Have their relative priorities agreed;
- Be understood by everyone involved.

This process of prioritization will reflect and take account of the nature of the dominant conversion process which we discussed in Chapter 3. Failure to prioritize will only lead to confusion and limit the success of your efforts.

STEP 2: FIND AND CHOOSE YOUR CRITICAL PERFORMANCE FACTORS
In order to complete this step in a manner which enhances our ability to improve the performance of our organizations we have to decide:

- What we are going to measure;
- Where we are going to measure it;
- When we are going to measure it.

Each of these will be considered in turn.

What
We identified and illustrated, in Chapter 1, the different ways in which efficiency, effectiveness and adaptability can be used to measure and monitor both the health and the potential for performance improvement of an organization. Efficiency, as we saw, is concerned with resource utilization

while effectiveness is concerned with measuring if the product or service is where the customers want it, when they want it. We also saw that adaptability is concerned with the ability of the organization to adapt to unusual, different or non-standard requests for product or service. Examples of these different ways of measuring performance, for an estate agent, would be:

- *Efficiency*: Number of potential client contacts per day.
- *Effectiveness*: Average fee revenue per contact or per cent conversion of contacts to sales.
- *Adaptability*: Per cent of non-conversion to sales because 'you haven't got what we want'.

Simple but effective techniques to help you to analyse your information and choose the right critical performance factors are described in Chapter 11 and bench-marking (Chapter 2) also gives guidance about not only the nature of these key factors but their desired levels.

Whatever is chosen to measure and monitor the performance of the organization it must be:

- Linked to the prioritized targets;
- Credible as a measure;
- Quick, easy and inexpensive to measure;
- A measure which motivates people to perform better and to go on improving.

These organizational 'pulse points' are key factors in the process of improving organizational performance. It is as if the organizational improvement process's version of our computer's *WSYIWIG: What you see is what you get* becomes

WYMIWYI: *What You Measure Is What You Improve*

Where
Where we measure these parameters and factors will make a significant difference to the quality of the feedback that they provide. As we saw in Chapter 3, this feedback is generally triggered by a measurement of outcomes (Figure 3.7) but can also be triggered by the measurement of inputs to the conversion process (Figure 3.8).

The proximity of our measurement to the conversion process can affect not only the timeliness of our subsequent actions but also their relevance, quality and effect. These measurements need to be close to the activity involved. This proximity gives us the opportunity to 'damp' the effects before they spread throughout the organization. It also means that the feedback, to those involved in the activity, will be direct and timely. For example, managing the electricity usage of a particular department or section would be difficult if the meter recorded the usage for the whole organization. A meter for that department would give direct and accessible feedback which can be related directly to actions taken. Quality guru Shigeo Shingo recommends[10], in the context of TQM, that measurement should take place:

• upstream;
• as close to the source of a defect as is possible.

In the context of improving organizational performance this piece of wisdom tells us to measure as close to the dominant conversion process as we can.

When
The frequency at which we take our measurements can also influence the quality and effectiveness of our consequent actions. As we saw in Chapter 3, too high a lag or too long a time between detection and corrective action or cause and effect, can cause undesired outcomes to continue and increase. On the other hand, too short a time or too rapid a response can create instability or 'hunting' and 'cycling'. However, these responses will both only occur when we have:

• decided what to do, and then
• implemented that decision.

The step of measuring and monitoring is a preparation for or precursor to those actions and, whatever the nature and speed of the consequent 'corrective' action, we do need to make sure that the information that is measured is:

• timely;
• measured at a frequency which reflects the rate of change of the environment itself.

For example, in the situation which we looked at earlier, there would be little value in measuring the department's electricity usage on a weekly basis when the usage on a Tuesday is 50 per cent higher than any other day. We would, of course, only find that out (and be able to do anything about it) if we measured on a daily basis.

Once we have chosen our target and decided the what, where and when of

131

our critical performance factors, we have completed our preparation. We are now ready to move to the next stage, that of measuring and monitoring.

Measuring and monitoring

STEP 3: IDENTIFYING THE MEASURER

The traditional ways that were used to measure and monitor both the health and the improvement capability of an organization were, as we saw in Chapter 1, often concerned with money measures. Simple examples of these include Return on Investment (ROI), Payback period and Discounted Cash Flow (DCF). Important as they are, these measures, and those who create them, are remote from both the customers and their needs and those who either interact with that customer or create the product which the customer desires. One of the major steps in the movement from quality control systems towards the TQM approach (see Chapter 4) is the acceptance that those who do it can also measure and monitor how well they are doing it. This shift to 'self-inspection', which we saw acting so effectively at Johnsonville Foods (see p. 123), is one which involves:

- Trust:
  - you have to trust that they will do it and do it when it needs doing;
- Training
  - you have to show them how to do it;
- Self-empowerment
  - they decide what to do about it and may even decide what to measure.

This principle of 'self-inspection' must be applied to the factors that we measure in our quest for organizational performance improvement. Those who measure should be those who also do and this process of 'self-inspection' should be formally recognized in role descriptions, training and time usage. Not only should these 'doers' measure but they should also monitor, and Chapter 11 identifies simple techniques such as Moving Average and CUSUM which can make a considerable contribution to the process of monitoring.

Once we have our measuring and monitoring systems set up and running, we then have to start to do something with the information produced. Before we move on to look at how we do that, let's take time to look at the overall process of performance improvement. This is illustrated in Figure 6.1 which shows how the difference between the current and desired situations is used to drive the cycle of performance improvement. As we can see this cycle involves:

- Starting from the measurement of the difference between our current and our desired position;
- Identifying the causes of this difference;
- Looking at options for doing something about it;
- Selecting one for trial or test;
- Reviewing the results of that trial and modifying the option as required.
- Implementing that action.

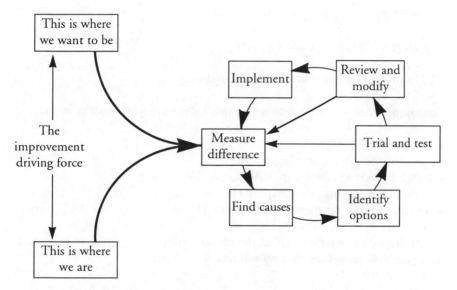

Figure 6.1   The performance improvement cycle

What we will now look at is how we identify the causes and the subsequent options and then choose the action that we wish to put on trial or test.

Identifying and choosing

STEP 4: IDENTIFY CAUSES

The cycle of interacting cause and effect is one that is well represented in many aspects of all our cultures. It is present in our religions, our sciences and in our political systems. In our application of this principle to the performance improvement process we have, so far, seen how we can measure and monitor the effect—what we are now concerned with is the identification of its cause.

This can be undertaken by either teams or individuals and by rigorous analysis or by less rigorous, but just as effective, 'creative' methods. However this is done, the objective should be the identification of the origin of the effect rather than the identification of a growing group or family of further associated symptoms or effects. This can require patience and time but it isn't necessary to know everything. As Johnsonville Foods CEO Ralph Stayer tells us[5]:

'Don't wait until you have all the answers'

and Shigeo Shingo[10] counsels that we:

'Don't delay improvement by overanalysing'

Techniques that we can use to speed this causal analysis process include:

- Pareto (see Chapter 11)
- Ishikawa diagram (see Chapter 10)
- Lateral thinking (see Chapter 10).
- Influence diagrams (see Chapter 11)
- Multiple Cause diagrams (see Chapter 11)

All of these can be used to effect the identification of the cause of the effect that you have measured and monitored.

STEP 5: IDENTIFY OPTIONS

At this stage in the performance improvement process, we are faced with the fact that, having identified the cause of the difference between our desired and current states, we now have to identify the options for what *might* be done about that cause. These options can be identified by using groups of people or by the efforts of individuals and can use logical rigorous analysis or other, perhaps more creative, methods.

One important factor in the success of this step is the realization that we are not facing a problem but, rather, we are being presented with an opportunity. This opportunity for change can enable us to create new ways of doing things and to discard the accumulation of bad habits that often blocks our route through to real and continuing enhanced efficiency, effectiveness and adaptability. It is important , however, that we do not limit this step, or indeed the overall process of performance improvement, to an incremental 'crawl' which inches its way along the path from organizational cradle to coffin. If we are going to find those efficient, effective and adaptable and sometimes revolutionary options then we have to cast off and break out of the old ways of both seeing and thinking about the operations of our organizations. Several ways of doing this are described in Chapter 10 and include:

- Brainstorming,
- Nominal Group Technique,
- Visioning.

When this is done we will arrive at a list of options or choices for our future actions. What we must now decide is which option we are to take.

STEP 6: CHOOSE
Once we have identified our options then we have to choose the one(s) which we are to implement, albeit only on a trial basis. The wisdom of Shigeo Shingo[10] tells us to 'think smart and think small' and thus choose, for implementation, those options which are:

- Simplest,
- Most efficient,
- Most economical.

Our own wisdom would suggest that we add, to that list, the criteria of:

- Most easily understood by others.
- Have most support from others.

Often the option which you see and enthusiastically present as the most elegant and simplest of options can also be seen, by others, to be a machiavellian plot to overthrow the whole basis of Western civilization. Communication is important throughout the whole of the performance improvement process but never more so than at this step. You have to sell your ideas and be able to listen to the comments and reactions of others: failure to do this will guarantee the failure of your favourite option. The importance of this apparently mundane process of communication is discussed in further detail in Chapter 8. We can also evaluate our options by numerate methods as, for example, by use of a Decision Tree (Chapter 11).

Whichever method is used to arrive at the chosen option, if that option is to succeed, it must have included the views of those who will be involved in:

- Implementation,
- Use.

What we now have to do is to begin the process of implementing the actions required to lead us to our goal or target.

Implementing actions

STEP 7: TEST AND TRAIL

The Russian revolutionary, Lenin, wrote that both nations and people generally took 'one step forward and two steps back' in their search for improvement. In our search for improved organizational performance we shall start by taking a small step forward. This small step shall be a trial or test of our chosen option. However, if this trial or test is to succeed then it must also:

- Provide a way for tapping into the creativity and support of those who work in and for the organization
- Create a visible statement of intent;
- Find and use the best way of managing the chosen change for that organization.

As such, this trial or test needs to be:

- Chosen with thought and care;
- Planned with care;
- Monitored.

We also need to be aware that this test or trial is, in the eyes of others, a change. That change can be seen as a challenge or as a threat and the successful management of change needs and demands different skills and abilities to those that we use in our day to day 'steady state' management roles and situations. These skills and abilities are examined in more detail in the next chapter but at this point in our journey we do need to take note of the fact that:

- People react in different ways to change;
- In order to manage change with success you need to:
  - involve all those who are affected by the change;
  - communicate with all those who are affected by the change and others who are not;
  - use teams to achieve the change.

As we noted earlier, the planning of this trial or test needs to be conducted with care and attention. An effective plan, as we will see in Chapter 12, is not a straightjacket or prison but a tool which is:

- Capable of accepting changes at all levels of detail;
- Clear and specific in its content;
- Easily understood by all who use or see it.

Such a plan will also provide:

- A common understanding of the project for all those involved;
- A basis for co-operative effort;
- A starting point from which the project can be monitored.

The contribution of the team to many aspects of organizational performance is considerable and there are few situations to which it will not be able to make a positive contribution. But teams do require support and the freedom and time to develop to their full potential. Their members will also need training and those in the organization around the team will need to understand the purpose and process of the team. These and other aspects of teams are explored in Chapter 9.

STEP 8: REVIEW AND MODIFY

If we are to manage this change we need to monitor its progress towards our goals or targets. This monitoring will have two phases:

1. The active and continuing monitoring which occurs during the trial itself.
2. A review which will take place after the trial is complete or has run for an adequate period of time.

The purposes of these phases are different. Phase 1 is about navigation or tactics. It takes place only while the trial is underway and provides information which enables us to manage or guide the progress of the trial. Phase 2 takes place after the trial or test and is concerned with such issues as:

- Did we achieve our targets?
- If not, why not?
- Did we have the right type and quantity of resources?

Both of these monitoring phases will provide us with the information that we need to review the option that we have trialled, and to decide if and how it needs to be changed. These changes can come about not only because of the performance of the option but also because of people's views about and reactions to that option. As we must keep reminding ourselves, to be successful the performance improvement programme must involve those who do as well as those who manage.

STEP 9: IMPLEMENT

As a result of this review we will have decided one of the following:

- That we want to implement a large-scale version of the option together with when and how we wish to do it;
- That we wish to modify and re-trial the option;
- That we wish to trial another option.

The second and third of these options require us to go back to Steps 7 and 6 respectively, to either set up and run another trial or to choose another option for trial. If, however, we have decided to move forward to the implementation of a large scale version of our trialled option, either in its original or a modified form, then we need to remind ourselves of the issues we noted in Step 7. These were that this implementation step needs to be:

- Planned, and
- Monitored.

The plan and its implementation needs to take account of people's:

- Differing reactions to change
- Need to be:
  - involved,
  - communicated with.

It will also be seen that teams whose membership reflects the structure of the organization and the skill demands of the task will make substantial contributions to the planning and implementation of this step.

As we have seen in this description of the building blocks which together create the process of successful organizational performance improvement, that process will only achieve its end points or targets by the thoughtful and careful application of a number of key topics and processes. The first of these, the management of change, is examined in the Chapter 7.

Summary
People are key to the ways in which we make our improved organizational performance happen. Their skills and abilities are essential to the ways in which we:

- Design,
- Generate,
- Undertake the changes that lead to improved performance.

Reviews of different organizations with records of successful performance improvement programmes indicate the common factors of:

- An overarching vision of where or what they want to be which is communicated to all in the organization;
- A leader who wants to work in partnership with the people of that organization;
- The commitment and enthusiasm of those people;
- The use of teams to focus that commitment and enthusiasm.

The building blocks of a successful performance improvement programme are:

- Preparing:
  - Step 1: identify your target;
  - Step 2: find and choose your critical performance factors and decide: *what* is going to be measured, *where* it is going to be measured, *when* it is going to be measured.
- Measuring and monitoring:
  - Step 3: identify the measurer.
- Identifying and choosing:
  - Step 4: identify causes;
  - Step 5: identify options;
  - Step 6: choose.
- Implementing actions:
  - Step 7: test and trial;
  - Step 8: review and modify;
  - Step 9: implement.

References
[1] Semler, R., *Maverick!: The Success Story Behind the World's Most Unusual Workplace*, Century, London, 1993.

[2] Semler, R., Managing without managers, in *Harvard Business Review*, vol. 67, no. 5, 1989.

[3] Pascale, R., *Managing on the Edge*, Penguin, London, 1990.

[4] Tichy, N. and R. Charan, Speed, simplicity and self confidence: an interview with Jack Welch, in *Harvard Business Review*, vol. 67, no. 5, 1989.

[5] Stayer, R., How I learned to let my workers lead, in *Harvard Business Review*, vol. 68, no. 6, 1990.

[6] Senge, P., *The Fifth Discipline*, Century Business, London, 1990.

[7] Pedler, M., J. Burgoyne, and T. Boydell, *The Learning Company*, McGraw-Hill, Maidenhead, 1991.

[8] Roddick, A., *Body and Soul*, Ebury Press, London, 1991.

[9] Goldhill, J., May the sales force be with you, in *Times Saturday Review*, 28 Sept. 1991.

[10] Dyer, C., 'On-line quality: Shigeo Shingo's shop floor,' in *Harvard Business Review*, vol. 68, no. 1, 1990.

7. Managing change

Change is the process by which the future invades our lives.

Alvin Toffler

Introduction

Change is not a new phenomenon: it has been a part of our lives and our organizations for a long time. The environment in which our organizations come to life, grow, mature and die is one which has never been quiescent, static or stagnant. As early as 2000 BC, the Chinese I Ching or *Book of Changes* struggled to give form and meaning to the process of change and around 500 BC, the Greek philosopher Heraclitus, reflecting upon this process, observed that 'everything flows and nothing stays still'. This theme of constant and ongoing change has continued to be a subject of comment and interest into modern times with views including Bob Dylan's 'the times they are a'changin' and Harold Macmillan's reference to the 'wind of change' which he saw blowing through Africa in the early 1960s. We need only look to the more recent changes in what used to be called the USSR and those that have taken place in the communist states of Eastern Europe to have the presence of change confirmed for our own times.

However, what is new is that:

- The rate at which that change occurs has increased;
- The magnitude of those changes are also increasing.

This accelerating process, which Alvin Toffler[1] calls 'the roaring current of change', is affecting our values, our families, the places where we work, the jobs that we do and many other aspects of our lives, as well as creating a volatile and sometimes bizarre environment for us to work and play in. An example of the increasing pace of this change for one aspect of technology is shown in Table 7.1. The increasing magnitude of these changes is illustrated by John Scully who comments[2] that we are experiencing a 'change of an entire economic system' and that the old centralized, mass producing and large-scale organizations are giving way to systems built around 'decentralization, customization and the critical judgement skills of workers who are empowered'.

In order to survive in this 'brave new world', both we, as individuals, and our organizations will need to be able to change ourselves. However, it is not

141

enough to be reactive and to be driven by these winds and currents of change. We have to be able to sense the changing currents and be able to read the volatility and turbulence of the technical, economic, social and political climates. As we saw in Chapter 2, the visions, goals and targets of our organizations need to reflect and grow from a comprehensive understanding of all these aspects of this volatile and changing environment.

Table 7.1   The accelerating rate of computing

4000 BC	Pictograms used to record herds of cattle and stocks of grain
2000 BC	Abacus invented
760 BC	Arabian use of Indian numerals and development of algebra and trigonometry
1632 AD	Slide rule invented
1642 AD	Pascal adding machine
1694 AD	Leibnitz calculating machine
1793 AD	Decimal system introduced in France
1812 AD	Babbage's steam driven computer
1890 AD	Hollerith tabulating machine
1946 AD	First electronic digital computer
1948 AD	Invention of Transistor
1951 AD	UNIVAC 1 operational
1960 AD	First tape drive
1964 AD	BASIC language invented
1975 AD	First personal computer
1989 AD	Virtual reality
1990 AD	Commercial handwriting recognition software
1996 AD	Voice recognition? The computer on your wrist?

This environment is one that we can no longer rely upon to be predictable and safe, and as a consequence we must, as Tom Peters[3] tells us, learn that 'loving change, tumult, even chaos is a prerequisite for survival'. And yet, because we often find change threatening, unfamiliar and disturbing, we try to avoid or even ignore it by assuming that it will not happen, despite all of the evidence to the contrary. The Hudson Institute's Leon Martel[4] describes this as acting 'on a basis of continuity'. That is we assume, when we plan for the future, that the present will continue: and of course it rarely does!

The process of improving organizational performance is, of course, a change-creating process in itself. We have seen, in earlier chapters, how this process can enable us to monitor the interactions between our organizations and currents and patterns of change present in the environment. We also saw how this enables us to develop, with other stakeholders, our vision of a future 'state of being' for our organization. This chapter looks at that process of change and, in so doing, examines the dimensions or characteristics of change itself, our reactions to it, the ways in which the change process can be managed. and its relationship to the process of improving organizational performance.

What is this thing called change?

A typical dictionary defines the noun change as 'the substitution of one thing for another', 'alteration' or 'variation' and the verb to change as 'to alter' or 'make different'. This process of alteration or variation is a very common one but one which can, nevertheless, have a significant affect upon our lives. For example, the changes in climate that we experience throughout the year make a considerable difference to our energy needs, the clothes that we wear, the sports we play or watch and the amount of time that we spend outdoors. In another example, we know that the composition of the elected bodies who govern us can often change as a result of an election. This can affect the tax we pay, the freedom we have to write or speak freely and many other aspects of our social and economic systems. These and other changes may be large, as when we change our jobs or our partners, or they may be small, as when we wear jeans to work instead of a suit. Sometimes we choose the changes we are exposed to and at other times we have no choice in either when they occur or what are their nature and contents.

One way of looking at two of the dimensions of change is illustrated in Figure 7.1. This shows us that change can be:

- Voluntary or involuntary,

and can have an origin or source which is:

- Internal or external.

A voluntary change is one that we undertake freely and willingly and without compulsion and one example of this might be the change in our holiday plans that results from our winning a large prize on the football pools or from a lottery. An involuntary change is, however, not undertaken from choice and is forced upon us by others. An example of this type of change might be the change in our holiday plans that results from a strike of airline employees or air traffic controllers.

The source or origin of these changes can also make a difference to the ways in which we react to or cope with them. Examples of externally

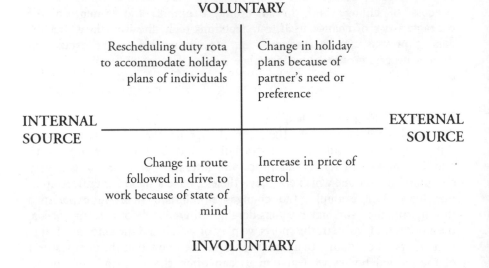

Figure 7.1 Dimensions of change

sourced changes include the changes in the price of petrol and other oil-based fuels and income tax that have become a part of our lives. These are also involuntary changes—we have little choice about whether or not we accept them—whereas a change in our plans for a summer evening which results from an invitation to a neighbour's barbecue is an example of a voluntary but also externally sourced and welcome change. For some of us, an externally sourced and involuntary change is one that we will resist and fight, irrespective of its nature and value, because of the absence of our freedom of choice. Indeed, wise and experienced change managers will be aware of and take account of this characteristic as we shall see later. Internally sourced changes are those which occur, for us as individuals, because of what we think or feel and can be our chosen reactions to both the pleasant and unpleasant features of the environment in which we work and play. For example, if we have previously been treated with inattention or discourtesy in a particular shop, then we will choose not to repeat that experience and shop elsewhere. In the context of our organizations, examples of internal changes include reorganizations or different ways of doing things. These can come about as the result of our plans and targets for the future. The process of organizational performance improvement is one example of a change which can be internally sourced as, for example, when we change the ways in which work is done. We do need, however, to be aware that while these internal organizational changes are voluntary for some members of those organizations, there will always be others who perceive them to be involuntary changes, and will resist and fight.

Another view of the change process is one which relates the changes undertaken to their influence upon the conversion processes which exist in all organizations. As we saw in Chapter 3, these processes exist within all our organizations and are concerned with the transformation of resources into products or services. Using this input–transformation–output model, we can classify changes on the basis of their influence and action upon:

- Inputs: examples of these changes, which are sometimes described as 'upstream' changes, are:
  - changes in workforce composition,
  - introduction of new technology,
  - change in cost of materials.
- Outputs: examples of these changes, which are sometimes called 'downstream' changes, are:
  - changes in customer expectations,
  - changes in consumer legislation,
  - up- or downswings in patterns of general business or economic activity.

Our knowledge of some of the changes that we experience tells us that they can involve patterns or cycles of upward and downward change and can also involve regular returns to their starting point. These are described[4] as cyclical changes. The weather and, it is said, economic growth rates are both examples of cyclical changes. This type of change is often:

- Short-lived,
- Limited in length, term or season,
- Recurrent and periodic in nature.

The responses that this type of change requires from us are often temporary and superficial in nature because we know that the change will, in its turn, change again and in time, return to its original starting point. All that we need to do is to go with or accommodate these temporary upswings or downswings as we would when riding an ocean wave.

Other changes, however, involve a more fundamental alteration or shift. These are called structural changes and are:

- Irreversible,
- Permanent in nature.

Examples of massive structural changes which were or are being experienced by all organizations include the Industrial Revolution, which occurred in the late 19th century, and the Information Revolution which we are currently experiencing. These structural changes are, by their nature, deeper, more fundamental and longer lasting than the cyclic changes. Our responses to structural change must reflect these differences and must, in their turn, be long-lasting and more durable than our responses to cyclic change.

Whatever the nature of the change, the key to successful change management lies within the way that we respond or react to that change.

Crisis or opportunity?

One of the common beliefs about change is that it only occurs when there is a crisis. It is argued that it is at these times that we, and our organizations, can most easily undertake radical shifts in our attitudes and beliefs. While there can be little doubt that threats which we see as endangering our survival are potent stimuli for change and action, research[5] on the causes of organizational change indicates that less than half of these changes are triggered by crises such as financial losses or loss of market share. The majority were proactive changes—shifts or moves such as developing market opportunities or embracing new technology—and were undertaken in order to create something new. When we look at the ways in which we behave as individuals we can also find examples of this passion to embrace change. We look for new products to buy in our shops, we take our holidays in countries that we have never visited before and we read books by authors who are new to us. We will also often, from choice, expose ourselves to social situations in which we will meet new people in new places.

Yet there are also circumstances in which our response to change is not positive and proactive. Many of these involve change which we find threatening and difficult and which we resist, often with considerable energy. The variety of ways in which we can display this resistance is also considerable ranging from feigned or real indifference through 'working to rule' to active sabotage. So why is this so and what are the characteristics or features of a change situation which make us embrace it instead of resisting or fighting it?

Reactions to change

Before we consider why our reactions to change differ it is important to note that these are often complex and often mixed. Rarely do we, and hence also rarely do our organizations, have a clear cut and polarized reaction to change. For example, we often feel excitement at the prospect of something new and unknown and yet, at the same time, we feel anxiety about losing what we have or the risk of failure at some future time.

In reality, we both seek and shun change: we are truly ambivalent in our reactions to it. As we shall see later in this chapter, it is this Janus-like behaviour that provides us with an essential key to the successful management of change. John Kotter and Leonard Schlesinger[6] of the Harvard Business School tell us that people resist change for the following reasons:

1. They fear the loss of something which they value. This need not be physical but can be related to status, power, prestige, etc.
2. They have have not understood the change and its implications. This often occurs when trust levels are low and communications are poor.
3. They don't think that the change makes sense. People often have different value systems and can also reach different conclusions from the same facts.
4. They are not able to cope with the level or pace of change. The change may be too demanding or fast in terms of the new skills and behaviour needed.

This resistance to change can also be based upon the presence of a real or perceived threat to economic security. As we shall see in Chapter 9, our need for food, shelter, clothing and warmth is basic in its influence on the ways in which we behave. A threat to any one of these will be met by resistance which is fierce, resolute and immediate.

Whatever our intial reaction to change might be, there are few of us who are able to cope with high levels of uncertainty for extended periods of time. Change creates new situations in which uncertainty abounds. This uncertainty might be about major issues such as 'what does this new job involve' or minor issues such as 'where do I park my car': all of these are about the risks and uncertainties of a new situation and all of these are stressful.

However, the reality of life is that we all have experienced, at one level or another, change in our lives, and have survived that process. Indeed, we often embrace change willingly and with enthusiasm since we believe that what is to come is more attractive and interesting than what we have. Whether this turns out to be true or not is beside the point; it is the existence of that incentive which triggers our proactivity towards change. Put simply, we will embrace change when we see it as being to our advantage to do so and we will reject and fight change when we see that it contains no advantage for us. This perception of advantage or gain is a major driving force in our behaviour and one that we have met before. As we saw in Chapter 6, it is that comparison between where we are and where we want to be that provides the driving force or fuel for the engine of change in the performance improvement process. What we need to look at now is how we can guide, control and manage that engine of change.

147

Force field analysis

It was an American social scientist called Kurt Lewin[7] who first expressed the view that the ways in which organizations, and people, behave can be represented as a balancing act or equilibrium condition. What are being balanced are the effects of the forces which act upon us. In any situation there are a number of these forces; some will seek to promote a change in our behaviour and others will seek to restrain or limit that change. For example, as I sit and write these words I am aware of a desire to get up and have a cup of coffee while sitting in my sunny garden. At the moment, that force for change is balanced by my need to continue writing this chapter, to do it well and to meet the time targets I have agreed with my publisher. So I continue to write. At some point, however, my need for a cup of coffee and a break from writing will become stronger and, as a result, I shall go and have my coffee. The force for change has overcome, albeit temporarily in this case, the restraining force. This balancing act or equilibrium is not fixed or frozen: it is dynamic and interacts with the environment in which we work or play though at any one time it can be portrayed by what is called a force field diagram.

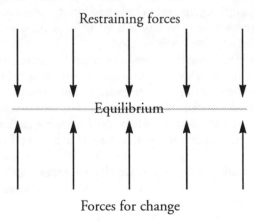

Figure 7.2   Force field diagram

If we want to change this equilibrium situation then we must act in one of two ways:

- Weaken one or all of the restraining forces;
- Strengthen one or all of the forces for change.

The resulting imbalance will mean that a shift or change occurs and a new equilibrium is established. The forces can be anything which acts upon or is relevant to the situation. They can be, for example, concerned with:

- *People* People's needs, attitudes, prejudices, behaviour or biases and the interactions between people;
- *Processes* The needs, structure, limitations and strengths and form of the conversion process;
- *Systems* The political, resource allocation and occupational systems of the organization.

Force field analysis is a simple, practical and proven way of deciding how you are going to guide, control and manage the change process. It has the following steps:

1. Identify the situation and the forces involved.
2. Identify the goal.
3. Decide:
   (i) What you are going to do.
   (ii) When you are going to do it.
4. Implement the above.

However, the quality and effectiveness of the outcomes from this process, which can be carried out by an individual or a group, are dependent upon:

- A clear and unambiguous identification of the situation or problem;
- A detailed and comprehensive identification of the forces acting in that situation;
- The presence of a practical and realistic plan for implementation.

Lewin suggested that the implementation sequence for the change process consisted of three separate though connected stages:

- Unfreezing from current position;
- Moving to new position;
- Refreezing in new position.

Each of these stages must be carried through to completion if the change process is to become stable and durable. For example, if we were to change the way in which client information is recorded and stored in a local authority social work department, then the first and unfreezing step would be to tell everyone that the system is changing. The movement step would involve the introduction of new record cards and storage equipment. The last and refreezing step in this simple example would be to ensure that all future client records were completed and stored on the new systems. If any one of these stages was not completed then the change would become unstable and the situation would revert back to the old record system. The application of force field analysis to a problem which some of us may have faced is illustrated below.

To move or not to move

Fred Higgins was facing a growing problem; and it wasn't going to go away! He and his wife Linda currently occupied a three bedroom semi-detached house in Norbury with their three children, two cats, one dog and a rabbit. Space was short and Fred had to do something soon before the house 'collapsed' or Linda left him. There just wasn't enough space in the house for everyone to do what they wanted when they wanted and the resultant territorial battles made the Second World War look trivial by comparison. One weekend Fred decided that he had just had enough and he went down to the pub with his neighbour Dave. He soon found himself telling Dave about the problems that he and Linda had with the kids. Dave, being a nice sort of bloke, listened for a while but soon grew impatient with Fred's moaning. 'What's stopping you doing something about it?' he blurted out, as Fred reached the end of another episode of woe. Fred responded by talking about the cost of mortgages, the cost and hassle of moving, etc. Towards the end of this monologue Fred noticed that Dave was doodling on the back of a beer mat. 'You're not listening' he said, to which Dave said that he was and showed him what he'd been drawing. It was a force field analysis and Dave told him that it should be able to tell him how to solve his problems. Either the amount of beer he'd consumed or the depth of his despair stopped Fred from saying something very rude and he allowed Dave to go on. Ten minutes later they had a force field analysis which looked like the diagram opposite.

Fred studied this for a while with a frown. Then suddenly he smiled. 'I know what we'll do,' he said. 'We'll build two bedrooms in the loft.' Fred had realised that he could reduce the effect of all the restraining factors in one fell swoop: by staying where they were and building upwards. So off he went to tell Linda, leaving bachelor Dave smiling enigmatically into his pint of beer.

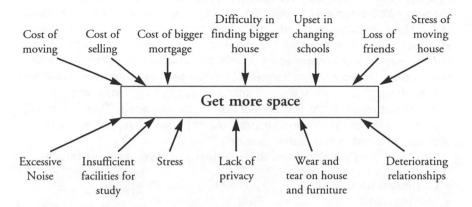

Restraining forces

Cost of moving   Cost of selling   Cost of bigger mortgage   Difficulty in finding bigger house   Upset in changing schools   Loss of friends   Stress of moving house

Get more space

Excessive Noise   Insufficient facilities for study   Stress   Lack of privacy   Wear and tear on house and furniture   Deteriorating relationships

Driving forces

Case Figure 7.1

So, having decided what we are going to change and when we are going to do it, we should now be ready to 'move mountains'. But are we: what about the people involved in that change?

Managing the change process
One of the key issues of the change process is about how we manage the people involved in that process. Organizations are people and, as we saw earlier, people react in complex and often contradictory ways to the process of change. They are, for example, often frightened by and anxious about the process of change. As Peter Senge[8] comments: 'People don't resist change. They resist being changed.'

Yet they also can be enthusiastic and proactive about change, welcoming it as an opportunity to experience new situations and emotions. As Anita Roddick[9] writes of the way in which the Body Shop chain is managed:

'One of our main responsibilities is to allow our employees to grow, to give them a chance of fulfilling themselves and enhancing the world around them.'

If we do not take into account the often conflicting needs, wants, fears and anxieties of those who are involved in or affected by this process of change, then our changes will fail to generate the results that we desire.

151

The importance and constancy of this problem of how to involve people in the process of managing change is reflected in the considerable variety of the views and comments about how to do it. As you would expect, these range from the academic and intellectual to the pragmatic and practical. However, when you examine this bouillabaisse of experience, advice and theory, you find that there are a number of themes or factors which are common to the successful management of change. The evidence is that if we follow these themes then we will manage our changes in a way that is effective and results in the achievement of our desired goals. These goals will then not only benefit the organization but will also be supported by those who are involved in the change process.

Stated in their simplest form these factors and themes are, as follows:

- Communication,
- Involvement,
- Teams.

What we will now do is to look at each of these themes in order to establish what they contribute to the process of managing change.

COMMUNICATION

The process of communication and its contribution to organizational performance improvement is looked at in some detail in Chapter 8. At this time, however, we need to note that communication is a two-way process— you have to listen as well as talk—and that it is also a process which, when carried out well, can make a considerable contribution to the way in which change is managed.

However, despite the fact that we communicate with each other all of the time, doing it well is not always easy and can involve some difficult decisions. For example, there may be situations in which communicating with all of those involved in the change process will take a long time and a lot of effort. There may also be circumstances in which prior experience or history has biased or prejudiced people's views and they are reluctant to trust or listen to those who propose the change. There can also be situations in which the very survival of an organization is at stake or the issues involved are of considerable commercial sensitivity.

So why do we need to communicate about the changes which we, as managers, believe to be necessary? To answer this we need to look at both sides of the communication issue. Let's look at the downside first: it takes time to involve and talk to people and when you've done it once they will expect you to do again. It also takes time to listen to what they say and what they tell you. All of that is time that could be spent trying to actually implement the change. I say 'trying' because that is all that you would be doing! Until you have really communicated with these people you cannot presume that you have their support and help, and you do need both of those to achieve your change.

The upside is that when you do listen, they will begin to talk about things which are important—both to them and to you—and what they say might, just might, include a good idea that you hadn't thought of yourself. Whatever the risk and whatever the cost, the principle is just the same: you need to tell them what is going on and you need to listen to what they say. In order to do that you have to plan your change programme in such a way that it contains time for listening and talking. The need for communication is a continuous and ongoing one (communication is not a one-off exercise) but is a worthwhile investment. As the Open University's Derek Pugh[10] says:

'Effective reasons for change are those that can be accepted by many of the interest groups and people who will be involved.'

Once you've started the communication process then you are probably going to be ready for the next step, that of including those people in your plans and in your thinking.

INVOLVEMENT

This is the process by which those involved in or affected by the change influence its content and its process. It does not involve management in abdicating their responsibility for taking decisions nor is it consensus management. What it does mean is that management creates a culture in which people feel free to ask about what is happening and management feel free to ask: 'What do you think?' without feeling bound to accept the answer unconditionally. If encouraged and allowed to grow, this involvement will lead to commitment rather than compliance and that commitment will get people involved in the process of creating something new. The detail of the method you use to encourage the growth of this involvement will differ with the different levels of your organization. Managers and supervisors may need, for example, to feel that they have a co-ordinating and facilitating role in the involvement of those for whose work they are responsible. They, in their turn, may need to be informed about the strategic implications of the proposed change and encouraged to work with others in different parts of the organization. One way of harnessing and supporting these twin horses of involvement and commitment is by the use of teams.

TEAMS

The team is a powerful weapon in the process of improving performance and that of managing change. The detail of how we can design, create and run effective teams is examined in detail in Chapter 9. What we need to note now, in looking at the role of teams in managing the process of change, is that these teams need to:

- Be multidisciplinary;
- Contain people from several levels of the organization chart;
- Have a clear well-defined objective;
- Be expected to generate results.

Bob Waterman[11] relates how this sort of team has made a significant contribution to the growth and development of several major US corporations including General Electric, Ford, Citicorp and First Boston Bank. Not only do these teams, which exist at all levels in these organizations, produce results but working in them also enhances and upgrades the involvement and commitment of the team members.

The experienced manager will use these factors of involvement, commitment and teams to enhance planning, control and management of the change process as we can see in the example below.

Too slow for comfort

The Orange Electronics Company wasn't facing a crisis: sales were good and rising and there were several new products in the pipeline. But Brett Johnson, who co-founded Orange some 3 years ago with James Righton, wasn't happy. As the order book had grown, so had the company and as a result it now took much longer to get things done. For example, Brett mused, why did it take so long to get that modification to the video circuit board from his doodle pad on to the shop-floor? What he knew was that unless they changed and were able to react quicker then they'd lose the client base they had built up. Brett wanted Orange to get bigger but he didn't want it to get slower. When James came back from one of his sales trips, Brett really poured out his heart about this problem. James listened quietly, nodding when Brett cited examples of how, since they had started up, the organization had got slower. Brett finished by saying that while he was sure that they needed to get back to the good old days of short lead times between idea and product what he didn't know was how to get there.

James smiled: 'You may be a genius with electronics, Brett', he said, 'but you don't know much about people.' James then told him about the seven golden rules[10] of change:

1. Always establish, with those involved, that we do need to change.
2. Don't just decide *what* you want to do, think out *how* you want to do it.
3. Talk to people: ask them what they think and get them involved.
4. Encourage them to tell you why they don't like your ideas or suggestions.
5. Don't be rigid: be prepared to change your ideas or your approach.
6. Once the change has started: check out progress and direction, and be prepared to use this feedback to introduce changes in detail or minor shifts in direction.
7. Publicize success—tell everyone about it—and use success to build success.

Brett looked at James thoughtfully: 'You know, James', he said 'I sometimes wonder why we are partners, but when you come up with things like that then I know. I'd better get down there and start talking to everyone.' James smiled. 'Remember rule number 2' he shouted as Brett rushed through the door, 'and wait until you've thought a bit more about how you want to do it.'

Change can only take place with the support and co-operation of others. Those who attempt to impose change on others put not only that change, but also their future relationship with others, at risk. They do so because they fail to gain the support and co-operation of those who are needed to carry out that change. Under these circumstances the net result is at least an NMP (Not My Problem) syndrome but also could be, if economic security is threatened, a level of resistance which is damaging and full of conflict.

Change and performance improvement

The process of organizational performance improvement is one in which change plays an integral part. The process is driven by the desire to move from a 'now' position to a 'want or need to be' position. This change process often, though not exclusively, comes about because of decisions or choices which are internal to the organization. In that sense it is internally sourced but if those decisions are to result in success for the organization then they must also take account of or reflect the state of flux of the external environment. For organizations, as well as people, the response to an involuntary and externally sourced change is often one of resistance and rejection. As we saw with IBM, the larger the organization, the stronger the resistance, and, in the end, the more devastating the results. Yet this need not be so! As we saw in Chapter 6, General Electric's CEO Jack Welch has transformed both the culture and profitability of this giant corporation from

155

one based on 'middle of the road' safety to one in which simplicity, dignity, renewal and the ability to respond quickly to the changes of the outside world are all prized values. It is worth noting that one of the mechanisms that Welch has used to create this change has been the 'work-out', a team-based process which aims to enlist the support, commitment and active involvement of all employees. It is also a process in which communication plays a key role.

These changes in GE are just one example of how the performance improvement process can be successfully applied to all organizations, big or small. This performance improvement process is not an isolated mechanistic process solely aimed at increasing profitability, rather, it is a dynamic, organic and people-involving process which lies at the heart of the cycle of organizational growth and development. It requires us to act upon our convictions, visions and desires and empowers those who do. For those who don't follow this road of self-empowerment, the safety based and limited actions will slowly and inexorably lead to the extreme unction, i.e. the last rites of a dying though still breathing organism.

Earlier in this chapter, we saw that communication is one of the key factors in the management of the change process. The next chapter examines the ways and means of this process which is vitally important to all aspects of management.

Summary

Change has been and will continue to be a feature of all our lives both at work and at play. However, these changes have become both:

- Faster, and
- Larger.

If we, and our organizations, are to survive and prosper then we must embrace that change process and learn how to manage and control it.

Change itself has several dimensions and these include:

- The voluntary or involuntary nature of the change;
- The internal or external nature of its origin or source;
- Its influence upon the 'upstream' or 'downstream' side of the conversion process.

Change can also be cyclic or structural in nature though most organizational change is not crisis-driven but comes about because of proactive decisions targeted at creating something new.

The response of both ourselves and our organizations to change are complex and mixed. We both fear and desire it and it is the perception that we will gain from the new situation that is a key factor in triggering a proactive response to change. Force field analysis, with its four easy steps, provides us with a proven and practical way of:

- Analysing, and
- Managing the change situation.

Key factors in this management process are:

- Communication,
- Involvement,
- Teams.

The successful performance improvement process is a change process which is:

- Dynamic,
- Organic,
- People involving.

It is also a change process that lies at the heart of the cycle of organizational growth and development.

References

[1] Toffler, A., *Future Shock*, Pan Books, London, 1970.

[2] Black, L., Renaissance manager, in *Independent on Sunday*, 2 May 1993.

[3] Peters, T., *Thriving on Chaos*, Pan Books, London, 1989.

[4] Martel, L., *Mastering Change*, Grafton Books, London, 1988.

[5] Wille, E., *Triggers for Change*, Ashridge Management Research Group, Berkhamsted, 1989.

[6] Kotter, J.P. and L.A. Schlesinger, Choosing strategies for change, in *Harvard Business Review*, vol. 57, no. 2, 1979.

[7] Lewin, K., *Field Theory in Social Science*, Harper, New York, 1951.

[8] Senge, P., *The Fifth Discipline*, Century Business, London, 1990.

[9] Roddick, A., *Body and Soul*, Ebury Press, London, 1991.

[10] Pugh, D.S., Understanding and managing organizational change, in *London Business School Journal*, vol. 3, no. 2, 1978.

[11] Waterman, R.H, *The Renewal Factor*, Bantam Press, London, 1988.

8. Communication

Communication is a continuous two-way process that influences both the culture and the health of the business.

David Drennan

Introduction

All managers need to communicate. There can be little doubt that this ability to communicate is an important, indeed vital, component of the kitbag of skills which enable managers to respond effectively to the multiple and diverse demands of this role. Our review of the process of change (Chapter 7) underlined the value of effective communication as a key factor in managing that process. However, this core skill or competence is one for which we are rarely formally trained or educated. Most of our training or education is aimed at acquiring the specialized knowledge that we need to do our jobs and to be, for example, good accountants, social workers or engineers.

Yet accountants, social workers, engineers, doctors, teachers, nurses, salespersons and, last but not least, managers are just a few examples of roles in which effective communication is important. Indeed, for some of these roles it might be argued that communication is *the* key skill or focal point.

The role of the manager is one of those jobs whose focal point is that ability to communicate or, to put it another way, undertake skilled interaction with others. Studies of the ways in which managers use their time indicate that managers can spend up to 90 per cent of their time talking to others and as much as a third of that time is spent in one to one meetings. With such a substantial commitment to the process of communication the manager needs to be able to undertake that process efficiently and effectively. The manager also needs to be able to use that communicative ability to enable, engender and facilitate the organizational performance improvement process. As Tom Peters[1] tells us, managers need to be able to both express the vision which empowers their staff *and* to be able to stay in touch with the needs of the real world in which that vision is being implemented. Yet communicating appears to be a process to which managers give little attention and which is often taken for granted!

Studies[2,3] indicate that not only do managers consistently underestimate the amount of time they spend in one to one communication but also that the efficiency of these communications is typically low with examples of information retention levels lying in the range 20 to 50 per cent. So, as communication pervades all that managers do, even small improvements in that process will benefit their working lives enormously. However, the development of this communicative skill and ability is not something that happens overnight. It is, initially, a part of the process of growth and development that we all experience. For example, children quickly learn to use language as a way of communicating and the average child's active vocabulary grows from 3 words at 12 months of age to over 2000 at 5 years of age. This growth in vocabulary is also paralleled by a growth in experience and understanding of the 'rules' of conversation. All of this takes place because of the child's pressing need for more precision and content in its communications. The patterns of this communication continue to change as the child grows, experiences the upheavals of adolescence and moves into adult life. By then, the common skills or core competences of communication will have become:

- The ability to receive and respond to a variety of information;
- The ability to present information in visual forms;
- The ability to communicate in writing;
- The ability to participate in both verbal and non-verbal communication.

The effectiveness with which managers demonstrate and use these abilities can make a considerable difference to their performance. In his or her initial management role the manager will be expected to be able to write reports, undertake presentations and to motivate staff. As experience and role responsibilities grow, these abilities will also extend to include those associated with interviewing, negotiating, appraising and counselling. The skilled and experienced manager will also be able to use a range of verbal and non-verbal skills that result in people being motivated, feeling valued and being given feedback.

All of this communication takes place within a social environment and as such is often described as a social skill. This chapter is about communication between people in the social environment in which they work and its relationship to the process of improving organizational performance. There can be little doubt about the importance of this process. Failure to communicate efficiently and effectively will not only limit the manager's role but also the roles of those with whom she or he communicates. Most managers communicate with a very wide range of people during their working day. These people might, for example, include the manager's:

- Boss,
- Fellow managers,

- Staff and team members,
- Staff from other departments,
- Customers, clients, patients,
- Union representatives,
- Suppliers of goods and services,
- Competitors.

The list could be endless! In addition, and all of these people:

- are also trying to communicate with that manager;
- are able to contribute or influence the process of organizational performance improvement.

So, given that the ability to communicate is an important and indeed, mandatory, skill for the manager, our first step in exploring this vital topic will be to define what we mean by communication.

What is communication?
A typical dictionary definition for the process of communication identifies that it involves the actions of imparting, bestowing and revealing to others. A more rigorous definition of this process might see communication as being concerned with passing information; and, doing so by means of previously agreed symbols, such as words and numbers. However, our own experience tells us that communication in the workplace is not just concerned with passing information but also any aspect of our interactions with others. It can be, for example, concerned with expressing praise or displeasure or opinions. It can also be about maintaining or initiating social relationships or merely passing the time of day. When we think about this process of communication we begin to see that we communicate about:

- Data or information,
- Sentiments, feelings and emotions,
- Standards, values and beliefs,
- Opinions, hypotheses, ideas and notions.

This tells us that when communication occurs ideas, information and feelings are conveyed from individual to individual. However, our experience also tells us that communication is not limited to one to one situations. It can also take place when an individual addresses a group, crowd or audience of people or when one group interacts with another group or within a group itself with several people involved in the process.

All in all, this process of communication is one which can be used in a wide range of circumstances and for a wide variety of purposes. It is also a very flexible process and is not limited to solely conveying information *or* ideas *or* feelings. *All* of these can be conveyed or transmitted simultaneously. When an individual communicates with another it is not just ideas or information but also feelings that are being conveyed. For example, someone may tell their manager that the report that they are doing for him will be a week later than the agreed date. The manager may tell them that he is not happy with that and that they will have to improve on that completion date. The manager not only says that the message sent is unacceptable but also expresses feelings about that message. Further thought will make us realize that the content of the message that the manager sends is not limited to the words spoken. For example, when the manager speaks, the tone of his voice will be part of the message that is sent. If those involved in this interaction can see each other then gesture, use of space, body contact and facial expression will also be a part of the message that is sent. One way of differentiating between the different parts of the messages that we send one another is shown in Figure 8.1.

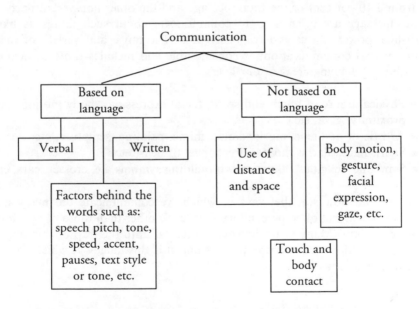

Figure 8.1 Classifications of communication

This figure indicates that communication can be classified initially on the basis of whether it is one of two types:

161

1. *Language based* or *linguistic* This type of communication will include all aspects of the use of language including:
   (i)   The words used and their verbal or written content and meaning.
   (ii) The tone, speed, volume, pitch and accent of speech, i.e. its paralingual content.
2. *Non-linguistic* This type of communication is not based on language but encompasses all bodily communication including:
   (i)   Body contact and touch (tacesics).
   (ii) Interpersonal distance and territory (proxemics).
   (iii) Facial expression, head movements, posture, gestures, gaze, etc. (kinesics).

All of these contribute to the ways in which we communicate with each other: whether we are conscious or unconscious of their presence and whether we choose to acknowledge that presence or not. Like it or not, we do communicate with each other by the presence or absence of our facial expressions, the ways in which we look at each other or move our bodies when speaking or listening and the gestures we make while talking and listening. In fact, the word content of our communications only accounts for around 10 per cent of the total message and the other non-verbal parts of the message are often used to communicate about such things as like–dislike, power, status and responsiveness. The range and variety of these non-verbal communications is considerable and includes those associated with the following areas of our lives:

- Physical: sense of touch and smell, facial expressions, body motions and proximity, gaze, etc.
- Artistic or aesthetic: music, dance, mime, painting, sculpture, etc.
- Signs: flags, alarms, horns, sirens, peel of bells, etc.
- Symbolic: religious, status or ego building symbols, i.e. crosses, cars, etc.

As we can now see, the ways in which we communicate are many and complex and can often be conducted at levels other than those of which we are conscious. Many of us, however, often fall into the trap of thinking of communication as a one-way process and it is this fallacy at which we will now take a look.

One-way or two-way process?
Communication is often thought of as a one-way process, as in telling someone something or listening to someone. But communication is not a one-way process. All communication is a two-way process, irrespective of

how it is undertaken. Even when that communication is primarily concerned with issuing instructions about what to do or where to go, the listener is providing the speaker with feedback. This feedback does not have to be in the form of words: it can be concerned with the expression on the listener's face, whether she is looking at the speaker and what her body posture is. All of these provide the speaker with feedback as to whether his message has been heard and understood and what the listener feels about that message or the speaker.

A model of this process is shown in Figure 8.2 in which the following interpretations will apply.

1. *Encoding* This will involve choosing the appropriate 'code' or language to use. It will need to be appropriate for the receiver and her or his skills, language and abilities. It will also need to be appropriate to the channel and medium used. Examples of inappropriate code might include the use of technical jargon which confuses the receiver or the use of very formal language at an informal social event.

2. *Decoding* This means interpreting the information sent. For example, this can mean being able to translate to another language or understanding what a nod or a wink means. It is often described as being a part of a larger group of processes, called cognition, and by which we process and make sense of all of the sensory inputs we receive. In the context of our social interactions, people who are skilled in this larger group of processes are often described as being able to 'size up' people and situations.

3. *Noise* This means any form of interference with the message which has the result of reducing the quality or strength of the message 'signal' or generating spurious, distracting or inaccurate information. This noise can be external (traffic noise, bad telephone line, a bad fax copy, a misspelled

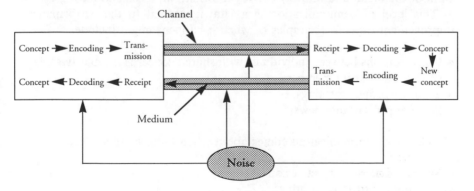

Figure 8.2   The communication process

163

or incorrectly used word) or internal (preoccupation with other messages, a headache, strong negative feelings about the transmitter).
4. *Channel and Medium* These are often confused or used interchangeably, Medium is generally seen to be the means of communication, i.e. spoken word or written word, and Channel to be the conduit through which the message passes, e.g. a book, note, telephone call, film.

The manager who is aware of the need for and value of effective communication will, in preparing his or her message, take into account a number of factors about the intended receiver. These will include receiver's language, proximity and availability. To be effective, the manager's message will use appropriate language in the verbal or written medium and a transmission channel, e.g. telephone, face to face, letter, which will give the manager a reasonable expectation that the message will be received and understood.

However, as we noted earlier, this is not a one-way process and the manager needs feedback in order to know whether and how the message had been received. This feedback, which may be limited to a nod or a grunt, can be just as meaningful and valid as the original message. For some of the face to face situations which the manager experiences this level of feedback is not only typical but also acceptable. For example, the manager may have given an instruction to someone to, for example, work overtime and only need her or him to acknowledge that they have heard what the manager has said.

But if we are to empower our people and encourage them to become involved in the process of organizational performance improvement then this feedback needs to change and become more than an acknowledgement of the message. When the feedback contains as much information (from the receiver) as the original message then the communication patterns change to that in which the transmitter and the receiver roles alternate and overlap. Both of them can and do fully convey information, ideas and feelings.

This level of communication is a vital ingredient to the performance improvement process. Examples of when it happens might include:

- Conversations between individuals with shared concerns or objectives, i.e. colleagues or team members;
- Team or project meetings;
- Some appraisal interviews.

This level of communication comes about when those involved have:

- Shared concerns, objectives and targets;
- Adequate trust in each other;
- A joint commitment to the generation of mutually acceptable outcomes.

164

The team is one of the mechanisms which meets these criteria and we shall take a more detailed look at teams and their contribution to the performance improvement process in Chapter 9.

Whatever mechanisms are used communication will only reach the levels we saw above if it has clear objectives. So let's take a look at why we communicate.

Why do we communicate?

We saw earlier that communication is about transmitting and receiving ideas, facts or feelings from individual to individual or group to group. It was also evident that, if we are to communicate successfully, we will need to use both our skill and our experience. Communication does not occur without cause or reason or in a disordered manner and, in common with all social acts, the act of communication will be subject to rules or norms. For example, if it is to be effective the nature of the communication must be such that it is perceived by others to:

- Have a purpose, objective or desired outcome;
- To be appropriate to the situation.

So what are these outcomes?

Obviously we communicate for a wide range of reasons for but generally because we want to influence other people and their attitudes and perceptions and ultimately their behaviour. That is, we want to affect the ways in which they:

- Think and feel about things, and/or
- Do things.

In order to achieve these objectives the manager needs to ensure that:

- Both she or he and the receiver have a full understanding of the message;
- The receiver responds in the required manner.

Most managers are involved in communication whose main purposes can be classified as instructing, influencing and exchanging information.

INSTRUCTING
The intent of an instruction is to change the ways in which people act or behave. Examples are:

165

- Complete this review by the end of the month.
- I am writing to instruct you to ensure the completion of this project on time and to budget.
- Write to me when you return.

INFLUENCING

Influencing is also about generating a clear and identifiable change in behaviour. However, the difference between influencing and instructing is that influencing:

- Is less explicit,
- Involves actions such as:
  - encouraging
  - suggesting

When the manager is influencing people then she or he is motivating (in a negative or positive way), persuading or encouraging. An example might be:

'If we attain our target this month, it would mean that you all share, under the new incentive scheme, in the benefits of this achievement.'

EXCHANGING INFORMATION

This involves both giving information and seeking information.

1. *Giving information,* i.e. informing people
   The receiver may need this information in order to, for example, make a better decision or to be better able to inform someone else, e.g. a customer. The information given might include:
   (i) Facts: 'Turnover was up by 10 per cent last month.'
   (ii) Ideas: 'Why don't we do it this way?'
   (iii) Interpretations based on facts: 'She persists in not reacting to falling sales.'
   (iv) Feelings about any or all of the above: 'I believe that, based on the evidence available, it is time for us to move into a new marketing strategy.'
2. *Seeking information* This is the opposite of giving information and can be achieved by:
   (i) Asking questions: 'How do you do that?'
   (ii) Giving information about needs: 'I'd like to know more about that.'
   (iii) Showing openness to receive information: 'Yes, I would like to hear about your holiday.'

The manager can, of course, combine all of the above types of communication. However, a decision will have to be made as to their main purpose and what is the most appropriate way of communicating.

How do we communicate?

As we saw in Figure 8.1, we communicate through a variety of communication mediums with an initial distinction being made between the use or non-use of words. The purpose of the communication will also influence both the medium and the channel used.

In the context of improving organizational performance the factors which influence the 'how' of communications are outlined below:

OBJECTIVES

The manager needs to be clear about whether persuading, informing, questioning or instructing is the objective. All of these will influence the choice of both the medium and the channel used. For example, the information used to monitor the efficiency of the conversion process will need to be recorded in writing with the use of clear unambiguous language. However, before deciding which make of computers to buy for departmental use the manager may choose to explore options or choices before taking a formally recorded decision and to do so verbally and face to face (rather than over the telephone) with individual colleagues.

NEEDS

The nature of the message (formal, informal, confidential, etc.), who is receiving it (boss, the project team, the machine-shop, etc.), the channels available and their cost (meetings, letters, telephone calls, faxes, conference calls), the need to record the content and/or the feedback, the need to ensure consistency of message: all of these, and others, significantly influence the 'how' of communications.

The medium that we choose for our communications can be: spoken word, 'body language', written words.

THE SPOKEN WORD

This is the most direct form of communication and can be done formally (interviews) or informally (discussions). We can also speak at length or briefly and in a manner which reflects our feelings and our own personal style. The use of equipment can enable the spoken word to be recorded or transmitted over long distances with neither speaker nor listener being able

167

to see one another. Speech can be used to communicate with groups or individuals. The use of the spoken word can make a major contribution to the process of organizational improvement. It can:

- Make people feel that they have been personally consulted;
- Lead to expression of feelings as well as ideas;
- Enable sharing and comparing;
- Facilitate non-verbal communication and immediate feedback when face to face.

Whether conducted face to face or not, the spoken word is a powerful tool in the process of improving organizational performance. The spoken word is complemented and supported by what is often, though incorrectly, described as 'body language'.

NON-LINGUISTIC COMMUNICATION
This means of communication operates in parallel with the verbal process and can reinforce, contradict or neutralize the spoken words. It is said to be often more effective at communicating feelings and emotions than either the written or spoken word though it is often not consciously used or perceived. Most of its forms require visual contact between those involved though one form (paralinguistic) relies on the tone, speed, stress, volume and pitch of the spoken word. The understanding and use of the non-verbal communication channel can make a significant difference to effectiveness of communications.

THE WRITTEN WORD
The written word is indirect in nature but as such can enable the writer to express his or her own ideas and feelings without having to respond to reactions and responses of other people. This indirectness can also enable the writer to put more thought into the choice of words used and the written message can be reshaped until satisfactory. As with the spoken word the written communication can be brief or lengthy, formal or informal and also, for the experienced writer, can reflect an individual style. Organizations often have 'rules' about the style and presentation of written material. The tangible form of the written communication means that:

- It can be easily copied and so provide physical evidence of transmission and content;
- It can be sent to a number of people at the same time.

Despite the innate nature of the communication process and its apparent ease, communications do not always go well. We have all heard about or experienced the misheard or misunderstood comment that caused a major row or the badly worded letter that lost us a major customer. The next section will take a look at the reasons for these failures in communication.

Communication difficulties

Communication is not always successful. The reasons for this can be as varied as the messages sent but examples might include illegibly written or printed letters, wrongly addressed letters, whispered comments which are misheard and misunderstood, shouted expressions of affection and messages with a warm content which are said without a smile. These and many others are examples of our inability to communicate effectively. So why does it happen?

There are a number of reasons which can prevent people from exchanging ideas and feelings as effectively as they might and these can be classified as follows:

1. *Lack of clear objectives* This leads to uncertainty of message, i.e. the transmitter can't decide what to say, and may be due to not knowing what or how the receiver needs to be told or not wishing to offend, upset or shock them.
2. *Faulty transmission* While the transmitter knows what he or she wants to say, the message is sent by the wrong medium or channel. An example might be sending a personal message in writing when a telephone call or a visit would have been more appropriate, tactful or understanding. Other examples might be that we speak too quietly or slowly, or use jargon or inappropriate language. The transmitter may also expect the receiver to absorb too much information in the time available or may not take into account the receiver's prior knowledge of the subject.
3. *Perception and attitude problems* These include problems related to false or unstated assumptions or misunderstood messages where the transmitter might use a word in one context or with one meaning while the receiver might use the same word in a different context or with a different meaning. Examples, albeit simple ones, of this would include words such as 'now', 'urgent' and 'quickly'. These problems can also occur when transmitter and receiver have viewpoints which are so radically different that it is not possible to generate a shared understanding by talking. History is full of examples of this but recent ones have included Israelis and Arabs and nuclear armers and disarmers. The inability or unwillingness of the receiver to understand or absorb the message is also part of this group of problems as is the behaviour of the

transmitter in withholding information from fear of consequences, for reasons of secrecy, deception or lack of trust.

4. *Environmental problems* These include:
   (i) Interference, i.e. distractions and noise.
   (ii) Lack of channels, i.e. no formal meetings, no telephone.
   (iii) Distance.
   (iv) 'Chinese whispers' or 'Telephone tag' phenomenon: the longer the message chain the more distorted the message.

All of these difficulties can be minimized and even eliminated if we preface and conduct our communications with thought and care about their 'how' and 'when'. The next section will take a look at when we communicate and how that can influence our contribution to the process of improving organizational performance.

When do we communicate?

The simple answer to this question is that we communicate whenever we interact with, meet, talk to or see others. As our organizations consist of other people, then the process of communication is, by and large, an ongoing and continuous one. Nor is this likely to change. Mike Pedler, John Burgoyne and Tom Boydell[4] in describing the 'Learning Company' of the future identify 'Internal Exchange' as one of eleven characteristics of such an organization and write of the need for managers to 'facilitate communication, negotiation and contracting rather than exerting top-down control' as a part of that characteristic. A Massachusetts Institute of Technology review of American industrial performance[5], conducted at the end of the 1980s, observed that communications in many US companies were restrained by 'steep hierarchical ladders and organizational walls'. This study also identified the need for greater employee involvement so that the employee becomes a 'full participant in the enterprise', with obvious communication implications. However, despite the need to improve overall communication, some of those interactions have attracted particular attention either because of their frequency or because of their consequences. The following sections will take a brief look at two of the more significant, in terms of the organizational improvement process, of these interactions.

These are:

• Presentations,
• Interviews.

Presentations

The presentation is a very effective and flexible way of communicating with people. It can be formal or informal and enable the presenter to reach a wide range of both audience size and composition. While almost all presenters will use the spoken word to reach their audience, these words are often supplemented by visual material involving the use of overhead projectors and transparencies, slides, flip charts, etc. Effective presenters will also make considerable use of gesture, gaze and facial expression to underline or reinforce what they are saying.

In today's business environment, there can be very few managers who do not get involved in the process of giving a presentation. However, few managers are born with a natural aptitude for doing so. Most of them find the process stressful and have to work hard to produce a reasonable effort: even then they are often aware of the faults and limitations of their efforts.

Nevertheless, a presentation does provide the manager with an opportunity to communicate. Presentations of a professional standard result in the ideas, concepts and information presented being understood and possibly accepted by the audience. Presentations of an unprofessional standard result in audiences which do not understand or accept the material presented and may even be antagonised by the way in which it was presented. The ability to prepare and deliver a presentation of a professional standard is therefore another important component not only of the kit bag of managerial skills but also of the manager's contribution to the process of organizational improvement.

It is, however, a process which is very often conducted in a very public manner and consequent success or failure can often result in the audience acquiring enhanced or diminished perceptions of the presenter's overall managerial abilities. As such, conducting a presentation is often seen as a stressful situation. This section will attempt to reduce the level of that stress by considering what the presenter needs to do in order to ensure that the presentation is conducted in a professional manner. However, it should also be understood that practise and experience are also needed to produce a permanent professional standard of presentation.

THE KEY QUESTIONS

Most managerial presentations are used to:

- provide information,
- influence others.

These different objectives have implications for a number of aspects of the presentation process including:

171

- The presentation material used,
- Scope of subject,
- Time required,
- Numbers of audience,
- Layout of the presentation space.

The key questions for all managerial presentations and presenters are:

- *Who is the audience?*
- *What are the objectives?*

The presenting manager needs to be clear about the answers to these questions before any presentation is undertaken. For example, failure to understand the needs and idiosyncrasies of the audience can result, in the extreme, in a presenter telling jokes about the Irish to an audience of Dubliners, jokes about the Scottish to an audience of Glaswegians or jokes about cricket to an audience of baseball managers: all high-risk strategies if the presenter's objective is to persuade or influence them on another issue! Uncertainty or lack of clarity about the objectives of the presentation will be equally disastrous and will result in a presentation which:

- Has several conflicting or overlapping objectives;
- Tries to cover too much ground;
- Leaves the audience confused and uncertain.

The importance of the presenter being clear about who the audience is and what the objectives of the presentation are cannot be overstated. Presenters ignore these at their peril and no amount of expertise in presentation method will make up for the absence of thoughtful and considered answers to this questions.

If we take a further, more detailed look at these key points we will find that their importance is also reflected in the need for the presenter to bear the audience in mind *all the time* throughout his/her preparation and presentation. The presenter will need to list what is known about them in terms of audience number, their job titles and responsibilities, and their interests, biases, prejudices and concerns.

While the presenter can assume that, for most managerial presentations, the audience will be made up of experienced adults who will assume, at least initially, that the presenter is able to speak with authority on the subject, they will also have many other things on their minds. This audience's concentration will also fade after around 10 to 15 minutes. As a result the presenter will need to capture and keep their imagination and interest. In general terms the audience will remember what the presenter says if it has a clear structure and pattern and if it is repeated.

As we saw earlier, clarity about the objectives of the presentation is particularly important. The presenter should write down, *in a single sentence*, the objective of the presentation. Examples might be:

To gain capital sanction approval for Project 34.
To persuade the Board to agree to relocate the offices to Bristol.
To get this department to do things differently.
To tell my team what the company results were like this year and why we need to do better.

The next step will require the presenter to decide the structure and content of the presentation. For example, there is a considerable body of research to support the view that audience understanding is directly related to the presenter's ability not only to prepare but also to structure, organize and sequence the material presented. Alternatives for the order of this material can include:

- Chronological order,
- Logical order,
- Descending or ascending order of importance,
- Descending or ascending order of complexity,
- Psychological order (from known to unknown).

The order used will depend upon the complexity of the material, the level of the audience's prior understanding and the outcomes desired. When viewed in the light of the process of exerting influence in order to improve organizational performance, an effective sequence of presentation might be:

- State proposal,
- Anticipate objections,
- Show evidence and proof,
- Provide practical evidence,
- Repeat proposal.

Antony Jay[6] identifies an alternative presentation structure as being:

- Preface (welcome, self-identification, intention, route map and rules),
- Situation,
- Complication,
- Recommendation.

It will also be evident that, whatever the overall sequence used, there also exists a need to present material in an order which facilitates the audience's

173

understanding. The impact of this material can be enhanced by the use of visual aids.

The preparation of this material is a key stage in the preparation of the presentation. As important, however, is the preparation of:

- the room in which the presentation takes place—layout, seating plan, lighting, heating and ventilation etc.
- the equipment involved in the presentation—overhead projector, screen, flip chart board etc.
- the preparation and rehearsal of the presenter.

Attention to all of these factors will make a significant and positive contribution to both the immediate and longer-term impact of the presentation.

A further example of a communicative interaction which often occurs during the process of improving organizational performance is that of the interview. The next section will take a brief look at the interview process.

Interviews

Information is an important input to the process of improving organizational performance and this can often be gathered or acquired by interviewing people. These information gathering interviews can be associated with the acquisition of any or all of the following:

- Numerate data: 'How many times did that happen?'
- Objective facts: 'On which day did he say that?'
- Descriptions: 'Tell me what you do with this invoice.'
- Subjective evaluations: 'Would you say morale is worse or better than last year?'
- Feelings: 'Do you like that way of doing it?'.

Conducted in a formal or informal manner, these interviews can provide material which is not only important but also vital to the process of improving organizational performance. For example Derek Pugh[7], while reviewing the process of organizational change, identifies the need to establish the need for change as being the first step in effective change management. Information gathering interviews are often a key stage in that initial step. Quality gurus Joseph Juran[8] and Philip Crosby[9] both write about the need to identify the facts about failure rates, critical components, quality costs and operator attitudes, among others, as a key and critical first step on the road to improved quality in both service and manufacturing

174

organizations. Again, information gathering interviews are often a key stage in that initial step.

The way in which these interviews are conducted can make a considerable difference to their outcomes. For example, a manager who is investigating a computer systems failure will not only display bias but also get limited answers to subsequent questions if she or he responds to a factual description by the operator of actions taken with the question: 'Why on earth did you do that?' rather than 'Can you tell me what/why you decided to do that?'. Closed questions like 'That was unsatisfactory, wasn't it?' generally produce limited answers.

The majority of information gathering interviews have a number of stages.

1. *Background information acquisition* This initial stage involves establishing a basic factual framework which establishes answers to 'what', 'how' and 'who'. This may involve organization charts, production records and/or a host of other documents—all of which are needed as background information.
2. *Preparation* During this stage decisions must be made about what information is needed from the interviews and how that information is to be acquired or accessed. These decisions will provide answers to:
   (i)   Who is to be interviewed and in what order?
   (ii) How long will the interviews last?
   (iii) Where will they be held?
   (iv) What questions will be asked?
   (v)   How will the answers be recorded, for example, notes or tape recorder?
3. *Interview* The quality of the information acquired will depend not only upon the questions asked but also how those questions are asked. The skilled interviewer will use probing, open-ended questions and silence and will manage the timing and duration of the interview.
4. *Analysis* After the interview it will be necessary to analyse both the information obtained and the effectiveness of the interview process.

As we saw earlier in this chapter, the information gathering interview is just one example of the communication interactions which occur during the performance improvement process.

Whatever the purpose, goal, culture, structure or ideology of the organization, the manager will need to communicate with those around him or her. In order to make a worthwhile and valuable contribution to the process of improving that organization's performance the manager must ensure that his or her communication style and abilities are compatible with the needs and culture of the organization. When that occurs the quality and

175

content of these communicative situations are able to make substantial contributions to the commercial success of that organization.

In Chapter 7 we saw that teams can make a considerable contribution towards the successful management of change. When successful, the team acts as a lens which focuses the commitment, creativity and enthusiasm of its members towards the achievement of a joint target or goal. The next chapter will examine the team phenomenon and the contribution which it can make to the process of improving organizational performance.

Summary

The ability to communicate effectively is not necessarily something for experts or specialists; nor is it an add-on optional extra. It should be an essential integral part of the working lives of all managers. Communication can be seen to be:

- A social skill with a purpose;
- Both linguistic and non-linguistic in nature;
- A dynamic and interactive two way process.

Communication which is not based on language involves the use of gesture, posture, space, touch, gaze and expression while language based communication is concerned with the use of written and spoken language including the paralingual aspects of speech. Models of the process of communication use the concepts of encoding and decoding with the use of medium and channel. Noise interferes with this process and can be implicit in the process itself or originate from without the process. The objectives of communication are to affect other's thoughts or actions by:

- Influencing, and/or
- Instructing, and/or
- Exchanging information.

The effective use of the linguistic and non-linguistic based communication to achieve these objectives will require the manager to possess an understanding of:

- the desired purpose(s),
- needs of the chosen medium and channel,
- needs of the receiver(s),
- the causes of failure in communication.

Presentations and interviews are two examples of the interactions that occur during the performance improvement process. For both of these processes, which have different and particular demands, the ability to communicate in a skilful manner is essential.

References
[1] Peters, T., *Thriving on Chaos*, Pan Books, London, 1989.
[2] Horn, J.H. and T. Lupton, The work activities of middle managers: an exploratory study, in *Journal of Management Studies, vol. 2, no. 1, pages 14–33.*
[3] Handy, C.B., *Understanding Organisations*, Penguin, London, 1976.
[4] Pedler, M., J. Burgoyne and T. Boydell, *The Learning Company*, McGraw-Hill, Maidenhead, 1991.
[5] Berger, S., M.L. Dertouzos, R.K. Lester, R.M. Solow, and L.C. Thurow, Toward a new industrial America, in *Scientific American*, vol. 260, no. 6, pages 21–29.
[6] Jay, A., *Making Your Case*, Video Arts, London, 1982.
[7] Pugh, D., Understanding and managing organisational change, in Mayon-White, W. (ed.), *Planning and Managing Change*, Harper and Row, London, 1986.
[8] Juran , J.M, *Managerial Breakthrough*, McGraw-Hill, New York, 1986.
[9] Crosby, P.B., *Quality is Free*, McGraw-Hill, New York, 1979.

9. Teams

A team is more difficult to study than a person

R. Meredith Belbin

Introduction

Improving the performance of an organization is an ongoing, continuous process which rarely comes about as a result of the efforts of a single individual. Despite the fact that our society has, from time to time, thrown up uniquely gifted and often charismatic individuals who are capable of moving whole organizations by the power of their vision and drive, the significant majority of the tasks which occur in these organizations require the co-operative efforts of a group of co-workers. One of the most effective tools for the harnessing and focus of those efforts is the team. As we saw in Chapter 7, the team is a vital component in the process of managing change. The team is not based upon the efforts or drive of a single individual, however charismatic, influential or insightful that person may be, but upon the complementary efforts of a small number of co-workers. As we will see in this chapter this powerful tool for organizational improvement is not driven by a leader but drawn forward by the commitment, of a number of mutually accountable individuals, to a shared purpose.

The activities of that team will be varied and often conducted away from the publicity which often attends the actions of the charismatic leader. They might include, for example, gathering information, implementing detailed actions or communicating with other groups. These activities, while often seen to be mundane, are nevertheless essential to the process of improving organizational performance. Indeed, without them, the vision of the desired future, whoever that is seen by, will be stillborn.

However, before looking at this team process, we do need to briefly visit the role of the leader. Our views of the nature and role of the organizational leader have changed with the passage of years from the traditional view that leaders were unique individuals who were born, rather than made, to the view that effective leadership results when the leadership style matches the needs of a given task and the needs of the work group. This latter view takes us to the position that there is no unique 'right' style of leadership but only styles which work better with certain groups undertaking certain tasks. Contemporary views of the role of the leader increasingly see this to be that of a facilitator or an enabler rather than a driver or a motivator. This shift reflects the increasing contributions made by those who 'are the organization' rather than those who are seen as or act as its figure-head. However, a detailed study of the subject of leadership, interesting as it may be, is one which is beyond the bounds of this book. Let it suffice to say that, however an organization or group is led, that organization or group is a collective of people and those people are present in that collective for other reasons than the money that they earn by being so. What then are these other needs and how can they contribute to the process of performance improvement?

Food, warmth and other needs

One of the more generally accepted views of these other needs is that proposed by Professor Abraham Maslow[1]. This view suggests that we all have five types of need. Maslow argues that these needs:

- Can be arranged in a hierarchy which reflects the order of their action upon us.
- Have their strongest influence on us when they are unsatisfied.

Thus we need to have our basic needs for food and water satisfied before we begin to seek job security and when that need is satisfied we will then seek to have our social needs answered. We will then seek to have our self-esteem needs answered and finally strive to answer our needs to fully express and realize our individuality (see Figure 9.1).

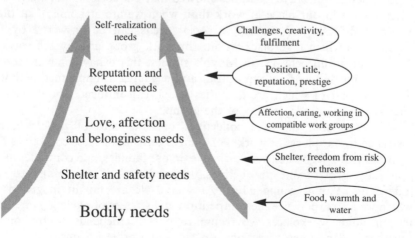

Figure 9.1 Hierarchy of needs

The importance of this view of our needs to the process of performance improvement process lies in its confirmation of the fact that we do not come to work for the money alone. We also come to work in order to satisfy our social needs and to do so by interacting with our co-workers in ways which are both satisfying and meaningful to us.

As Rensis Likert[2] puts it, we:

'want appreciation, recognition, influence, a feeling of accomplishment and a feeling that people who are important to us believe in us and respect us.'

You will also recall that we noted[3] in Chapter 1 that the organizations in which we attempt to satisfy these needs:

'exist to achieve purposes that individuals cannot achieve on their own.'

This means that not only do we join these organizations to satisfy our needs but that we only do so when we cannot satisfy them elsewhere.

In short, for all of us, as individuals, these organizations are primarily mechanisms for answering needs as well as being mechanisms for converting resources. To be so, these organizations have to contain and use social systems as well as those systems concerned with resource allocation and resource conversion.

This is a great deal more than an abstract theoretical concept. The influence of the social interaction which takes place when a number of people come together is considerable. This was first identified as early as the 1920s and 1930s when Elton Mayo's[4] studies showed that our social needs are no less when we are in our place of work than when we are at home or at play. These studies showed that these social needs can be answered by the interactions which take place within the work group and by the ways in which that group behaves. In Mayo's studies, this behaviour was seen to include adjusting work group output and engaging in unplanned activities or actions, all of which are activities which can influence the efficiency, effectiveness, and adaptability of the group.

Our experience of these collectives or assemblies of people is not restricted to our places of work. Personal experience of these collectives and their influence begins at a very early age, in our families, and continues as we gradually grow from the helpless dependency of an infant to the independence of a young adult. At school we are taught in groups in which we also experience the competition and stresses of playing games and in our adult workplaces we recognize our interdependence by joining together in departments, sections, divisions and project teams.

The continuing existence and variety of these assemblies, throngs or groups of people tells us that the collective unit is not a recent event or an outcome of the Industrial Revolution. It is, in fact, a universal experience which has appeared, and will continue to appear, in all of our societies. As such, this collective social unit can be viewed as:

- A natural phenomenon;
- An essential part of all our lives.

Tribes, families, clubs and companies

As we have already seen these collective units can be described in a variety of ways. This variety includes those collective nouns of which tribe, family, group, club, company and firm are just a few examples. But are these collective units all the same or do they behave and work in different ways ?

We can begin to answer this question by taking a look at behaviour patterns that are both common to and different between two typical and commonly occurring collections of people. These are:

- A group of people travelling together to London to see a play;
- The crowd entering a London main line railway station at rush-hour.

The first and most obvious difference is that of size. The rush hour crowd consists of a large and unlimited number of people while the group will be, either by choice or some membership requirement, of a limited size. The next difference is to do with what the sociologists term the 'shared views, social customs and beliefs' of these two assemblies. Those of you with experience of London main line railway stations at rush-hour will be aware that the people in the crowd do have a broad and general purpose in common: to get on the train, to get a seat if possible and to get home. However, each of the individuals who make up that crowd will rarely be aware of any further detail of the objectives of the other people around them and will not have shared or discussed those objectives with them. They will often only become aware of the objectives or purposes of others when those clash with their own objectives, e.g. in conflicts over space or seating. They may have an objective in common but it is not a shared one and that common objective will probably be limited to that of getting on the train. Indeed, as the crowd approaches the train, its apparent physical unity will begin to fragment as will any commonalty of purpose. Some of its members will wish to sit at the front and some will wish to sit at the back of the train. Others will wish to sit in different positions (facing forwards or backwards) or will wish to get off at different stations. It is very rare for crowds of this nature to display anything but the most limited of purposes in common and even rarer for them to undertake actions which require more than basic co-operation.

However, the assembly of theatre-goers which we have called a group will have a set of shared characteristics or objectives and will be prepared to act together in order to achieve these. For example, the group could consist of a number of people travelling from, say, Croydon, to see a play in London's West End. That objective may have required or encouraged co-operative action in order to get the tickets and to get to the theatre. This co-operative behaviour will have its rewards for group members. These rewards, for example, might include a group discount for the theatre tickets or the security of travelling together in an unfamiliar part of the city. These rewards will undoubtedly also include the social interchanges and interactions that will take place within the group. These interactions and exchanges may be facilitated by prior experiences of travelling or working together. It is also possible that the group may have an identity such as that of a social club or supporters club. However, those who make up both the crowd and the group will need to be in close physical proximity if they are to function effectively within those collectives. The rush-hour crowd consists of a number of people who are physically close to each other—as a result, for example, of attempting to get on the same train—while the group of theatre-goers will have chosen to travel together to a mutually agreed destination. In one case, the crowd, the proximity results from the coincidence of individual objectives while in the other, the group, the proximity occurs because of mutual agreement and choice.

By this time it will be evident that the major and significant difference between the group and the rush-hour crowd is that the group members:

- Have a shared objective rather than an objective in common;
- Undertake joint activities in order to achieve that objective.

This characteristic of sharing is one which also occurs when people come together in the collective unit that we call a team. So is a group the same as a team? Again, we can begin to answer this question by looking at the ways in which they both behave.

Groups or teams?

The word 'team' is often used in everyday life to describe a number of people who do something together and the typical dictionary definition for a team states that it consists of a number of people who work together. However, these joint or mutual activities can include playing together. The word 'team' is, for example, frequently used in sport: we often talk about football or rugby or hockey teams which compete against each other in order to win games, competitions, cups and leagues. We also often use the word 'teamwork' to describe the sort of activities that take place when a number of people work together on a common task or collaborate to overcome a problem which is common to all of them.

We saw earlier that a group consists of people who share certain characteristics and it is now evident that a team consists of a number of persons who are working co-operatively together. These definitions begin to give us an understanding of the differences between these collective units.

Before we examine those differences in more detail it is worth taking a look at the nature of groups. The variety of groups which exist is considerable. For example, the social scientists who study groups point out the differences between what are called *primary* groups and *secondary* groups. Primary groups:

- Have lots of face to face interaction;
- Encourage association and co-operation;
- Have a fundamental influence on 'social nature and ideas' of individuals.

Secondary groups involve:

- Large numbers of people;
- Limited face to face interaction and co-operation;
- A declared common goal or objective which is often of lower priority than individual goals.

An obvious example of the primary group is the family but it can also exist in the workplace as a small collection of workers with some shared interests, experience or knowledge. The size of these primary groups is usually limited due to the need for face to face interaction. Typical examples of secondary groups, in which this face to face interaction is limited include US Senate, UK Parliament, political parties and large committees. In the workplace, departments and divisions are typical examples of secondary groups. Both these types of groups can be created or designed and as such are generally described as *formal* groups. Many of the groups which exist in our workplaces are formal in nature and are:

- Created with a specific purpose or desired outcome in mind;
- Hierarchical with a formal leader and often with other designated roles for group members;
- Usually permanent but can be temporary;
- Often subject to changes in individuals involved but less often to change in the roles involved.

Examples of formal groups would include departments, work groups and project control or co-ordination groups though the later will often cease to exist on completion of the project. Roles within these formal groups can be the subject of written definitions, i.e. job specifications, and the group composition and structure is often described in organizational documentation such as an organization chart. The formal leader or co-ordinator of such a group will be responsible to the boss of the organization for the group's performance. Formal groups can be said to exist primarily to satisfy the task needs of the organization while *informal* groups exist primarily to satisfy the social and emotional needs of the individual. These can exist within formal groups or on their own and generally come into being because of chance or the choices and preferences of the individual members. They often act as informal communication networks or 'grapevines'. Examples of these informal groups can be a coffee club, a car pool or a lunch group.

So where are the differences between groups and teams and what is the significance of these differences to the performance improvement process? As we saw earlier, the team is a collective unit in which collaboration or working together is emphasized. However, these teams can also be formal in that they are created with a specific purpose or desired outcome in mind, as in a sports team or project team. They can also be permanent or temporary and can often be subject to changes in individuals involved. While teams are generally formal in nature they can also exist as in the informal state, should a common need arise. However, it is the comparison between the collaborative nature of the team and the limited shared characteristics of the group that provides the key to the more fundamental differences in their nature and operation. McKinsey's Jon Katzenbach and Doug Smith reviewed[5] some 50 teams operating in over 30 different organizations. Their conclusions indicate that while groups have a formal leader role, leadership in teams is often shared and can be rotated from individual to individual. Similarly, while team members are said to be answerable for their actions on both an individual *and* a collective basis, group members are said to be only individually accountable. All in all, these studies indicate that teams:

- Work together to generate collective, rather than individual, outcomes;
- Often have 'untidy' open ended discussions designed to solve problems.

whereas groups :

- Generate individual, rather than collective, outcomes;
- Have tidy, efficient meetings which delegate work to others;
- Act indirectly and by the exertion of influence on others.

These studies also indicate that teams are concerned with outcomes which are:

- Specific,
- Measurable,
- Meaningful to team members.

As such the team provides us with a powerful mechanism for improving organizational performance.

So how do we design, create and run a team that will enable us to make a positive contribution to the efficiency, effectiveness and adaptability of our organization? In order to answer that question we have to look at a number of characteristics of the team. These will include the team's:

- Size,
- Internal interactions and processes,
- Composition,
- Purpose.

LARGE TEAMS OR SMALL TEAMS?

The size of a team and the effect which that has on the ways in which the team operates has been the subject of a considerable amount of research. Before we take a look at that research it is worth reminding ourselves that teams are very much about mutualism and co-operation. This means that factors which erode or put at risk those characteristics can only be accepted if they bring with them some compensating characteristic or capability. Indeed the research indicates that the 'right' size of team is a compromise between the higher levels of skill and knowledge diversity and creative conflict which larger groups engender and the higher levels of participation, cohesiveness and involvement that occur in smaller groups.

For example, members of small teams tend to work well together and display higher levels of satisfaction with their membership of the team while large teams inhibit the involvement of some members and generate issues about leadership. Nevertheless, as the size of the team increases, the range and diversity of skills and abilities present within the team also increases. While this can make a positive contribution to the quality and diversity of discussions, it is also evident that introverted members can become increasingly inhibited and potential dissenters less willing to speak for fear of being thought 'deviant'. Another result of increasing team size is an increasing gap between the frequency of contributions from members as, with more members, each individual has, on average, less chance of contributing.

The results of this can include:

- Communication patterns which are less interactive due to the larger numbers involved;

- Discussions which display less sensitivity to minority issues;
- A tendency for the way in which team decisions are taken to shift away from consensus decisions involving all members towards majority decisions which exclude minorities.

The net result of all of this and other research indicates that the maximum team size should not exceed 10 members. In situations where participation and involvement are key issues, a team size of between 5 and 7 members is seen to be optimal. These small numbers encourage co-operative working with contributions from all members. Size is not, however, the sole factor in determining the efficiency of a team and the next section will take a brief look at the nature and range of the interactions that go on inside a team.

How does a team work?

An effective team is rather like a scaled-down version of an organization. As such, it is a mechanism which converts the activities of individuals, who are working towards answering their own needs, into a cohesive, dynamic and interactive unit which works towards the achievement of compatible goals or outcomes. So how does that happen?

Cranfield's Professor Andrew Kakabadse[6] tells us that what goes on inside a team, i.e. its social interactions and dynamics, can be said to fall into the following three groups of behaviour patterns.

1. *Behaviours concerned with the task* These are concerned with harnessing the collective skills and abilities of the group towards the chosen or given task. Behaviours such as decision-taking and managing, giving and seeking of information and opinions, agreement and disagreement, testing understanding and summarizing all fall into this set of task-related behaviours.
2. *Behaviours concerned with morale and harmony* These are concerned with the quality and level of interaction taking place within the group, i.e. the group process rather than its outcome. Peace-keeping, harmonizing, providing feedback are all examples of these maintenance-related behaviours.
3. *Behaviours concerned with individual member's goals and needs* These are related to the individual's needs and wants and are concerned with issues such as power, status, prestige, belonging and friendship. Examples of these self-related behaviours include point scoring, withdrawing, seeking recognition, attacking and defending and trivializing.

Some samples of the behaviours associated with these types of behaviour are given in Table 9.1

Table 9.1 Samples of team member behaviours

1. Those concerned with the team task

Initiating	'I suggest that we take a look at the information that we have now before we try to identify what our future choices are.'
Seeking information	'Can we complete the indoor redecoration in time for the Social Club dinner dance on 23rd December?'
Summarizing and decision management	'I believe that we have now heard all the available information and been able to express our views about their relevance and accuracy. I suggest that we now begin to think about what we are going to do.'

2. Those concerned with maintaining team morale, cohesiveness and harmony

Peace-keeping	'I do see that you both have strong feelings about this issue. Can we try to find some common ground?'
Giving feedback	'I do like the overall feel of your proposal but I am a little unsure about some of the detail.'
Encouraging	'Well done.'

3. Those concerned with individual team member's goals and needs

Defending	'I really cannot understand why you are attacking this idea since you yourself suggested something very similar last week.'
Withdrawing	'No comment.'
Point scoring	'I must express some surprise that you as a marketing man feel able to comment on some of the chemical formulation of our new perfume. Perhaps I should give up chemistry and take up marketing!'

Teams are not static or fixed in the ways in which they operate. Since they are made up of people and since, by and large, people are able to learn and develop, then it follows that teams will also change, grow, learn and develop. In the initial stages of a team's existence, time is needed for the members to get to know each other and assess each other's strengths, weaknesses, beliefs and value systems. This can lead to alliances and subgroups being formed. But even these are not static or fixed and they will dissolve and reform as the group changes and develops. Several studies of this development process indicate that it has a number of sequential stages and one version[7] of these stages identifies those of:

- *Forming* A time of inhibited, guarded, watchful, polite behaviour when team members are beginning to get to know each other;
- *Storming* As confidence grows, conflicts over personality, approaches, standards and beliefs emerge, giving rise to opting out behaviour and feelings of demotivation;
- *Norming* Team organization, systems, standards and procedures are established in this stage as are understandings about individual skills and abilities—high task focus evident;
- *Performing* Cohesiveness, mutual support, flexibility and productivity.

Whether a team will move, or needs to move, through all these stages to the mature performing stage will depend upon the nature of the task and the time available. For example, with a short time scale high-priority task, there may not be time to allow or encourage the full development process to occur. This does not necessarily mean that the group is ineffective since it may well achieve its task targets but the interpersonal conflicts and barriers will not have been tackled and will, if the group were to remain together, emerge with a subsequent 'regression' of the group back from the 'norming' to the 'storming' stage. In some groups a cyclic pattern of 'norming' → 'storming' → 'norming' can occur. Even when time and organizational support is available for this development process, the transition out of the above 'storming'/'norming' cycle or just the 'storming' stage alone can be dependent upon the pressure to produce outcomes and the abilities of the team members. The ability and willingness of a team to develop to the stage where it is capable of mature performance is dependent upon a number of factors. Some of these are external to the group, for example, the nature and time scale of the task or the willingness of the organization to allow the group to develop. However, others are internal to the group, and there is evidence that the individual characteristics and abilities of the team members and their ability to work together are crucial to the effective functioning of a team.

Who shall we have on our team?
While teams, in common with other forms of collective, are natural phenomena, they rarely spring into existence spontaneously. Most of the teams which exist in our organizations are formal in the sense that their

members have been selected and formal in the sense that they are created with a specific task or job in mind. It is also common practice to select team members on the basis of the job that they do while not in the team. The net result of this process of team selection often turns out to be a team which is representative of the organization's management group. Unfortunately, this does not always mean that the team will be effective or efficient in the way in which it operates. This external role basis for selection will not, for example, guarantee that the team members are compatible with each other. Nor will it provide any basis for confidence in the team's ability to grow and develop through the stages that we identified in the previous section. In short, all that selection on the basis of position or role will guarantee is that the team members are conversant with the demands of the external role which they occupy!

What we need when we choose our team members is some way of predicting how they will function in the team. We have already seen that the behaviour of team members is a response to the differing and sometimes opposing:

- Needs and demands of the task;
- Needs and demands of the team;
- Own needs.

Our experience tells us that some people are comfortable and effective in team situations while others are not. We will probably also be able to recall situations where a good team collapsed when one member left or moved on or when, on moving from one team to another, a team member failed to repeat the promise and performance shown in the first team.

Selecting a winning and effective team is a complex and difficult task, as can be seen in the example below, but it is one for which there are guidelines and maps to help us.

The wrong committee

The Consultancy and Short Course committee of the Business School was not performing well. The revenue from the short courses had fallen and these were now limited to the 'how to manage money' programmes which had been designed some years ago and run for the local authority. Consultancy work had always been limited in scope and revenue and was now being eroded further by the efforts of a new branch of a major commercial management consultancy which recently started operations in the local town. The Dean of the Business School, John Chamberlain, who chaired this committee, had been told by the University Vice Chancellor that more income was needed and needed soon! The committee consisted of the head of the management department, Don Stunning, and the directors of the undergraduate and postgraduate academic programmes which the Business School ran. It met monthly and its individual members often produced extensive position papers based on their views of the state of management education and the visits of Stunning and his colleagues to other Business Schools in both the UK and abroad. And yet these efforts were failing to produce the required results.

As he thought about this parlous state of affairs, John Chamberlain suddenly remembered what had been said to him some years ago by a member of staff who had left the Business School to go back into industry. What he was told was that the Business School would never succeed until its members of staff were able to convince the outside world that their lectures and courses were based on not only sound theory but also sound experience of business as it really operated. John thought about his committee and realized that very few of them had any experience of the practicalities of business and even less had any experience of marketing. He also realized that none of Don Stunning's trips had involved talking to clients: actual or potential. The next day he started to change the composition of the committee and to bring in the few staff members who had business experience. He also decided to commission a marketing consultant to review how they might increase the revenue from these courses and consultancy: the cost was small compared to one of Don Stunning's trips.

By the end of the next term it was evident that his efforts had been worthwhile: plans and programmes were evolving at a frantic pace and the revenue had started to increase. John Chamberlain began to feel that he now had a team rather than a debating group.

Early research into the ways in which teams functioned identified the presence of team roles which did not reflect or were not related to the external roles which team members carried out. These internal roles were related to the ways in which team members behaved in the team. Most of these studies indicated that there were at least three of these roles present in all teams. These could be described as:

- Strong fighter role;
- Logical thinker role;
- Friend/helper role.

However, our own experience will tell us that these are not the only roles seen in teams. Charles Handy[8] suggests that there are also the roles of:

- The comedian, who often defuses conflict or tension;
- The organizer, who looks after the arrangements and chores for the team;
- The commentator, who will, not always constructively or popularly, make remarks about the activities of the group;
- The deviant, who typically challenges and disagrees with the group consensus.

Dr Meredith Belbin[9] has taken this work a stage further and developed a 'blueprint' for the composition of the 'ideal' team. Belbin examined, via the use of psychometric tests, the characteristics of teams involved in playing management games. The objective of this research was to establish if there were any common characteristics among those teams which were successful and those which were unsuccessful. Successful teams were found to be made up of people with an adequate range of individual characteristics to ensure that some eight different team roles were carried out. The original outlines and titles established for these roles were:

- *Chairman* Described as being 'calm, self-confident and self-controlled', this role clarifies group objectives and sets agendas.
- *Company worker* A hard working practical organizer who turns other team members' ideas into manageable tasks.
- *Shaper* 'Outgoing and dynamic', this role is the task leader, uniting ideas and shaping the application of team effort.
- *Plant* 'Individualistic and unorthodox', this role is the ideas generator for the team but can be detached from practicality.
- *Resource investigator* Often described as the fixer of the team this role has high communicative skills and social acceptability.
- *Monitor–evaluator* The analyst of the team who tends to be 'sober, unemotional and prudent'.
- *Team-worker* 'Mild and sensitive', this role listens and communicates well and often smoothes conflict.
- *Completer–finisher* A perfectionist who has to check every detail.

According to Belbin, each individual team member has a preferred team role. She or he will also have a secondary role which she or he will act in if the preferred role is occupied by a more powerful individual or if no other is able to act in that secondary role. The original roles defined by Belbin were later modified to include a *Specialist* role and to change the role title for the *Chairman* role to *Co-ordinator* and the title for the *Company worker* role to *Implementer*. The *Specialist* role is described as one which views the team

191

task or objectives through the medium and with the limitations of their area of individual expertise.

The presence of all these roles in a team is said to result in a balanced and effective team which:

- Makes the best use of its resources;
- Has the ability to bounce back from disappointments;
- Displays adaptability;
- Contains creative capability which is limited to a few members;
- Has limited dependence on key members.

The Belbin approach to team composition management has developed self-assessment questionnaires to enable individual optimal roles to be identified. In more general terms, if we are to have effective teams, we need to recognize that these teams will have to be made up of people who:

- Are chosen for their interpersonal skills as much as their functional skills;
- Are able to adjust their team role and function to complement those of others in the team;
- Provide a balanced range of both external and internal roles.

Relevant information about potential team members and their potential or demonstrated ability to meet the above criteria can be acquired from:

- Performance in other teams;
- In company training courses;
- Appraisal procedures;
- Team role assessment questionnaires.

Creating and developing an effective team for organizational performance improvement is not a quick or an easy task. It is, however, a worthwhile one. The effective team will generate outcomes of a quality and quantity which are in excess of the sum of their individual capabilities and in so doing will make a major contribution to the performance improvement process. The genesis of such a team will lie in the choice of its members from a basis of their value to the team rather than their functional external role. The composition of this team must also reflect its purpose or goals and it is this aspect of teams and their contribution to the process of performance improvement that we shall now take a look at.

What are we going to do?

Teams do not exist in a vacuum: they exist within organizations and as such are subject to a variety of external pressures and constraints which influence both what they do and how they do it. For example, the team which is asked to quickly solve a pressing and urgent problem with the distribution of perishable products will be working in a different environment and at a different pace to a team which has been asked to identify the probable computing needs of an organization in the early 21st century. The characteristics of the purpose or task of the team that can significantly influence the composition and effectiveness of that team are outlined below:

THE CHARACTER OR NATURE OF THE TASK

This character or nature will influence many aspects of the team's operation and even its composition. These will include the time-scale, depth and quality of the team's work and the functional external roles represented. For example, a task which involved reviewing the technical aspects of high technology production equipment would involve a team that had a strong external functional bias towards members with relevant technical knowledge and production backgrounds. Similarly a task which needs to be completed quickly may well require the choice of team members who have worked well together in previous teams and who can consequently bypass some of the forming stage of development. Tasks which are defined in an unclear or ambiguous manner will tend, even with the best of teams, to produce unclear and confused outcomes.

TASK OUTCOME CRITERIA

If they are to be carried out in an efficient and an effective manner, all tasks need to have measurable outcomes. In the light of earlier comments about the organizational conversion process it is perhaps not surprising to find that these outcomes can be either tangible or intangible. They may be the production of a report or a set of recommendations, a change in operating procedure or some conclusions resulting from the acquisition and manipulation of information. Whatever their nature, if they are to make a positive contribution to the effectiveness and efficiency of the team, these outcomes need to be:

- Measurable;
- Realistic;
- Credible;
- Understandable.

Teams: a conclusion

In overall terms there should be little doubt about both the capability and the potential contribution of teams to the process of improving organizational performance effectiveness Their use is wide spread and the variety of their names—quality teams, multi-disciplinary problem-solving teams, project teams, self-managing teams—illustrates their power and flexibility. The power of this instrument for change is such that there are few situations to which it will not be able to make a positive contribution. But teams do require support and the freedom and time to develop to their full potential. Their members will also need training and those in the organization around the team will need to understand the purpose and process of the team. These and other needs are shown in Table 9.2.

However, given that these can be met, then your teams will empower your people and provide the drive and energy to improve the performance of your organization.

Table 9.2   Needs of successful teams

Successful teams need:
Challenge and urgency
Specific and attainable goals or objectives
Recognition and reward
Autonomy
Support and understanding
People who have and can use:
− interpersonal skills
− functional skills
− problem-solving skills
− decision-taking skills

At the beginning of Part 2 we started our review of the practicalities of improving organizational performance by identifying the key steps in that process. This review continued with a look at how that change process is managed and the contributions made by both effective communication and teams. This process will not, however, be without its problems and Chapter 10 takes a look at some of the more effective ways of identifying solutions to those problems.

Summary

The significant majority of improvements in organizational performance come about through the co-operative efforts of numbers of co-workers who

194

share purpose and commitment. The most effective channel for these complementary efforts is that of the team. Unlike the group, the team is a mechanism which is concerned with:

- Collective rather than individual outcomes;
- Outcomes which are :
  - specific,
  - measurable,
  - meaningful to all team members.

To be effective the team requires:

- To be limited in size (maximum of ten);
- To consist of members who are able to balance with their own needs:
  - the needs of the task, and
  - the needs of the team;
- To consist of members who:
  - are chosen for their interpersonal skills as much as their functional skills;
  - are able to adjust their team role and function to complement those of others in the team;
  - are able to provide a balanced range of both external and internal roles.

The structure and composition of this team will also be affected by :

- The task's character or nature;
- The criteria against which team outcomes are evaluated.

References
[1] Maslow, A., A theory of human motivation, in *Psychological Review*, vol. 50, pages 370–396.
[2] Likert, R., *New Patterns of Management*, McGraw-Hill, New York, 1961.
[3] Stewart, R., *Managing Today and Tomorrow*, Macmillan, Basingstoke, 1991.
[4] Mayo, E., *The Human Problems of an Industrial Civilization*, Macmillan, New York, 1933.
[5] Katzenbach, J.R. and D.K. Smith, The discipline of teams, in *Harvard Business Review*, vol. 71, Mar-Apr, pages 111–120.
[6] Kakabadse, A. and R. Ludlow and S. Vinnicorbe, *Working in Organisations*, Penguin, London, 1988.
[7] Tuckman, B.W., Developmental sequences in small groups, in *Psychological Bulletin*, vol. 63, No.6, pages 384–399.
[8] Handy, C.B., *Understanding Organisations*, Penguin, London, 1985.
[9] Belbin, M.R., *Management Teams: Why They Succeed or Fail*, Butterworth-Heinemann, Oxford, 1992.

10. Problem-solving

Problems are only opportunities in work clothes.

Henry J. Kaiser

There is no such thing as a problem without a gift for you in its hands.

Richard Bach

Introduction
While the process of improving organizational performance can itself be viewed as a problem-solving process—the 'problem' being the difference between where we are and where we want to be—in fact the range and nature of problems involved in that improvement process itself are considerable. In reality, problems are ubiquitous: they are a constant and pervasive feature of our lives, both inside and outside our organizations. They can have their roots or origins in situations which are minor or major and can also lead to, irrespective of their origins or causes, major or minor consequences. These consequences can affect or influence the lives of large numbers of people or they can impinge upon the life of a single individual. These problems can be defined or expressed in terms of numbers as, for example, when we overspend our budgets or they can be expressed in terms of abstract concepts such as, for example, what is 'right' or what is 'wrong'. The common view of problems is that they are 'negative' or 'bad'. Certainly there are problems that contain or imply consequences which we find undesirable or unacceptable as, for example, when we are faced with an unexpected and large bill. Problems can, however, be 'positive' or 'good' in that they involve us in decisions about choices whose outcomes are all acceptable, as for example when we are faced with a choice about what to do with an unexpected bonus or pools win.

They can also be concerned with our feelings about one other. Organizations consist of people and all of these people are involved in a web of complex and ever-changing social interactions and relationships. These interactions or relationships can be transitory or long lasting and can involve or exclude any part of the whole gamut of our emotional repertoires. We can like, care for, be irritated by, be rude to, fear, be angry with, be indifferent to, hate and love those with whom with we share our places of work, and they can and do respond in like or different ways. Our individual inputs to this seething and everchanging network of human contacts and

196

connections are contained in the ways in which we behave, look, speak, sound move and even smell; and all of these are perceived and interpreted by others.

This process of perception is a complex one which is coloured and biased by our views, beliefs and expectations. Edward de Bono[1] states that perception 'refers to the way that we see the world' and points out that we see 'mainly what we are prepared by experience to see'. Other research[2] suggests that we employ two different kinds of mechanism in processing the information that comes to us via our sight, hearing, touch and smell. These are the mechanisms of:

- Filtering by which we accept or reject the information which we receive;
- Pigeon-holing by which we select 'favoured' responses even when there is limited evidence to justify that choice.

These mechanisms add certainty to our lives as well as helping us to cope with the massive influx of information that we continually receive. However, they also limit the information that we accept and interpret to that which our experience leads us to expect. In so doing they reinforce our biases and prejudices. This occurs, for example, when we ignore or refuse to accept input about a colleague's state of mind when it conflicts with that which our prior experience has led us to expect. So someone who is angry with a particular situation may have his or her anger ignored because they were not angry when it last occurred or because you've not seen them angry before. We also demonstrate the presence of these biases and prejudices when we, often with limited or incomplete information, fit people into 'slots' or models or categories, and in so doing make judgements about their likely future behaviour. Examples of these slots or models are present in such statements as:

'Short men are always aggressive'
'Women cannot be logical.'

In reality, there is substantial evidence to refute both these examples. However, our biases and prejudices will continue to influence our behaviour until we are willing to modify what we think, from our prior experience, is likely to be true or to happen. This dependence upon prior experience not only limits the quality and content of our contact with the world of the 'here and now' but it also leads to problems.

This selective filtering of the reality of the world around us can also be present in the ways that we view the behaviour of our organizations and the numerical symptoms of that behaviour. As such, its influence upon the process of performance improvement is considerable. We may, for example,

197

choose to not see the significance of factual information, which our monitoring provides, because it does not 'fit' with what we expected to see.

This situation is further complicated by the fact that the ways in which we see and interpret the behaviour of both others and our organizations are influenced and determined by our expectations and needs. Each of us brings to each situation a very individual 'bundle' of experiences, beliefs, attitudes, expectations, values and objectives. It is, therefore, not surprising that different people will often interpret the same situation or the same information in different ways. As a consequence, their interpretations and perceptions of the problem will differ. These different views can include a number of dimensions:

- *Significance* As in: 'This is the key issue' or 'This isn't important'.
- *Polarity* As in: 'This high wind is dangerous' or 'Isn't this high wind exhilarating?'
- *Presence* As in: 'I find him very rude' or 'I don't have a problem with his behaviour'.

The objectives of this chapter are that we should take a look at:

- The nature and characteristics of problems;
- Some of the more effective ways of identifying potential solutions.

We shall look at these as they occur within the context of the performance improvement process.

What is a problem?
We have already seen that problems can vary significantly in terms of their nature, origins and consequences and that our individual experience, knowledge, beliefs and needs can influence their significance, polarity and presence. Typical dictionary definitions of a problem are that of a 'difficult or doubtful question' or something which is 'hard to understand or deal with'. These definitions suggest that a problem is something which is:

- Ill-defined,
- Expressed in ways which are difficult to understand, or
- Lacking in certainty.

But is this always so? As we saw earlier, some problems come about because people or organizations behave or react in ways which are different to those which we expect and it is the unexpected nature of this behaviour rather than the degree of its definition or clarity which initiates our response. There are also problems which are well defined and clearly stated and about which we are able to do little. The famine in Ethiopia is one example of this type of problem. However, our experience tells us that in many situations, particularly those we meet in our organizations, the data available about the problem is limited and often of uncertain accuracy. It may also not be possible to either identify or compare all the alternative solutions for the problem.

This begins to give us the view that problems are what they are because of the conflict between our needs and desires and the actuality of the 'real' world. For example, an unusual request from a customer is a 'problem' because we have not anticipated or planned for it and a down-turn in sales is a 'problem' because we desired or needed steady or rising sales. In both of these situations we are 'face to face' with a situation which differs from the one which we desire. If, however, we do not wish to respond to this difference, then we do not have a problem. If we do wish to respond or react to the difference but we are not sure how or when to respond, then we do have a problem. This sequence is illustrated in Figure 10.1.

This emerging picture also suggests that our problems lie on a spectrum or continuum at one end of which we have structure, certainty and clear alternatives whereas, at the other end, we have uncertainty, lack of structure and no clear alternatives. One expression of the extremes of this continuum is that given by Dr E.F. Schumacher, who wrote *Small is Beautiful* in the 1970s. Schumacher[3] suggested that there are two types of problem which he described as:

1. *Convergent* These have an optimal and unique solution and the alternatives will converge towards this.
2. *Divergent* These do not have a 'correct' solution and evaluation of the alternatives serves only to underline and contrast their contradictions.

The difficulty that we have with the divergent type of problem is often not with the methods used to try to solve it or even the data used but with the nature and construction of the problem itself. For example, a divergent problem, in the context of the performance improvement process, would be 'How do we delight our customers?' for which there are many, many potentially successful solutions. In the same context a convergent problem would be 'How do we increase our productivity?' for which there will be a unique answer.

Some of the characteristics of this continuum are shown in Figure 10.2.

Many of the problems which we face in the 'real' world are closer to the divergent or soft end of this spectrum than the hard or convergent end. Whatever the level of our problem's 'messiness' or its 'hardness', if we desire

Actual situation
Desired situation
Is there a difference?
No
Yes
Do you want to do something about that difference?
No
Yes
Do you know what to do and when to do it?
Yes
No
You do not have a problem
You do have a problem

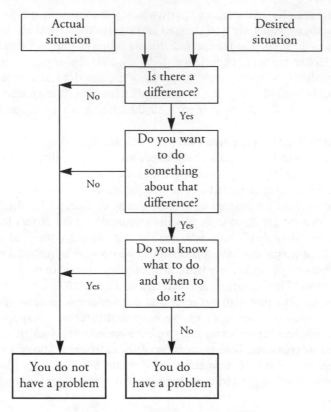

Figure 10.1 Do you have a problem?

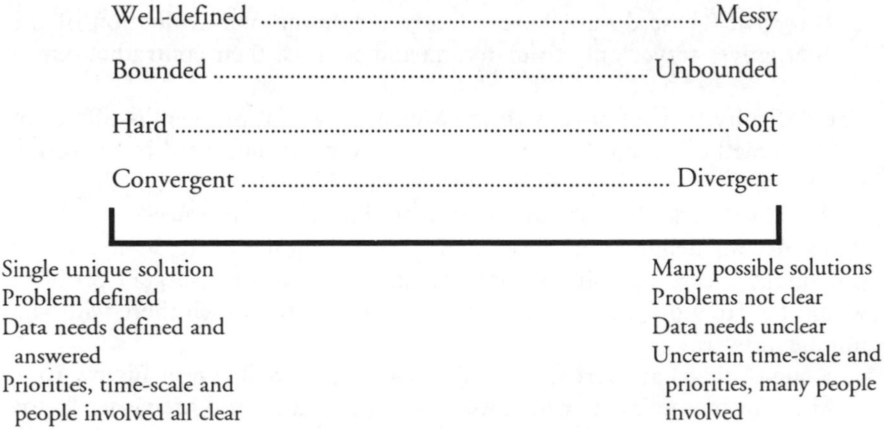

Well-defined .... Messy
Bounded .... Unbounded
Hard .... Soft
Convergent .... Divergent
Single unique solution
Problem defined
Data needs defined and answered
Priorities, time-scale and people involved all clear
Many possible solutions
Problems not clear
Data needs unclear
Uncertain time-scale and priorities, many people involved

Figure 10.2 Problem spectrum

to do something about that situation then we will need to identify actions which give us some hope of generating a solution.

How do we solve this problem ?

The first step towards solving our problems lies in our defining the problem. But how much definition do we need? In a perfect world we would, in solving our problems, have:

- All the data that we needed;
- A logical and rational way of analysing, processing and evaluating that data;
- A clear understanding of the problem;
- A clear understanding of the basis on which the choice of a solution shall be made.

These would give us a total definition of not only the problem but also our objective and route for arriving there. But in the real world of our organizations we have to cope with:

- Information which is limited in quantity and quality;
- Difficulty in upgrading that information because:
  - of the lack of resources;
  - the cost of upgrading might exceed the likely benefits;
  - the problem is perceived to have a lower priority than other problems.

Nobel prize winner Herbert Simon recognized this when he wrote[4] of the 'limited rationality' of organizational decisions and concluded that we, and our organizations, often settle for 'good enough' decisions based on limited information. Simon calls this process 'satisficing' and says that most people do not attempt to find the best solution to their problem but look at alternatives until they find one which meets a set of minimum criteria. This solution is then accepted as satisfactory and the search is stopped.

What we need to ask is whether we need to know all the facts, details, implications and subtleties of a problem before we can solve it and whether we can cope with a less than complete picture. Part of the answer to this question lies with:

- How often the problem occurs;
- The problem's potential consequences.

For example, a recurrent problem is one that we are likely to need to know more about because it keeps happening and also perhaps because our previous attempts to solve it have failed. However, while infrequent or occasional problems would appear to be less demanding, in terms of data needs, this can and does change when we look at the consequences of the problem. For example, a problem which occurs only once every hundred years would appear to be one that would not demand much of our attention. If, however, that problem results in the deaths of two million people, then it will warrant and receive more attention. This marriage of frequency of problem occurrence or, to be more accurate, its likely future occurrence, and the consequences of that occurrence is an important one. It will give us, even if we have to estimate or guess both the consequence and the frequency, a basis on which to prioritize our response to that problem. If this product of frequency and consequence is high then we will need further data in order to define and solve the problem. If the product is low we can then either:

- Decide a solution from the data we have;
- Defer solving the problem to a later time;
- Decide not to solve it until it either:
  - occurs more often, or
  - has greater consequences;
- Decide to ignore it and hope that it will go away.

The other part of the answer to the question of how much data do we need will often, in the 'real' world, lie in the answers to:

- How much data do we have now?
- How much more data can we get and at what cost?

As we have seen earlier, our organizations often limit the scope and outcomes of the decision-taking process in ways which:

- Reflect the anticipated value of outcomes. For example: why spend more money on data gathering than we will gain in increased profit?
- The nature and accuracy of the input data. For example: why spend time and resource on evaluating uncertain data?

In our earlier 'perfect world' we would follow a problem-solving sequence in which we:

- Defined the problem,
- Specified our objectives,
- Identified the measures for these objectives,
- Identified the alternative solutions,
- Evaluated these alternatives,
- Chose a solution,
- Adopted that solution.

But, as we have already seen, people don't always solve problems in logical or rational ways. For example, we may, in the terms of the above sequence, 'jump' to a preferred solution, without evaluating the alternatives, because of strong leadership or the compatibility of this solution with our organization's long-term vision. We may also 'move backwards' in this sequence because we need to redefine the problem. This can come about if none of the alternatives considered 'satisfice' or if we have a conflict between two alternatives.

Our own experience will also tell us that we often arrive at solutions to our problems in ways other than the logical and rational 'perfect world' approach that was outlined above. Some of these are based on the use of our intuition. This word is used to describe the process we follow when we arrive at decisions or conclusions without explicit or conscious logical thought. While intuition has been often strongly associated with creative effort as, for example, in August Kekulé's identification of the structure of the benzene ring in a dream, its use in our business decisions has been less well documented (or accepted). Nevertheless, there is evidence which indicates that we do use our intuition under these circumstances and often to good effect. Weston Agor[5] writes of studies which indicate that top executives in major corporations such as Chrysler, Burroughs and General Motors use intuition and value its results. These 'gut decisions' are, however, often disguised with a cloak of logic and data in order to enhance their acceptability.

These views of the 'non-rational' ways of solving problems include an identification of the different roles of the right and left hemispheres of our brains. While these hemispheres control the movements of the opposite sides of our bodies, they also handle information in different ways. The left hemisphere, which controls the right side of our body, processes information in a linear sequential manner and the right hemisphere, which controls the left side of our body, processes all input information simultaneously. The implication of this, as far as problem-solving is concerned, is that we have access to two ways of processing information: an analytical, linear and logical left-brain way and an intuitive and experiential right-brain way, and this right-brain way can be and is used to some effect.

Henry Mintzberg[6] argues eloquently that :

'The important policy level processes required to manage an organization rely to a considerable extent on the faculties identified with the brain's right hemisphere.'

However, just as we learn in our schools and universities the patterns and ways of analytical left-brain thinking, we also need to learn how to access the patterns and ways of right-brain thinking. Joel Levey[7] describes a number of relaxation and mediation techniques and identifies over 30 studies confirming increased hemispheric synchronization and increased creativity as a result of the use of these techniques.

The ways in which we solve our problems are complex and often unordered. The remainder of this chapter will examine some of the ways by which we can add to the quality of our problem-solving processes without becoming inhibited or limited by a doctrinaire adherence to a process or methodology.

Nominal group technique

This is a problem-solving method which involves the use of a group of people to find potential solutions to an identified problem. It is productive not only in terms of the number of ideas generated but also the quality of those ideas. The process works by involving all the members of the group and by using group consensus to evaluate and rank all the ideas generated. The outcome is a group agreement about the action which needs to be taken.

These are the steps.

Step 1 The team leader presents the problem or opportunity to the group. This must be done in a manner which does *not* suggest a preferred solution.

The process and ground rules are also explained at this stage.

Step 2 Working on their own, everyone writes down a list of potential solutions for the stated problem.

Step 3 Everyone, in turn, reports a single idea from their list which is recorded on a flip chart or board. The name of the person who suggested the idea is not recorded and no comments or evaluations are made during this stage which continues until all the ideas on everyone's list have been put forward.

Step 4 During a brief discussion any clarification of ideas needed is given and similar ideas are amalgamated if the owners of the original ideas are agreeable.

Step 5 Each group member then identifies his or her top five ideas and writes these down on a piece of paper which is given to the leader.

Step 6 The leader amalgamates these individual rankings and generates a top five list for the group.

Step 7 These five are reported to the group and then discussed. Another vote is taken to identify the idea(s) to be actioned.

Experience indicates that most people find difficulty in reporting their ideas briefly and without commenting on their merits. The control of the group leader is important here as the discipline of quickly moving on to the next person for each new idea reduces this difficulty. It is also important that the group stays together while the team leader or someone else is analysing the options to find the group's top five.

Brainstorming

This group technique has two separate stages:

- The generation and recording of ideas;
- Assessment of these ideas.

The stages are kept separate in order to focus the attention of group members on the process of creating, without assessment or evaluation, as many potential solutions as is possible. If the process works then the solutions suggested at this stage will include many which are bizarre, impractical or unconventional rather than being limited to 'practical' or 'sensible' solutions. Some of these solutions will have been 'sparked off' by a chain reaction as one person's solution triggers a related solution from someone else which in its turn triggers another solution from a another group member and so on.

The steps of brainstorming are simple and straightforward but must be observed if you are going to tap into people's creativity. They are:

Step 1 Identify who is going to act as group recorder. This role involves:
  (i)   Making sure all rules are observed.
  (ii) Making sure all ideas are written down on flip charts or a large board.
Step 2 Write the problem down clearly and in a place where everyone can see it.
Step 3 The recorder spells out the rules and makes sure that everyone understands them. They are:
  (i) Generate as many ideas as you can.
  (ii) All ideas will be recorded accurately and without editing, censorship or comment.
  (iii) Ideas can relate to or be triggered by the previous ideas or can, at any time, start a new chain of thought.
  (iv) All ideas are accepted including the unconventional, weird and bizarre ones.
Step 4 All of the ideas are written down in a numbered list so that everyone can see them all of the time.
Step 5 Everyone is free to state their idea and it *must* be written down.

205

Comment or evaluation in any form, verbal or non-verbal, is not allowed.

Step 6 When all ideas have been generated the written and numbered ideas are categorized, by the group, as follows:

Good

Possible

Bad

Unusual

Similar ideas can be grouped together using their numbers to identify them.

Step 7 For all the 'good' and 'possible' ideas, further categories of similar ideas are created.

Step 8 Fit the 'unusual' ideas into these categories or create new ones.

Step 9 Check to see if the group has any further ideas under each of the above categories.

Step 10 Ask each group member to pick the category which they think is the most promising. and to say why.

Step 11 Discuss the various options and choose the one(s) to proceed with.

As a technique, brainstorming is more informal and relaxed than the nominal group technique. It does however require more discipline from all involved, particularly in the avoidance of comment and evaluation during the ideas creation phase. Once group members get the hang of the ideas generation process they normally enjoy it. It is important that the recorder also takes part in this process and is not seen as an arbiter or judge. It is also important to ensure that categories designated as 'bad' are only done so after thorough group discussion, since they are discarded and not discussed further after being so labelled.

Lateral thinking

The traditional ways of describing the ways in which we think and, indeed, the ways in which we are taught to think are based on what is called 'vertical' or logical thinking. These involve our attention moving in a logical and sequential manner from one thought to another, each thought being in a chain of continuity with its preceding and following partners.

This 'vertical' thinking is :

- Selective,
- Based on:
  - judgement,
  - proof,
  - 'right' and 'wrong'.

Vertical thinking looks for unique 'right' answers and uses information only for its meaning in the process of looking for that answer.

Lateral thinking, which was identified by Edward de Bono,[8] looks for what is different—rather than what is right or wrong—and uses information to trigger off new ideas. Chance intrusions are welcome to the lateral thinking process which is described as being 'to do with changing perceptions and finding new ways of looking at things'. Simple illustrations of lateral thinking are given below.

Lateral thinking[8]

How do you weigh an elephant?
Bury the weighing machine and let the elephant walk on to it.
Put one leg on each of four small scales.
How do you increase the profitability of a railway system passenger traffic?
Make additional charges for low volume lines.
Make extra charges for peak hour travel.
Charge for occupancy time rather than journey length.
Charge for in-journey entertainment.
How do you reduce supermarket theft?
Charge on basis of difference in entry and exit weight.
Vary price discounts on weekly basis to reflect theft rate.
All food free but charge for entry.

There are two basic processes for lateral thinking:

- Escaping from:
  - dominant or polarising ideas,
  - the prison of the 'right' answer,
  - conventional entry points,
  - concept prisons,
- Provoking by:
  - being 'wrong',
  - making unjustified leaps,
  - using an idea as catalyst rather than an answer,
  - separating idea generation from idea evaluation.

The objective of lateral thinking is that of unlocking our creativity and as such it is used with, rather than as a substitute for, vertical thinking. Edward de Bono observes that, in practice, lateral thinking is used to create the ideas which are then evaluated by vertical thinking.

Visioning

Visioning is a simple technique which uses our ability to create mental images. This we do continually, either consciously or unconsciously, and we use these images to recreate past events or to express our desires about future events. These images often contain potent stimuli to both our minds and our bodies. For example, the image of a tasted lemon can cause our mouths to wrinkle and our saliva to flow and images associated with aggression can cause our body to secrete chemicals which prepare us for fight or flight and which result in raised heart rate and muscle tension.

The contribution of visioning to the process of solving problems is that of establishing future goals. It is not, however, concerned with how those goals can be achieved. Nevertheless, as we have seen in earlier chapters, the gap between our current and desired position and the vision of a desired future is one which drives the process of performance improvement. As such it can contribute a considerable amount of energy towards the process of problem-solving. We have also seen, in earlier chapters, that the process of performance improvement is one which is dependent upon the efforts of those who work within our organizations. Visioning can provide a view of a desired future which is both contributed to and shared by all who work in that organization.

The process of visioning can be carried out in a number of ways. All of these, however, have at their core our ability to bypass the constraints of language by the use of visual images. The process of creative visualization is a multi-faceted one and can involve the use of all our senses and all our creative capabilities. We can, for example, visualize objects whose texture, smell, taste and appearance can be changed at our whim. We can also visualize other people and their behaviours in circumstances and locations which do or do not involve us. By using this potent capability we can create, with considerable detail, an image of how we wish things to be.

Robert Burnside[9] describes the application and results of visioning in two quite different organizations. While both of the methods used had at their core the individual's ability to visualize his or her desired future state, they differed considerably in the degree of structure or formality involved. In its more formal form visioning involves the use of a defined task or scenario such as:

'Imagine the content of a newspaper article in the year 2000 which describes, in detail, the reasons for the organization's success.'

A less formal version of the process will use guided imagery techniques, which when supported by relaxation procedures, can ask people to, for example:

'Imagine that they are in their workplace in the year 2000, and ask them to look at how that workplace is structured, what they are doing in it, how other people are looking and behaving and what they are doing.'

Both of these visioning processes will take place in small groups and over a limited period of time. At the end of the visioning period people are asked to record in words or pictures the significant images or feelings that they experienced. These are then shared and discussed until the group has a view of what was common between all the member's visions. This common vision is then shared with others in the organization, such as other groups, or reported to those who are co-ordinating or facilitating the visioning process. When repeated with other groups, a consensus vision will emerge from this process. This can then be used as a jointly developed target or goal towards which the whole organization wishes to move others in the organization.

Despite its apparent esoteric and 'new age' appearance visioning is an effective and powerful way of:

- releasing people's creative potential;
- generating a consensus vision;
- empowering people to contribute to the future of their organization.

The Ishikawa diagram
The Ishikawa or 'Fishbone' diagram was developed by Dr Kaoru Ishikawa (see Chapter 4) in 1943 as a management problem-solving tool. It is regarded as one of the most powerful of the techniques available to solve problems and has been used in a wide variety of circumstances including quality circles.

The diagram (Figure 10.3) has, as its starting point, a box which is located on the right-hand side of a sheet of paper. Inside this box is written the problem to be solved. An arrow is then drawn across the sheet pointing towards the box and four further arrows are drawn pointing towards the main arrow. Each of these side arrows represents a family or group of causes which could have lead to the problem (or effect). The cause families for these side arrows are those associated with:

- People, i.e. those who are involved;
- Equipment and machines which are involved;

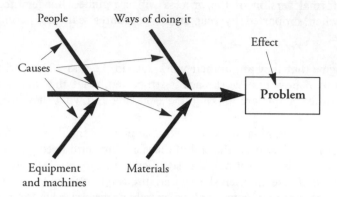

Figure 10.3 Fishbone diagram

- Ways of doing it, i.e. the method used;
- Materials which are converted or consumed.

The technique can be used by a group or an individual and has the six steps.

Step 1 Define problem.

Step 2 Draw fishbone with problem written in the box.

Step 3 Label the side arrows either with the general tags of Materials, Equipment and Machines, People and Ways of doing it or more specific tags which reflect the problem but still fall into these groups.

Step 4 Identify possible causes and write these on the diagram as a branch on the relevant side arrow.

Step 5 Continue with the identification of possible causes until all of these, even the improbable ones, have been written down.

Step 6 Review the diagram and decide which of the causes are to be investigated first.

The diagram results in a thorough and often penetrating identification of all possible causes. It does not, of course, tell you which of those possible causes actually took place, but if generated with care, it does give you confidence that all the possible causes have been listed. It is often worthwhile sticking to Ishikawa's original side arrow headings of Men, Materials, Machines and Method in order to make sure that the review of causes is comprehensive and methodical. Figure 10.4 shows the application of this technique to a problem which I often meet.

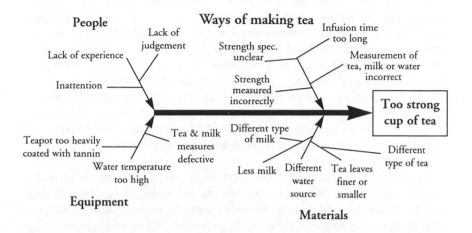

People   **Ways of making tea**

Figure 10.4   Ishikawa diagram: causes of strong tea

Problems or opportunities?

Problems, as we saw earlier, occur when we become aware of a conflict or difference between our needs and desires and the actual state of the 'real' world, and don't know what to do about it. These problems are the results or symptoms of our ongoing and continuing interaction with the environment around us and, as we saw in Chapter 2, it is this interaction which provides us with some of the information that we need in order to identify the goals and targets of our organizations. We also know that it is these goals which are used, by comparison with the current position of the organization, to fuel the engine of the performance improvement process.

Problems occur all of the time and it is often easier and more comfortable to desensitize ourselves to their message by ignoring them. We do this, for example, with our customers when we respond to their complaints by making them feel uncomfortable or unreasonable or when we ignore the rising failure rates of our conversion processes. In fact, these complaints are our customer's gifts to us—they care enough to tell us that we didn't meet their expectations—and when we are given that gift we are being given an opportunity to change.

Problems, wherever they come from and whatever their size or consequences, are opportunities for change and when we meet them we are, as it were, on the cusp of the change process. However, we don't have to accept these opportunities or gifts. Many of the day to day problems that we meet in our organizations are small enough for our rejection of their gift not to cause a collapse or major crisis, but they don't disappear. Those problems that we ignore will return to us—in a different form or wearing different data 'clothes'—because, when viewed at an organizational level, they are symptoms of either the need to change or of the existence of change itself. Our acceptance of their gift may not move mountains but it will, as we saw in the first pages of this book, start that process of accumulation which will lead to the creation of large and significant improvements in performance. This improved performance will, in its turn, provide the opportunity for all of those who work in these organizations to have choices about bigger and more significant, or even radical, changes in the ways in which their work is carried out.

Throughout the whole of the process of organizational performance improvement, there exists the need to analyse information. This analysis can, for example, lead to choices about what to measure and monitor or what option to implement. The next chapter examines some of the tools that can be used to undertake that analysis.

Summary
A problem can:

- Have trivial or significant consequences;
- Involve or affect small or large numbers of people;
- Be expressed in numerical or conceptual terms.

Problems can, for the same circumstance, reflect our individual biases, perceptions and prejudices in terms of their:

- Significance,
- Polarity,
- Presence or absence.

Problems occur because of:

- The conflict between our needs and desires and the actuality of the 'real' world;
- Our uncertainty about what to do about this conflict.

These problems lie on a continuum with the extremes of:

- Uncertain definition, timescale and priority with many possible solutions, and

- Single unique solution with clear, well-defined problem, time-scale and priority.

Solutions for problems are rarely generated by rational logical processes but by other processes which are often complex and disordered and include:

- The limited rationality of 'satisficing',
- The use of intuition,
- Right-brain processes.

Techniques which can be used to generate potential solutions to our problems include:

- Brainstorming,
- Nominal group technique,
- Lateral thinking,
- Visioning,
- Ishikawa diagrams.

All problems are opportunities for change and we ignore them at our peril.

References

[1] de Bono, E., *Word Power*, Penguin, London, 1977.
[2] Broadbent, D., Relation between theory and application in psychology, in Warr, P.B. (ed.), *Psychology at Work*, Penguin, London, 1976.
[3] Schumacher, E.F., *A Guide for the Perplexed*, Abacus, London, 1974.
[4] Simon, H.A., *Administrative Behaviour*, Macmillan, London, 1960.
[5] Agor, W.H., The logic of intuition: how top executives make important decisions, reprinted in Henry, J. (ed.)(1991) *Creative Management*, Sage, London, 1991.
[6] Mintzberg, H. Planning on the left side and managing on the right, reprinted in Henry, J. (ed.), *Creative Management*, Sage, London, 1991.
[7] Levey, J., *Relaxation, Concentration and Meditation: Ancient Skills for Modern Minds*, Wisdom Publications, London, 1987.
[8] de Bono, E., *Lateral Thinking for Management*, Penguin, London, 1971.
[9] Burnside, M.R., Visioning: building pictures of the future in Henry, J. and Walker, D. (eds), *Managing Innovation*, Sage, London, 1991.

11. Analytical techniques

Question: How are you at Mathematics?
Answer: I speak it like a native.

Spike Milligan

Introduction
We have already seen that the first step in the process of performance improvement is that of measurement and monitoring. Once this has begun, then we can begin to identify not only the shapes and contours of our organizations but also the causes of their behaviours or interactions with other organizations and the external environment.

However, in our review of organizational performance we will not only be dealing with facts but also with opinions, comment and feelings. The analysis of this pot-pourri of information is often a difficult task which can be made more so by the influence of prejudice or bias hidden under the mask of 'common sense'. But, as Albert Einstein[1] said, common sense is a 'collection of prejudices acquired by age eighteen' and if we are to change the ways in which our organizations operate then we need to undertake our analyses of their behaviour with:

- Minds that are open;
- An approach which is systematic and thorough.

There are, however, two issues that often arise from this need to analyse the key factors which characterize the health and vitality of our organizations. These are:

- How do we identify those factors?
- How do we monitor them?

This chapter is concerned with providing some tools to enable you, as the reader, to generate your own answers to those questions. It will do so by the description and illustration of a number of analytical techniques. These techniques have been chosen from the tool kits of the operations management and research specialists. That choice, however, has been strongly influenced by the need for these techniques to be:

- practical and pragmatic;
- capable of use in the everyday world of business;
- simple and straightforward in use;
- capable of use by someone with either:
  - limited formal training in advanced mathematics, or,
  - limited memory or recall of their training in advanced mathematics,
- capable of use without computer support.

These techniques are tools—that is, they are implements to be used by those who work—rather than abstract theoretical or academic concepts. None of them are new or unprecedented: they show, as do all good tools, the polish and patina of regular and careful use. However, as with all tools, the skill is in their use, and that will lie with you.

Pareto analysis

The principle on which the technique of Pareto analysis is based was found, during the late nineteenth century, by an Italian economist called Vilfredo Pareto. He was studying the patterns of wealth and income distribution present in Italy at that time and what he found was that the majority of both the wealth and the income was concentrated in the hands of a limited number of individuals. Pareto found that, at that time, around 90 per cent of the country's income went to 10 per cent of the population. He argued that this type of distribution is not just restricted to wealth or income but also occurs in many other situations. He then derived the Pareto principle which, in general terms, says that, in any group, the significant items are in the minority—'the vital few'—and the majority of the group are of relatively minor significance—'the trivial many'.

When applied as a technique, the analysis based on this principle is targeted at helping the user to find the minority of items in any group which are the most significant in terms of their effect, significance or consequences. This effect or consequence might be any one of a host of possibilities, and might include for example:

- cost,
- turnover,
- energy usage,
- number of complaints,
- staff time usage,
- any other relevant factor.

For example, when applied to the analysis of staff time usage in a hospital

215

accident and emergency department, Pareto analysis, which is also often called the 80/20 rule, tells us that the minority of patients (around 20 per cent) absorb the majority (around 80 per cent) of the staff time available. These patients are involved in life or death situations which require rapid and effective action while the remainder suffer from non-life threatening, but nevertheless inconvenient, complaints. In inventory or stock control, as the ABC technique, Pareto analysis tells us that not all stock items are of equal importance. Some of these items (A items) have very high turnover or sales revenue and as such require careful and tight control of stock levels, reorder quantities, etc. at frequent (weekly or monthly) intervals. In this approach to stock control, the B and C items are seen to be progressively less important in terms of sales turnover or revenue and as such are subject to quarterly and annual stock checks or analysis respectively.

In short, Pareto analysis can help the user to identify those items or problem areas in which the minimum of effort will produce the maximum gain. So how do we do it?

The first step is to assemble your data. Since we are considering relative performance or effect, absolute accuracy is not that important. What is important is that the data for all of the group items are all as accurate as each other and that this level of accuracy allows you to discriminate between the individual performances or effects of these items. At this time you will need some idea about the factor that will be used to contrast the contribution or effect of the individual items, but it need not be a final definition or one which causes other data to be excluded.

The second step is that of confirming or re-identifying the factor that will be used to contrast the contribution or effect of all the items that make up the group. This must be measurable but can also be generated by multiplying or adding or subtracting data for individual items. For example, the annual sales revenue items will be generated by multiplying sales volume by item price while the profit might be generated by subtracting total production costs from total sales revenue.

The third step involves generating a table for the data in which you:

- arrange the data for the comparison factor in descending order, i.e. with the largest at the top;
- generate the total of the comparison factor;
- calculate the individual percentages of that total for each item's comparison factor value;
- calculate the cumulative percentage values.

The fourth step involves identifying those items whose cumulative percentage lies below the 80 per cent level in the table generated in Step 3. These are the 'vital few' and can be shown graphically by plotting these cumulative percentages against the cumulative number or percentage of items. It is these significant items which you will subject to more detailed analysis or monitoring. The object of that further analysis and monitoring is to identify and eliminate the causes of problems or weaknesses and to identify, build upon and add to the strengths of our organizations.

Table 11.1 contains a simple example of Pareto analysis and Figure 11.1 is a plot of the resultant data. If we look at Table 11.1 we can see that a minority of the items account for the majority of the total of annual revenue. In this example:

- Items f and d account for 76.59 per cent of this total;
- Items f,d and g account for 89.53 per cent of this total.

Either of these groups of items can be the focus of further analysis and monitoring since their ability to contribute to sales revenue is some seven to nine times greater than that of the remaining items. From this simple example we can see that Pareto analysis will enable the manager to identify those factors, activities or areas whose contribution to the performance improvement process will be significant. We can also see that Pareto

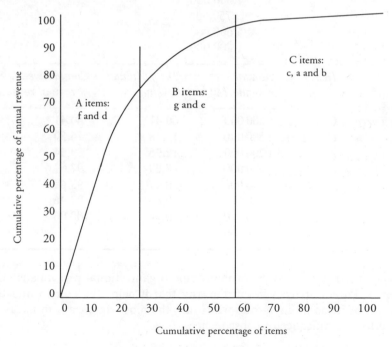

Figure 11.1 Pareto distribution

analysis can tell us which factors, activities or areas require frequent monitoring and, as importantly, which do not.

Table 11.1 Pareto analysis example

	Item	Unit price (£)	Annual sales (000's)
Step One	a	30	2.67
	b	12	4.18
	c	450	0.2
	d	75	20
	e	1500	0.5
	f	800	7.0
	g	200	6.0

	Item	Annual revenue (£)
Step Two	a	80,100
	b	50,160
	c	90,000
	d	1,500,000
	e	750,000
	f	5,600,000
	g	1,200,000

	Item	Annual revenue (£)	% of Annual revenue	Cumulative % of annual revenue
Step Three	f	5 600 000	60.41	60.41
	d	1 500 000	16.18	76.59
	g	1 200 000	12.95	89.54
	e	750 000	8.09	97.63
	c	90 000	0.97	98.60
	a	80 100	0.86	99.46
	b	50 160	0.54	100.00
	Total:	9 270 260		

When used in the process of improving organizational performance the power of Pareto analysis lies in the way that it helps the user to find the minority of items in any group which are the most significant in terms of their effect, significance or consequences.

Input–output diagrams

Input–output diagrams, as we saw in Chapter 3, are used to portray the flows of resources in and out of the conversion process. Their creation focuses the attention of the manager on both the nature and the range of these inputs and outputs. These, of course, have to balance each other. For example, an input of wood to a furniture factory will become the outputs of the finished furniture and the waste material, of sawdust, offcuts and low quality and reject furniture. Similarly, for a transport system, the inputs of vehicles, passengers, fresh and energetic drivers and fuel at one location have to be balanced by the outputs, at another location, of worn vehicles and track/roadway, the exhaust emissions of the vehicles, and stressed and/ or fatigued drivers and passengers.

The key step in generating an input–output diagram is that of making sure that you have identified all the inputs and all the outputs for the process. Failure to do so will not only mean that you have an incomplete diagram but will also mean that you have a diagram of limited value to you.

The power of the input–output diagram, when used in the process of improving organizational performance, lies in the way that it demands that the user identifies all of these inputs and outputs. This ensures, for example, that a subsequent Pareto analysis or efficiency or effectiveness ratio are based upon key factors which have been chosen after a comprehensive review of all the potential relevant factors.

The need to be comprehensive in the creation of these diagrams is illustrated by Figure 11.2 which shows the input–output diagram for the process of making a cup of tea. It is worth noting that this diagram begins the process of performance improvement by providing leads or questions about factors which could:

- Improve efficiency:
  - Reduce excess milk, excess infusion and excess hot water;
- Enhance effectiveness:
  - When and where is tea made?
- Improve adaptability:
  - How do we ensure tea is to 'required' strength every time and for every customer?

Frequency diagrams

These are pictorial representations of the number (frequency) of items or events of each size or type (variable). The information about these items or events is usually collected together in groups and the frequency distribution is represented, in tabular form, as follows:

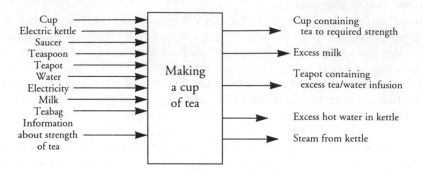

Figure 11.2 Input–output diagram

Salary (£/year)	Number of employees
≤ 15 000	11
> 15 000 ≤ 20 000	24
> 20 000 ≤ 25 000	35
> 25 000 ≤ 30 000	46
> 30 000	12

This information can also be presented as diagrams and these can take a number of forms, all of which have the purposes of displaying, explaining and making useful the information contained in them. Examples of frequency diagrams for the above salary data are shown in Figures 11.3, 11.4 and 11.5.

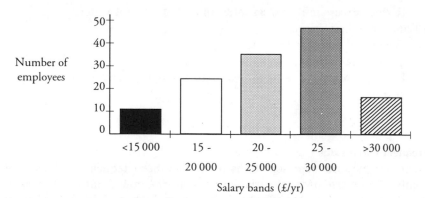

Figure 11.3 Salary histogram

All figures in £ per year

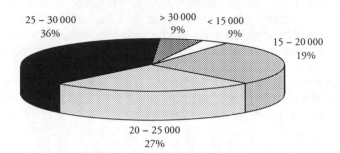

Figure 11.4   Salary pie chart (all figures in £/yr)

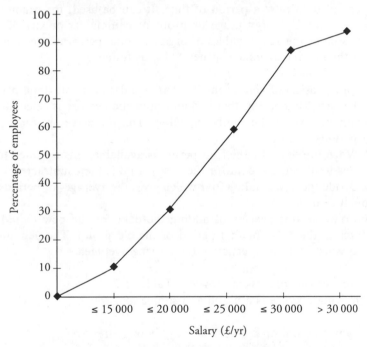

Figure 11.5   Salary frequency distribution curve

When used in the process of improving organizational performance, these frequency diagrams can enable the user to identify the minority of items in any group which are likely to be the most significant in terms of their effect, significance or consequences. They can also be used to draw conclusions

221

about the potential future 'behaviour' of that group by the comparison of the actual frequency distribution with a number of theoretical models. One example of this use, whose detail is beyond the scope of this book, is the supermarket queuing situation reviewed in Chapter 3. These and other diagrams are also powerful tools in your communication with others. The type of diagram used will, in part, depend upon the purpose of this communication (see Chapter 8). The histogram (Figure 11.3) and the frequency distribution graph (Figure 11.5) are both targeted towards the display of the distribution of the data while the pie chart (Figure 11.4) is focused towards a comparison of that data.

Moving averages
The moving average is a simple way of monitoring or measuring the movement of data over a period of time. It can be used, for example, to monitor a trend in energy usage or profit or complaints or any of what might be seen as the key variables of organizational performance. The way in which the moving average is generated is as follows:

Step 1 This consists of getting the key variable data for four time periods.
Step 2 These are added together and an arithmetic average is calculated by dividing the total by the number of values. This is the average for the first four periods.
Step 3 When the data for the fifth period is available, this is added to the previous total and the data for the first period is then subtracted.
Step 4 Divide the new total by four which gives the average for periods two through to five.
Step 5 Continue this process of adding the data for the new period and subtracting the data for first period of the old group. The new total is then divided by four to generate the moving average.

An example of this process is shown in Table 11.2.
The moving average is a useful and simple tool which:

• Helps you to monitor key variables by showing trends;
• Damps or smoothes out any seasonal variations or violent fluctuations in data.

The moving average can be presented in graph form with the usual convention being to locate the average in the middle of the period which it represents. Since the moving average is of the same magnitude as the original data for each time period, these can be plotted on the same graph.

Table 11.2 The moving average

Period	Energy usage (Kwh/ton)	Moving average total	Moving average
1	6.2	–	–
2	6.7	–	–
3	6.9	–	–
4	5.8	25.6	6.4
5	5.9	25.3	6.33
6	6.1	24.7	6.18
7	6.05	23.85	5.96
8	6.2	24.25	6.06

Cumulative sums

The cumulative sum or CUSUM technique is also used to detect and identify trends in measured data. It can be used, for example, to monitor trends in the key variables of organizational performance such as sales/employee or output/machine. One of its strengths is its ability to detect early shifts or movements in data and for this reason it is often used as a control chart in quality control situations. The technique involves the comparison of the measured data to a previously established target or norm and the subsequent plotting of the cumulative sum of the differences.

The steps in this process are:

Step 1 This consists of establishing the target for monitored factor. It can be a desired value or an historic average.

Step 2 The first measured data is subtracted from this target value giving a difference which can be either negative or positive.

Step 3 This difference is used to begin the cumulative sum of these differences.

Step 4 Steps 2 and 3 are repeated for subsequent measured data and the value for the cumulative sum is plotted.

A simple example of the application of this technique is shown, for the data that we used to illustrate the moving average technique, in Table 11.3 and Figure 11.6.

Table 11.3 The CUSUM

Period	Energy usage (Kwh/ton)	Difference	Cumulative sum of differences
1	6.2		
2	6.7	}	Target fixed at average
3	6.9		for periods 1–4, i.e. 6.4
4	5.8		
5	5.9	−0.5	−0.5
6	6.1	−0.3	−0.8
7	6.05	−0.35	−1.15
8	6.2	−0.2	−1.35

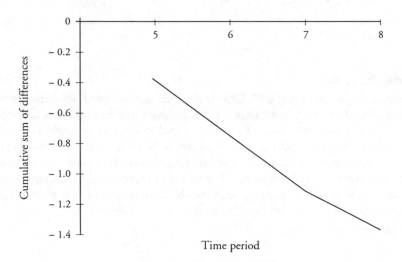

Figure 11.6 CUSUM graph

The CUSUM plot has an advantage over the moving average plot in that a change in measured value triggers a change in the slope of the CUSUM plot:

- When it happens, and
- In a way which is not damped by the 'smoothing' influence of an averaging process.

However, care must be taken in the choice of scales for the CUSUM plot as a large difference could push points off the plot. In the application of the CUSUM to quality control situations, a 'V' mask is often used to help interpret the significance of the slope of the plot. The design and use of this mask is described in detail elsewhere.[2]

Simulation flow charts

These are models of events in the real world. They can be about physical events, such as those, for example, which occur when an order consisting of several items is selected from stock and packaged, or they can be about the way we manipulate and use intangible things such as information or data. Their value to the performance improvement process lies in their ability to portray any sequence of events and, in so doing, to enable us to analyse that sequence for bottlenecks or problems.

In order to build this model we must first identify its:

- boundaries,
- components

For example, if we decide we are going to model the ways in which the products of an organization are transported from the warehouse to the retail outlets that sell them to the customer, then our model will start at the outlet of the warehouse and finish with the delivery of the goods to the retail outlet. If we want to study the effects of a change in this system by, for example, introducing another warehouse, then we must also include that potential component in the model.

The list of these components for this transport system will include:

- loading bays,
- lorries,
- drivers,
- destinations.

Similarly, the model of an ante natal clinic will include:

- mothers to be,
- receptionist,
- nurses,
- doctors,
- examination rooms with equipment,
- waiting spaces, etc.

These models are drawn in the form of a flow chart and you may need to draft this several times before you get it right! The flow chart will display the information that you have or have discovered, for example, by talking to the people who are part of the system or who use it. The level of detail in the flow chart will depend upon what you are going to use it for. If, for example, you are using the flow chart to identify blocks or groups of activities and the ways in which these interact, then the level of detail will be low. If, however, you are preparing the flow chart as the first step towards a computer simulation of the system, then the level of detail will be high. In the end, the boundaries and the level of detail of the flow chart are a decision for the user and his or her needs. An example of a flow chart is shown in Figure 11.7 which portrays part of a system for the processing of enquiries and generation of estimates by a manufacturer of office partitions.

The process of generating a simulation flow sheet is one which calls for logic and clarity rather than mathematical skills. As such both the process of its generation and the end result can make a major contribution to the process of improving organizational performance.

Decision trees

A decision tree is a method for helping you to make decisions under conditions of uncertainty. While it will not stop you making the wrong decision it will help you to be clearer about:

- What your choices are,
- What the consequences of those choices might be.

In order to understand how the decision tree works we must first take a brief look at probabilities. Probabilities are concerned with the possible outcomes of events. For example, if we toss a coin there is an equal chance or probability of it falling heads or falling tails. Probability is measured on a scale of 0 to 1 and the higher the value, the greater the chance or probability of the outcome occurring. If we have only two possible outcomes from an event—the coin will fall heads or tails—then the probability of each event is equal to (1 − the probability of the other event). That is to say that the sum of the probabilities of those outcomes, whatever their number, is 1.

In many business situations the amount of data available is limited and as a consequence the probabilities that we are dealing with are estimated or subjective probabilities. These are based on our skill in 'reading' or understanding complex or ill-defined situations and involve us in using our judgement to arrive at an estimate of the probability of an outcome.

Decision trees are often used in business situations when the outcomes of actions are unsure or unclear and as a consequence often use subjective probabilities. The steps in setting up a decision tree are as follows:

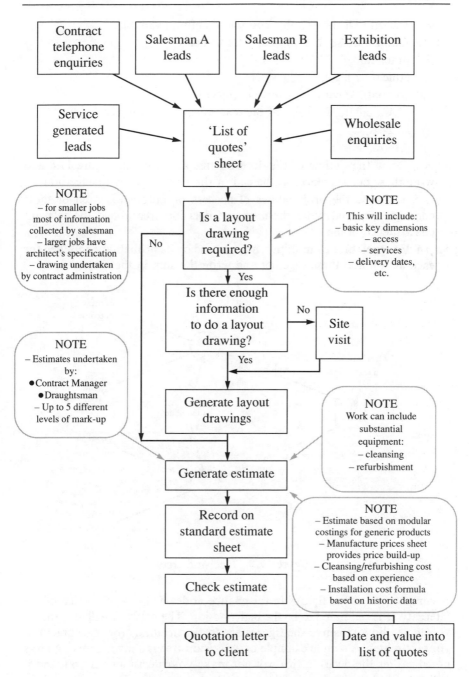

Figure 11.7 Estimates and quotations flow chart

Step 1 Identify all the possible courses of action available.

Step 2 Choose those that you consider to be:
(i)   practical,
(ii) ethical or legal,
(iii) compatible with your overall objective

Step 3 Calculate, for each of these actions, the consequences of:
(i)   success,
(ii) failure.

Step 4 Draw the outline of the decision tree as shown in Figure 11.8 and write these consequences at the end of the relevant consequence branch.

Step 5 Estimate the probabilities of success or failure for each of these consequences and write these on the decision tree above the relevant consequence branch.

Step 6 For each branch multiply the outcome by its probability and then for each action add these together and write the sum in the chance node.

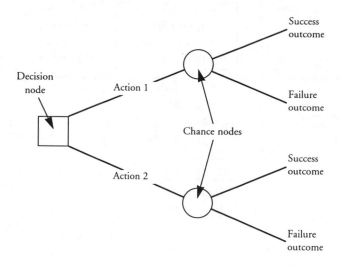

Figure 11.8   Decision tree

A comparison of the figures in the chance nodes will tell you which of the alternatives is estimated to be the better action. The network will also enable you to see how sensitive the figures are to the accuracy (or inaccuracy) of your estimates. A simple example of a decision tree is shown above. As was noted earlier the decision tree will not make your decisions for you, and it will not guarantee that you will never make a wrong decision, but it will help you to evaluate your choices and to gain a better understanding of their possible implications. As such it is a technique which will contribute to the process of improving organizational performance.

What, where, when, who and how?

One way of acquiring the open mind and the systematic approach which are so important to the analysis of the ways in which our organizations behave is by the use of a questioning technique. There are several versions of this technique and most of these appear to be rooted in the Method Study approaches which were popular in the 1960s and 1970s. They are all focused on the act of revealing the hidden problems or opportunities which lie covered by our daily routines and practices.

The extended credit dilemma

Mike Wills, the owner-manager of the Rocky Hills Food Company, had a problem. He had been approached by one of his larger customers, Ron Dunning, to provide help with his expansion plans. Dunning, who ran a successful chain of pizza restaurants, was asking Wills to extend his credit from 30 days to 60 days during the period in which he was opening a new restaurant. Wills knew that if this new restaurant was successful he would get more business from Dunning. However, he also knew that Dunning was likely to take all his business elsewhere if he didn't get the help he needed. What should Wills do?

He turned to his accountant, Dick Meadow, for help. Meadow used to work for one of the larger automobile manufacturers and reckoned he knew all about taking risks. So, they sat down together and worked out what they knew about this risk. They estimated that if the new restaurant was a success the value of Dunning's business with them would increase from its current level of $20 000 per year to around $35 000. If, however, the restaurant didn't succeed they estimated that Dunning's business would fall to $10 000 per year. Taking in to account all that they knew about Dunning they thought that the chances of Dunning succeeding were high (0.7) as were the chances of him taking his business elsewhere (0.8) if they didn't give him the extended credit. Dick said that one of two actions were open to Mike:

1. Give the extended credit for the next 12 months and risk the new restaurant failing.
2. Withhold the extended credit and risk losing Dunning's business.

229

Dick then drew what he called a decision tree which looked like this:

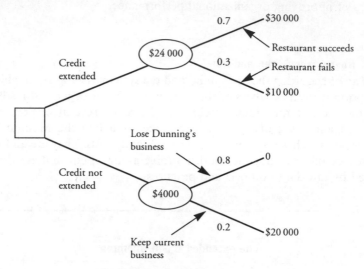

Case Study Figure 11.1

He also told Mike that he ought to give Ron Dunning the extended credit as the expected return was $(30 000 × 0.7 + 10 000 × 0.3) while the return from not giving him the extended credit was $(20 000 × 0.2 + $0 × 0.8).

They need to be applied with determination and persistence in order to ensure that they reveal all the information that is needed for you to solve the problem or grasp the opportunity (see Chapter 10 for other problem-solving techniques). The version which is described here is based on that identified by Professor Keith Lockyer[3] and has the following steps:

Step 1 What? This initial step is targeted at identifying what is being done.
Step 2 Where? This step aims to identify where the above actions are being undertaken.
Step 3 When? The target here is the timing or sequence of the events.
Step 4 Who? This step will tell us who is undertaking these actions.
Step 5 How? We need to know how these actions are carried out.
Step 6 Why? This involves repeating the first five steps **but** asking 'why?' at each step. For example, why are those actions identified in Step 1 being carried out or why are they being carried out in the manner identified in Step 5?
Step 7 What are the alternatives? This again repeats the first five steps **but** asks, at each step, about alternatives. For example, how else could the

action be carried out (Step 5) and who else could do it (Step 4).

Step 8 The way forward. This final step again repeats the first five steps **but** decides what should be done, where and when it should be done and by whom and how it should be done.

We saw at the beginning of this section that this technique focuses on the exposure of the hidden problems or opportunities which lie covered by our daily routines and practices. As you can see from the above sequence its final act is the generation of a way forward, a set of prescriptions for future more effective and more efficient action. Below is an example of how that can be done.

The Case of the Hairless Doll

Mike Fish, the production manager of a doll and toy manufacturer, was aware that the customer complaints about the top of the range doll—a blonde haired Princess Diana look-a-like called Glynis—were high and rising. Most of these seemed to be about Glynis's hair falling out and his attempts to find the source of the trouble had failed. So, faced with falling orders and the ire of his managing director, he called in the firm of AP Management Consultants. AP, who had an impressive reputation for trouble-shooting and fees to match, soon got to work. They asked all sorts of questions about what the operators did, when and how and even who did it and then, as if that wasn't enough, they began to ask questions like 'why was it done that way?' and 'why did we do that then?' The problem was, as Mike soon realized, he didn't have answers to some of the questions and for others the answer was that they had always done it that way.

So, when the senior AP consultant, John Long, asked for a meeting he began to get anxious. What John told Mike was that, from the answers to their questions, his team of consultants had built up a picture which indicated that the operators assembled the dolls in different ways. Some of them were inserting Glynis's golden locks and then applying glue and others were applying glue before the insertion. Mike began to get worried—which was the right way? John made it worse by telling him that he didn't know either but then said that together they now had to decide how it should be done. He also mentioned that he had noticed that the complaints about arms coming off were rising. Mike buckled to with a vengeance, and, with the help of John's team, soon had a standard assembly procedure written, tested and in operation. Glynis dolls were pouring off the assembly line and complaints had plummeted to an all time low, just in time for the Christmas market.

Then Mike noticed that the complaints figures for their number 2 line—the Teddy Bear called Fred—were beginning to rise. Still, he thought, now we know what to do and he began to write in his notebook 'What did they do?', 'Where did they do it?', 'When did they do it?' ...

Influence diagrams

These are one way of 'mapping' the relationship between the factors or groups of factors that influence and affect the ways in which organizations behave. The influence diagram attempts to represent the dynamics of these relationships. It does so by representing the influences at work by arrows whose direction represents the direction of the influence and whose thickness represents its strength.

The aims in producing an influence diagram should be:

• To show the major influences;
• To do so in a way which draws the eye to the patterns of those influences in the system.

Figure 11.9 shows an influence diagram for some of the external influences acting upon a university business school.

Multiple cause diagrams

While these are similar to influence diagrams, they do contain more information than an influence diagram. However, as with influence diagrams, their objective is to:

• Help you to sort out and refine your ideas;
• Identify cause and effect chains.

Multiple cause diagrams are primarily about explaining why something has happened and the arrows in the diagram are used to indicate that one factor or event leads to or follows on from another. The usual process for generating these diagrams has the following steps:

Step 1 Identify the outcome for which you want to establish the causes and write this down on the bottom of your piece of paper.
Step 2 Identify the main factors which affect this outcome and write these on the paper above the outcome and linked to it by arrows.

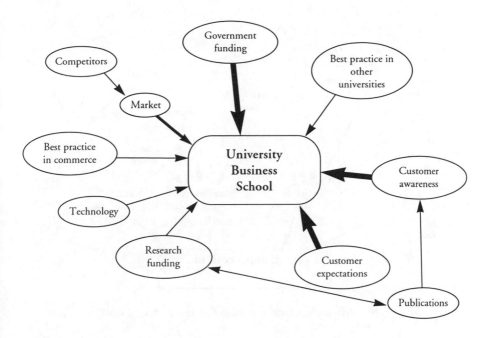

Figure 11.9   External influences on University Business School

Step 3 Identify the factors which affect those generated by Step 2: write
these above the Step 2 factors and link them to them by arrows.

Step 4 Identify the factors which affect those generated by Step 3: write
these above the Step 3 factors and link them to them by arrows.

Step 5 etc. Continue until you have identified all the factors. Then, finally,
check the diagram to make sure that it:

(i)   contains all the relevant factors;

(ii) has these in a correct relationship to each other.

Multiple cause diagrams are very powerful tools and can make a significant
contribution to the process of performance improvement.

The use of this technique is illustrated in Figure 11.10.

We saw at the beginning of this book that the process of organizational
performance improvement is made up of a continuous stream of multiple
small actions which accumulate to create a significant shift in performance.
However, despite the power of this incremental process, there are situations
in which a large step or jump needs to be made. These are often called
projects and Chapter 12 looks at how these projects must be organized,
planned and managed in order to be effective.

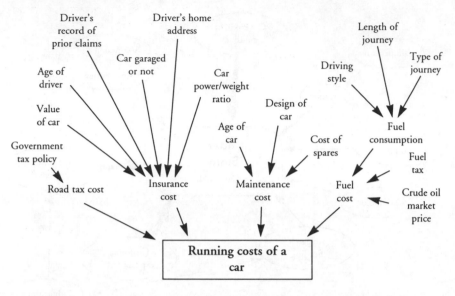

Figure 11.10   Multiple cause diagram for the running costs of a car

Summary

This chapter has briefly reviewed a number of techniques designed to help the reader to:

- Identify, and
- Monitor

those factors which are key to the process of improving organizational performance. The criteria used to choose these techniques included their:

- Practicality and capability for use in the everyday world of business;
- Simplicity and ease of use by someone with limited current or prior training in advanced mathematics or limited memory or recall of their training in advanced mathematics;
- Use without computer support.

The techniques reviewed were:

- Pareto analysis: used to identify items of or areas in which the minimum of effort will produce the maximum gain;

- Input–output diagrams: used to identify all inputs and outputs and so help the identification of key factors for Pareto analysis or efficiency and effectiveness ratios;
- Frequency diagrams: used in the analysis of data and the communication of information;
- Moving averages: used to detect change or trends in data which might be subject to seasonal or other swings;
- CUSUM: used to detect early shifts or movements in trends or data;
- Simulation flow charts: used to model systems or sequences and to help analyse those for bottlenecks or problems;
- Decision trees: used to help make decisions under conditions of uncertainty;
- What, where, when, who and why: a questioning technique aimed at revealing the hidden problems or opportunities;
- Influence diagrams: a way of mapping the relationships between factors or groups of factors;
- Multiple cause diagrams: a way of identifying cause and effect chains.

All of these techniques can, when used with thought and skill, make considerable contributions to the process of improving organizational performance.

References
[1] Einstein, A., *Scientific American*, Feb, 1976.
[2] Wetherill, G.B., *Sampling Inspection and Quality Control*, Chapman and Hall, London, 1977.
[3] Lockyer, K.G., *Factory and Production Management*, Pitman, London, 1974.

12. Project management

God is not dead but alive and well and working on a much less ambitious project.

Anon

Introduction

The process of generating performance improvement is a continuous and ongoing process which consists of small incremental steps. Nevertheless, there are occasions and circumstances in which it is necessary to take a large step, or even a leap, forward. These large steps are often called 'projects' and this chapter is concerned with looking at the ways in which these projects can be managed in order that they, too, can make a contribution to the process of performance improvement. There is considerable diversity amongst the projects of our organizations. These can be concerned with change in the physical resources that those organizations use, such as building of a new office block or factory, or concerned with changes in the less tangible resources such as the introduction of a quality manual based on BS 5750. They can also be concerned with distributing information, such as publishing a book, with influencing people in order to change their behaviour or views and opinions, such as a political election campaign.

These projects can also vary considerably in size, cost and duration. At the upper end of the range are the very substantial and ambitious national projects such as the Russian and American space programmes, the Concorde supersonic plane, the Channel Tunnel and the Aswan dam. At the lower end, our organizational projects might be concerned with the installation of a drinks vending machine or the design and introduction of a new academic programme.

Our experience of these projects is not limited to the workplace and our personal projects will include moving house, having an extension built, organizing a holiday or even choosing and buying a new car. In short, these projects can be concerned with any aspect of our work or play and Figure 12.1 illustrates one dimension of this diversity.

Yet despite the enormous variety of their size and cost, these projects all have a number of key features or characteristics in common. Not only do these key characteristics mean that projects are different from the other activities which we carry out in our organizations but also that projects must be organized, planned and managed in ways which are different to those

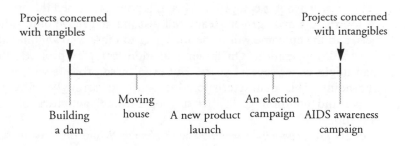

Figure 12.1 The project spectrum

that we use in our day to day activities. In order to establish why this is so we will first take a look, in this final chapter of Part 2, at what these common features or characteristics are.

What is a project?
We have already seen that a project can:

- Be large or small;
- Involve any number of people from nations to individuals;
- Last for years or days.

Faced with the very wide range of these factors it seems to be asking a lot to ask you to accept that all of the projects that we have identified above have a number of limited, but nevertheless key, common factors. But that is the case and these are the common and key characteristics:

1. *All projects are, in some way, unique* All projects will contain factors or elements which are unique to that project. Some projects will be singular, one-off, never to be repeated events while others will be concerned with lesser degrees of uniqueness. For example, the project which built the Thames Flood Barrier was a wholly unique project while the uniqueness of a project to build standard dwelling houses outside Chester will be limited to those factors associated with that particular site. That is, while the houses are not unique, the site is. All projects are, in some way, and to greater or lesser extents, unique. In this respect, they differ considerably from the repetitive day to day activities of our organizations.
2. *All projects exist for a limited and defined period of time* All projects have defined 'deadlines' or target completion dates. This means that the project has a limited lifespan—it does not go on for ever—and will reach

237

a point in time when it is complete. When this point is reached the project ceases to exist, its management team will disband and move onto other projects, and the outcome will be handed over to those who will manage its day to day operation. On larger and more complex projects, this lifespan might cover several years. But even these projects will reach an end-point. This characteristic also contrasts strongly with the repetitive and continuing day to day operational activities of our organizations.

3. *All projects are primarily concerned with change* While the day to day operations of our organizations are primarily concerned with continuity, predictability and stability, the activities of a project are almost exclusively concerned with change—with knocking down the old and building up the new. As we saw in Chapter 7, the skills required to manage this change environment are quite different to those needed for the relative stability and predictability of the organization's operations.

4. *All projects have defined outcomes or targets* All projects have well-defined goals, targets or sets of desired results. These might be, for example, the completion of the building of a house or the publication of a book. These are often divided into sub-goals or sub-tasks in order to help the planning, control and management of the activities which lead to these goals. For example, the goal of making a cup of tea can be divided into subtasks of switching on the kettle, getting the milk form the refrigerator, etc., etc.

5. *All projects undertaken by the use of a variety of resources* One of the characteristics of a project is the transient and short-lived nature of the resources involved. The building of a house will, for example, require periods of intense activity from bricklayers, electricians, joiners, tilers, plasterers and painters. These periods of activity will rarely overlap with each other but will be interdependent. For example, the painter cannot start his activities until the joiner, the plasterer and the tiler have completed their activities. They, in their turn, cannot start their activities until the electrician has completed her activities, and so on. The transient nature of these resources is also present in the equipment needed for the projects, in this case, the diggers, scaffolding, cranes, etc. In a well-managed project these will appear when needed—not before—and leave when their task is complete. This also contrasts strongly with the fixed nature of the resources used in the day to day operational activities of our organizations.

As we can see from the above, the characteristics of a project are quite different to those of the routine day to day activities of our organizations. Projects have defined end-points and outcomes and are concerned with uniqueness, change and the use of transient resources, while the routine operations of our organizations are concerned with stability, continuity and repetition.

Our review of these common but key characteristics of all projects should, by now, have brought us to the point where we can begin to think about a simple definition of a project. It is not surprising, in the light of the considerable variety of projects created by our organizations, to find that the literature of project management contains a variety of definitions of projects. Some of these definitions speak eloquently of human endeavour while others speak of specific outcomes or simply beginnings and ends. The definition that we shall use, however, is a straightforward one which states simply that a project is:

'a one-time activity with a well defined set of desired end results'.[1]

When we apply this definition to the examples that we have mentioned, we find that they all fit—they all display a degree of uniqueness, are one-off events and have defined and limited outcomes. So how do these projects contribute to the performance improvement process?

Performance improvement and projects

As we saw at the beginning of this book, performance improvement is not a 'one-off' or a 'once and for ever' exercise. It is, if it is to be effective and lasting, a continuous and ongoing process which is integral to the culture of the organization. We also saw that effective improvement in performance in all organizations is created and sustained by continuous incremental change—by building on success and by taking one step at a time.

So how does a project, as a one—time activity, contribute to this process? A performance improvement project may, for example, be concerned with the transfer of good practice or procedures, from one part of an organization, to the whole of that organization. It may also be about the creation of new facilities or the introduction of new technology in a part of that organization or with the introduction of new ways of doing things or the measurement and monitoring of new data. All of these situations are 'one-time' events with defined outcomes or end results. Yet these projects, as change creating events, can be a way of changing performance, of building on the good or eliminating the bad.

However, from our knowledge and experience of the performance improvement process, we will also be aware that successful performance improvement projects are only likely to take place because of, or as a result of, the measurement and monitoring process. As we saw in Chapter 6, that process tells us what the causes of our current performance are. This knowledge enables us to identify the options for changing that performance, and a project *may* be one of those options.

The use of projects for performance improvement does, however, contain dangers and risks. The most significant of these results from a key characteristic of all successful projects. That is that they are managed, run or operated by specialist teams of experienced project experts. We will see later in this chapter that the skill needs of the project manager role are different to those of the operations manager and the presence or absence of these skills can make a significant difference to the success of the project. However, the presence of a specialist project team will mean that the project will be run efficiently and effectively.

The presence of that team will also mean that the majority of those people who 'are that organization' are *not* involved in the project. Indeed, they may even be actively excluded from the project by the nature of the project management process. When this happens, not only is the project separated from the 'heart' of the organization, but it also does not tap into, or use, the abilities, skills and capabilities of the majority of the members of that organization. As a result, the project is likely to be limited in scope or potential. It will also need an additional 'selling' exercise to ensure its acceptance, and ultimately its support, by this majority. We have seen throughout this book that the process of improving organizational performance is dependent upon the efforts of the people who are the organization. As a consequence, this separation, which is so typical of the project, does place a considerable limitation upon the use and value of the project in the performance improvement process.

Despite these considerable risks, there are situations where project management can make a contribution to the performance improvement process. Examples would be the use of project management skills to ensure the speedy and economic rearrangement of an office—once the new layout had been agreed by all who use the office or the use of project management skills to ensure the speedy, timely and economic production of a one-off organizational broadsheet—once its content and purpose had been agreed.

This means that we can view the project and its management as tools to be used in the process of improving organizational performance. But, as is so with all tools, you have to know not only *how* to use them but also, and perhaps more importantly, *when* to use them.

However, having accepted the limitations and risks of projects in the context or the performance improvement process, what we now need to do is to take a look at how these projects are:

- Structured,
- Managed,

240

- Planned,
- Controlled.

Projects: bones, heart and lungs

Most managers fall into the trap of thinking about a project only in terms of its outcome or performance. For example, we might think of our earlier example of the rearranged office in terms of the outcome of the relocated desks and other furniture. However, the 'desired end results' of all projects have other characteristics and these can also exert a significant influence upon the efficiency and the effectiveness of the project process.

The characteristics or dimensions of the desired end results of all projects are:

- The nature of their outcomes or performance;
- The time taken or needed to achieve that performance;
- The costs of all the resources used in the project.

For example, a project concerned with the building of a dwelling house will be defined in terms of its:

- Performance or size, shape, facilities, capacity etc., e.g. four-bedroom, two bathroom, timber frame ranch house with patio, outdoor swimming pool and barbecue;
- Cost, e.g. $60,000;
- Duration, e.g., to be ready for use by 1 December, 1996.

These three dimensions of time, cost and performance are *the* significant factors for all projects. As such they must be:

- Clearly defined at the onset of the project;
- Monitored throughout the project;
- Carefully managed and controlled during the project.

Indeed, the importance of these factors is such that it can be argued that the failure to define all three at the onset of the project will result in a failed project. These characteristics also interact with each other and are interdependent. For example, a shortage of time left to complete a project might be compensated for by taking on extra labour—at additional cost—or reducing the work content by changing the outcome or performance. Similarly, an increase in the outcomes or performance of the project may require increases in both time and money to compensate.

241

It is also evident that, however well defined these 'desired end results' might be, the project process itself is not a fixed or static one. Projects can grow, from small beginnings, to become large and impressive endeavours which mature and ultimately die. This project life cycle is, in fact, a process which displays some of the characteristics of organic systems or organisms and the stages of this cycle trace the following process of development and change.

1. *Conception* During this stage the project is identified, its feasibility reviewed and initial estimates of cost generated. This stage will also involve an initial definition of performance and time. The end of this stage will be marked by a 'go'—'no go' decision based on the above information and the decision to 'go' will lead to the next stage of growth. A 'no go' decision will lead to the use of other processes for the improvement of performance and many projects die at this early stage of life.
2. *Birth and growth* During this stage the detailed design of the project outcome is developed and decisions are made about who will do what and when. Cost and time estimates are also refined. Both this and the earlier stage involve a relatively low, though accelerating, pace of activity.
3. *Maturity* This is the stage in which the planned work takes place. It is also the stage with the highest activity rate and as such it requires effective monitoring, control and forecasting procedures which will tell the project manager what:

   (i) has or hasn't been done or spent;
   (ii) ought to have been done or spent;
   (iii) will need to be done or spent in the future.

   At the end of this stage the project will have reached completion and the outcome should have been handed over to those who will use it.
4. *Old age and death* This stage involves a slower pace of activity involving the review and audit of the project and, ultimately, the break up of the project team.

Not only do the rates at which things are done change throughout this life cycle but also the demands and needs of the stages for resources or effort will differ and change. The maturity stage, with its focus on getting things done, involves the peak level of resource demand as is illustrated in Figure 12.2.

What also changes throughout this cycle is the relative importance of the three project dimensions of time, cost and performance. During the conception stage all of these will have equal importance but once we move into the birth and growth stage, time begins to edge ahead of performance

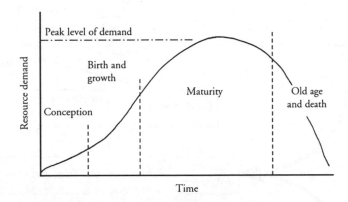

Figure 12.2 Resource demands in project life cycle

with cost taking third place. This probably reflects the fact that most of the scheduling and planning decisions are taken during this stage. Throughout most of the maturity stage, performance will be the key issue, but by the end of this stage all of these dimensions will have assumed equal importance and this ranking will continue throughout the final old age and death stage.

Despite the risks and limitations of the project process which we noted earlier, we can now begin to see how that process might be used in the larger process of improving organizational performance. We saw in Chapter 6 how the steps of first, measurement, and then, cause detection, lead to the step in which we identify our options for action. One of these options may be based upon or need the skills of project management. Figure 12.3 shows the interaction between the performance improvement cycle and the project life cycle and shows how a project, as one of the options for performance improvement, fits into the cycle of this process.

We have already mentioned that the way in which a project is managed is different to the ways in which we manage the day to day routine operations of our organizations. We shall now take a look at the demands and skills of the project manager role and the ways in which project teams are organized and run.

Project managers and project teams

One of the popular caricatures of the project manager is that of a driving, driven, hard-nosed individual who will sacrifice all to gain results. Other views of organizational project managers and the criteria for their selection might include:

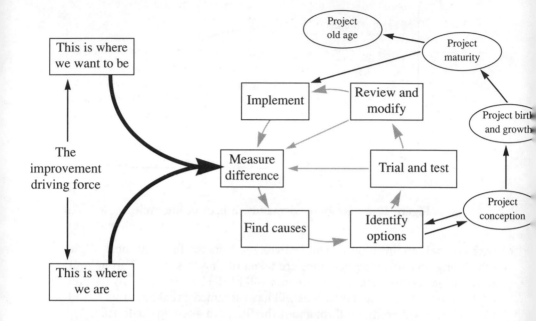

Figure 12.3 The project life cycle and the performance improvement cycle

- Someone who is currently available;
- Someone who can keep the project team happy;
- Someone who can keep senior management happy;
- Someone who can walk on, or part, the waters!

But not all project managers are selected on these criteria or behave in those ways. The primary function of the project manager role is the management of the way in which the 'desired end results' are reached and the selection of the individual to carry out this role must be based upon their ability to achieve those end results or outcomes. The project manager has to balance the demands from:

- The client,
- The project,
- The project team.

For projects concerned with the improvement of organizational performance, the client will be the organization itself, or some part of it, as represented by senior managers or others. This client will need to know that the project:

- Is being managed with due regard for the importance of its outcomes;
- Is using resources efficiently and effectively.

The project manager must ensure that these needs are met. She or he must also ensure that the project integrity is maintained by balancing the conflicts, arguments and rivalries which can easily lead to an erosion of the original definition of the project outcome, cost and duration. As the leader of the project team the project manager must also lead and motivate her/his team of project staff who:

- Will only be members of that team for the duration of the project;
- May have been 'borrowed' from other departments or functions.

The project manager's role as a team leader will also need to cover the selection of that team—in order to ensure that the relevant functional skills are present—and the transfer, at the end of the project, of these team members into other roles. The complexity and often conflicting nature of these tasks together with the need to be able to manage what are often considerable but fluctuating levels of resources means that the project manager's job demands a rare mix of skills and abilities. High among these demands is the ability to communicate. Project managers have to spend time explaining to, informing, selling to and persuading a wide range of people which can include senior management, contractors, team members, clients, functional departments, union members and many others. They need to be skilled in the 'arts' of listening, informing and persuading. The ability to organize is another skill which is high on the list of those needed for effective project management.

This is a cluster of competencies or skills which results in the project and the project team:

- Having clearly defined subgoals or targets;
- Being planned at a detailed and comprehensive level;
- Having clear priorities which are adhered to throughout the duration of the project and the crises and problems that occur during that project.

As we saw earlier, project managers lead teams of specialized personnel. These team members are almost always on the team because of their functional skills rather than their team skills. For example, a project team for a new office building will contain staff who are skilled in the civil engineering, structural engineering and environmental engineering aspects of the project. They are in that team primarily and sometimes exclusively because of their expertise in those specialist areas. Similarly a project for the production of information leaflets on the effects of smoking will need a team

245

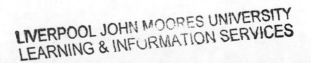

which contains medical expertise, writing skills, printing knowledge and costing/cost-control skills.

The project manager will need to be able to:

- Understand and communicate with these specialists;
- Gain their trust;
- Turn this group of individuals into a team.

The project manager will lead this team and, in so doing, will need to be able to:

- Motivate its members;
- Display and use a number of leadership skills including:
  - delegation,
  - flexibility,
  - decision-taking.

One of the common illusions that people often have about project managers is that they need to be technical experts in the subject concerned with the project that they are managing. There is little, if any, evidence to support this view of the project manager role. What is required is that:

- The project manager has an understanding of that subject or area of technology that is adequate enough for him/her to:
  - ask the 'right' questions,
  - understand the answers given;
- The project team includes full-time or part-time members who can provide an 'in depth' understanding of that subject or area of technology.

Despite the variety and range of projects present in our organizations, the role of the project manager is often one which is filled by secondment or on a part-time basis. It is not, however, a role for amateurs or those seeking a quiet life. It is a demanding and worthwhile role which requires skill, training and experience if it is to be carried out effectively. It is also a role which can make a major contribution to the organization.

How will we organize our project?
The transitory nature of projects means that the ways in which they are organized is rarely the subject of much thought or discussion. Yet this feature of projects can make a significant difference to their success or

246

failure. If it is to be successful then the project must be organized in such a way as to meet the needs of:

- The client,
- The project and the project team.

The needs of the client, for example, will be met when:

- Short linkages exist between client organization and project organization;
- The client is able to exert considerable influence over the project decisions;
- Project team members owe allegiance to the client organization.

The needs of the project team will be met when:

- The project manager has full and unconditional authority;
- All members of the project team are fully and directly responsible to the project manager;
- The project team has:
  - a clear and separate identity,
  - the ability to communicate and take decisions effectively and rapidly.

It will be obvious that there are many circumstances in which these needs are in conflict. As a consequence the choice of the organization used for a project is often a compromise. This compromise can take into account many factors including:

- Time span, cost and complexity of the project;
- Importance of project to the client and to the project team;
- Innovative nature of project.

For example, a low cost, short time span project which is concerned with the transfer of existing systems or procedures from one part of an organization to another, is likely to be one which is strongly influenced by the needs of the client. As such it is likely to:

- Have part-time team members;
- Have a structure which reflects that of the client organization;
- Be integrated into the existing organization management and control systems.

On the other hand, a project which is high cost, long time span and concerned with the introduction of new technology is likely to have:

- A stand-alone project team;
- Its own management and control systems;
- A structure which is related to the needs of the project.

The three main types of project organization and their relationship to the needs of the client and the project are illustrated in Figure 12.4 and the advantages and disadvantages of these are summarized in Table 12.1.

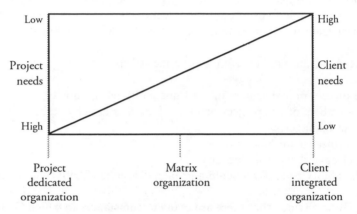

Figure 12.4   Project organization spectrum

The outlines of these types of structure are as follows:

PROJECT DEDICATED STRUCTURE

In this type of structure the project and the project team are separate from the rest of the organization—they exist as a self-contained unit with its own resources, staff, premises, etc. The communication with the rest of the organization is usually through the medium of progress reports which are delivered at regular intervals, e.g. monthly or two weekly, but can also occur after or before crucial project activities. This self-contained project unit will often report to a senior management position which is high enough in the client organization to eliminate functional bias or conflict.

MATRIX STRUCTURE

This structure is usually seen as a compromise—a middle position—between the extremes of the project dedicated and the client integrated structures. In its simplest form it is structured as shown in Figure 12.5 with the project manager drawing the resource he or she requires from each of the organization's functional departments.

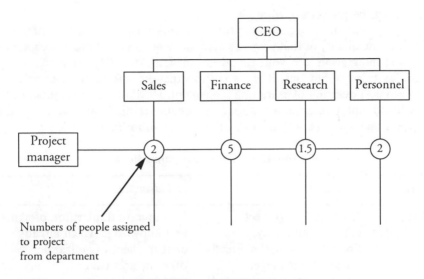

Figure 12.5 Matrix structure

This form of project management has been seen, in the past, as an effective and efficient way to manage organizational projects. However, its popularity has declined for reasons which include its considerable potential to degenerate into disorganized chaos and the fact that its team members have to work for two bosses: the functional boss and the project boss.

CLIENT INTEGRATED STRUCTURE
This type of organization is often used because the client organization needs to integrate the project into the existing structure of the organization. This is usually done on the grounds that it enables the project to tap into and use the functional skills and experience of the organization. For example, if the project is one which has strong engineering 'flavour' then it is placed under the supervision of the engineering department and a project which is mainly about changing the quality standards and procedures is placed under the supervision of the quality department. While the appeal of this integration is considerable, it also has the effect of reducing the ability of the project to induce change. This 'dead hand' effect may be considerable where the project is concerned with changing attitudes, norms or standards.

Given the variety and the complexity of both our organizational projects and our organizations how do we go about selecting the 'right' organization or structure for our project?

Selecting the project organization

Choosing the 'right' organization for your project can make a big difference to both the quality of that project's management and its ultimate acceptance by and integration into your organization. Unfortunately there aren't any 'golden rules' about this; it is, as is the situation with many management decisions, a question of exercising judgement. However, that judgement can be based upon information about the characteristics and nature of the project task and one way of doing that is shown in Figure 12.6.

Table 12.1 Project organizations

Type	Advantages	Disadvantages
Project dedicated	High level of project manager authority. Project team works directly for project manager. Good communication and decision-taking. Structure simple and flexible.	Can involve duplication of skills and knowledge which already exist in client organization or other project teams. Sytems and procedures may not be compatible with client's.
Matrix	Project is focus of dedicated project manager's activities. Communication and decision-taking as good as project structure. Access to resources and skills of client organization.	Balance of power and resource allocation can be delicate. Demands very high skill in negotiating from project manager.
Client integrated	Flexibility in use of staff. Access to client organization resources, skills and knowledge. Continuity of systems and procedures.	Can mean very low level of project manager authority, clashes with aims and targets of client organization. Poor communication and decision-taking.

However we structure the project team and organize its relationship with the client, we shall still need to plan or schedule the tasks and activities involved in the project.

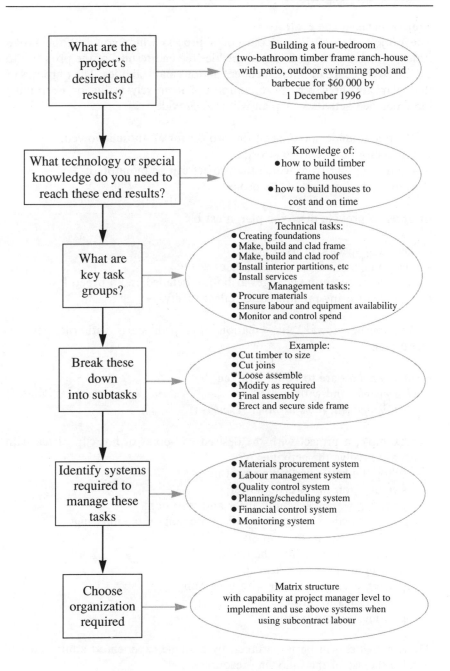

Figure 12.6 Choosing the project structure

Project planning and control

The project plan is the outcome of a process which converts the broad statement of intents contained in the 'desired end results' of the project into a detailed sequence of interdependent actions and activities. The purposes of that plan are, however, more complex than merely listing or portraying these detailed activities. A plan will also provide:

- A common understanding of the project for all those involved;
- A basis for co-operative effort;
- A starting point from which the project can be monitored;
- An overarching view of the project.

In order to provide these the plan must be:

- Clear and specific in its content;
- Easily understood by all who use or see it;
- Capable of accepting changes at both a detailed and a broad level;
- Capable of being monitored to reflect reality.

The journey toward the creation of a plan starts with the steps of identifying:

- *what activities* are to be undertaken, by
- *what people*, and with
- *what equipment, tools or other resources.*

For example, a project with the desired end-point of hot cup of tea with milk, will involve the activities of:
- filling the kettle and plugging it in;
- switching on the electric power;
- getting a teapot, teacup, saucer and teaspoon;
- getting a teabag and putting adequate milk in the milk jug;
- placing teabag in the teapot;
- pouring hot water into the teapot;
- pouring milk into the teacup;
- placing teacup in saucer with teaspoon;
- allowing tea to infuse;
- pouring tea into teacup.

These activities will be undertaken by a single experienced adult and will involve the use of the following resources:

a teabag	a saucer	water
milk	a teaspoon	a kettle
a teacup	a milk jug	electric power
	a surface to stand these on	

Already you will see that the simple process of listing these activities and their people and equipment demands begins to give us some sense of how this project might be planned and controlled. For example, you might be asking yourself whether the activities listed are in the right order or whether we would save time or money by limiting the amount of water that is boiled.

The next step in the planning process is to:

- estimate the time taken for these activities;
- identify their dependency patterns.

Your estimates of the time taken for the activities involved need only, at this stage, be concerned with the relative duration of the activities. For example, in our cup of tea project we know, from experience, that the longest activities are:

- boiling the kettle,
- infusing the tea.

If, however, you don't have adequate experience to make this judgement, then you need to ask someone who has that experience. We will, however, know that the kettle cannot boil until:

- it has been filled and plugged in;
- the electric power has been switched on.

That is that the activity of 'boiling the kettle' is dependent upon the completion of the activities of 'filling and plugging in the kettle' and 'switching on the electric power' before it can take place. Once we have worked out these dependency patterns and made an intial estimate of the durations of the activities then we can generate the first draft of the plan.

The simplest forms of the project plan are:

- The Gantt chart,
- The Critical Path network.

While a detailed study of these planning and scheduling tools is beyond the scope of this book and is the subject of many specialist texts we shall take a look, in outline, at these planning tools.

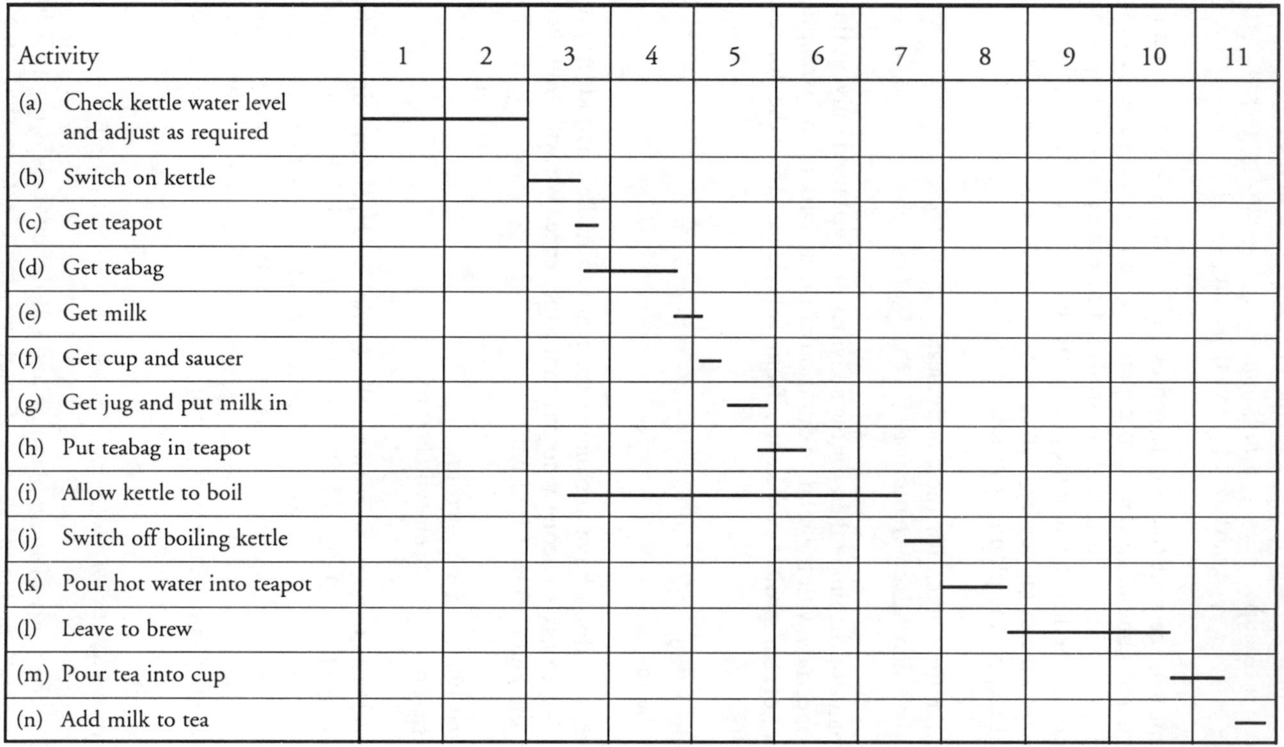

Figure 12.7 Gantt chart for cup of tea project

Gantt charts

This form of project plan, which was developed by Henry Gantt in 1917, is based on the use of a horizontal line for each activity. The length of that line is proportional to the time taken to complete that activity and all of the lines are displayed on a single chart whose horizontal axis is divided into units of time. The use of the Gantt chart for our cup of tea project is shown in Figure 12.7. This chart uses an arbitrary time-scale in order to show more detail but could have been graduated in seconds or fractions of a minute. For most organizational projects the Gantt chart will use a time-scale based on units of days or even weeks for the bigger projects. A Gantt chart, with its time-scale base, provides a picture of a project which:

• Can be easily understood;
• Shows the relationship of the activities.

It can be used to monitor progress by the filling in of activity lines or troughs (see Figure 12.8):

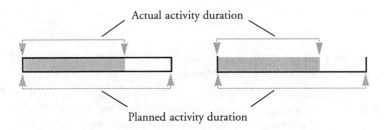

Figure 12.8

It can also be used to indicate key project points or milestones by the use of symbols such as ◆.

The Gantt chart is probably the most popular of the project planning methods. It is easy to understand and can be presented in a variety of forms ranging from a proprietary wall chart using adhesive strip through the hard copy output of modern computer software to a hand-drawn chart. The ease and speed with which it can be updated is high, particularly with the wall chart or computer produced charts. Another of its major advantages arises from its diagrammatic and logical nature which means that it can be generated with very limited prior training. However, Gantt charts cannot deal easily with complex projects or with projects which contain high levels of uncertainty about durations or completion times. These are best dealt with by the other major type of project planning tool.

Critical path networks

The second most common group of project planning methods are those based upon the critical path network. These, which were all developed toward the end of the 1950s, have a variety of acronyms which include:

- PERT (Programme Evaluation and Review Technique);
- CPM (Critical Path Method);
- CPS (Critical Path Scheduling);
- CPA (Critical Path Analysis).

All of these use networks to display the order of and interconnections between the activities of the project. These networks are of two types which differ in the ways in which they represent a project activity. These are:

- *Activity on arrow networks* The activity is represented by an arrow between a start node or point and an end node or point (see Figure 12.9):

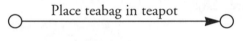

Place teabag in teapot

Figure 12.9

- *Activity on node or precedence networks* The activity is represented by a box and is linked to other activities by arrows (see Figure 12.10).

Figure 12.10

In this book, for reasons of brevity and simplicity, we shall only provide examples of the activity on arrow network type and Figure 12.11 shows one of these. This is an activity on arrow network for the cup of tea project, again with arbitrary activity durations for illustrative purposes When we take a close look at this network we can see a number of interesting features.

1. The nodes are identified by a circle which is divided into three parts. In a completed network these would be used to record further information (see Figure 12.12).
2. Some of the arrows are dotted. This means that the activities at each end of the dotted arrow are interdependent. That is, you can't pour out the tea until you have got the cup and saucer.

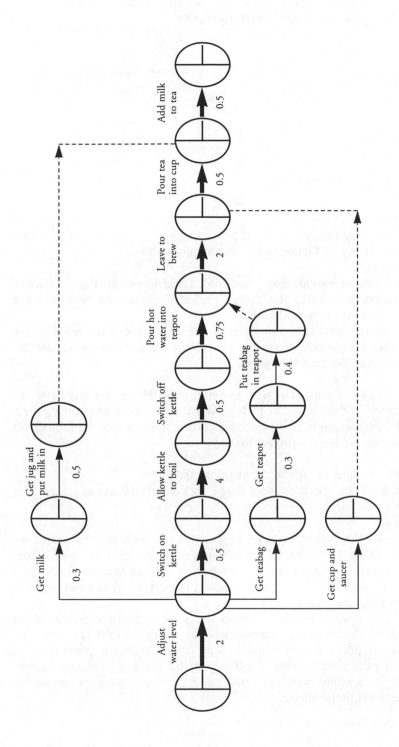

Figure 12.11 Making a cup of tea: activity on arrow critical path network

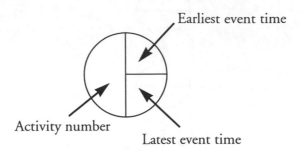

Figure 12.12 Node information

3. Some of the arrows are heavy and bold. These arrows are the sequence of activities which define the overall project duration. As such they are called the project 'critical path'.
4. Some of the activities take place at the same time. For example, the teamaker can get the teapot and the teabag and put the teabag into the teapot while the kettle is boiling.

The details of the construction and operation of these and other networks are described in detail in other texts[1,2]. While network-based planning tools are more complex, in both their construction and operation, than the Gantt chart they do enable the project manager to:

● Quickly examine the implications of changes;
● Make decisions about changes based on a good understanding of their implications.

This enables the project manager to examine the trade-offs between cost, time and money. However, the network planning tool has less visual impact than the Gantt chart and requires considerable training and experience for it to be used efficiently. For these reasons it is used, in its computer driven form, on large and complex projects.

This final chapter in Part 2 brings us to the end of the review of the practical issues involved in translating into the real world the ideas and concepts we identified in Part 1—with the subsequent generation of improved performance. Part 3 will summarize the key points and issues involved in creation and implementation of the process of improving organizational performance.

Summary

Projects are:

- unique,
- concerned with change,
- have defined outcomes and end-points,
- use a variety of transitory resources.

Despite their one-off nature projects can contribute to the performance improvement process as one of the options available to management to change the performance of an organization.

Efficient projects require a team of experienced trained specialists led by an experienced and capable project manager. The major risks associated with the use of project management for the performance improvement process are:

- the non-involvement of the majority of people in the organization;
- the need to sell the project to these people.

All projects have a life cycle with the stages of:

- Conception,
- Birth and growth,
- Maturity,
- Old age and death.

These stages have different rates of activity and resource demands. The ways in which projects are organized include:

- Project dedicated organization,
- Matrix organization,
- Client integrated organization.

Which organization is used will depend upon a number of factors including:

- The knowledge or technology demands of the project;
- Its time-span, complexity and cost;
- Its importance and implications for:
  - client,
  - project team;
- Innovative nature of the project.

Project planning is an important task which converts outcomes into detailed actions and provides a plan which must be:

259

- Clear, specific and understandable;
- Capable of change and being monitored.

This plan also provides a basis for:

- Co-operation,
- Common understanding of the project.

The basic steps in the generation of such a plan involve the identification of:

- What is to be done,
- By whom,
- When,
- With what resources.

Project plans are of two types:

- Time-based Gantt charts
- Critical path networks

Each of these has its particular advantages and disadvantages.

References
[1] Meredith, J.R. and S.J. Mantel, *Project Management: A Managerial Approach*, Wiley, New York, 1989.
[2] Lockyer, K.G. and J. Gordon, *Critical Path Analysis and Other Project Network Techniques*, Pitman, London, 1991.

Part 3
Coda and Summary

This is not the end.
It is not even the beginning of the end.
But it is, perhaps, the end of the beginning.
Winston Churchill

Coda and Summary

That knowledge which stops at what it does not know, is the highest knowledge.

Chuang Tzu

The need to outperform others has its roots deep in our history as a species. Desmond Morris writes[1] that, some 15 million years ago, the 'naked ape' came face to face with the need to outperform both the carnivores and the herbivores in the heightened competition for food that resulted from climatic change. Richard Leakey and Roger Lewin tell[2] us that even then there was competition between at least three different ape-like creatures, all of whom appeared to use tools, walk upright and live together in social groups. Nobel Prize winner Konrad Lorenz[3] points out that the emergence of the concept of individual property—as distinct from the communal property of the nomadic hunter-gatherer groups—was probably paralleled by the emergence of more complex hierarchical social groups and the need to compete for territory. The emergence of the industrial society, which began in England in the 1760s and in America in the early 1800s, started a process which has continued up to modern times and which has competition—for raw materials, labour, markets and organizational power—as an integral element of its structure. Our views of this competition and the subsequent need to outperform others have evolved and grown more complex and sophisticated with the passage of time. However, from Adam Smith's[4] belief in 'self-interest' through H. Igor Ansoff's[5] view of competitive strategy as a statement of a firm's 'intention to succeed' to the 'extended rivalry' of Harvard University's Michael Porter[6], the theme remains the same—that the prize goes to those who outperform all others. The events of the early part of the last decade of the twentieth century have, if anything, underlined that message with industrial (IBM et al.) and political (USSR et al.) giants tumbling into disarray and social and technical change sweeping through all our lives.

The central core or theme of this book has been that your response to that fiercely increasing competition should be proactive rather than reactive; that you should move towards and embrace it rather than building higher walls and stronger gates to keep it out. To do so and embrace competition whole-heartedly is, of course, an act of faith and courage, and yet we daily undertake such acts in our lives, as for example, when we drive on the freeways or motorways of our urban transport systems. It is not, however,

263

an act into which we should leap without thought or preparation and it is that thought and preparation which has provided the meat and bones of this book. Nevertheless, as we noted at the beginning of our journey through these pages, the process of successful performance improvement will remain ritualized and moribund without the presence and commitment of managers who need and want to improve the performance of the organizations in which they work. That need to change and grow, to do it better, is not an optional ingredient in this process, rather, it is like the yeast in our bread, *a must*, a basic requirement, a foundation stone of successful and effective performance improvement.

These pages have been intended as a guide to those managers and their key points have been:

1. Performance improvement is a continuous and on-going process which is driven by the gap between where you are now and where you want to be.
2. Performance improvement is a 'people centred' activity—success will only come from the whole-hearted involvement of all the people who are the organization.
3. Performance improvement starts and continues with the timely measurement and monitoring of key 'pulse' factors which are credible and understandable.
4. Performance improvement requires the 'what', 'where', 'why' and 'how' of the organization to be understood, probed, explored, discussed, debated and, above all, challenged, even the sacred cows of yesteryear.
5. Performance improvement means accepting and embracing change, rather than holding it at arm's length.
6. The ultimate judge of your performance and whether it has improved or not is the customer, and they all deserve to be delighted.

The achievement of real and consistent performance improvement which satisfies and delights the customer is one which provides a 'win' for everybody—customers, managers, CEOs, employees, shareholders, etc. It is also one which is not only a satisfying and worthwhile experience but also results in organizations which are healthier, more adaptable and more pleasant to work in.

As we have seen in the pages of this book, that goal is not achieved overnight; it involves a journey which requires the steady, consistent application of thought and energy. The intention has been for this book to provide an outline chart or map for that journey. The result has, however, adequate detail for you to set out on your own journey, the creation and direction of which lies in your hands.

References

[1] Morris, D., *The Naked Ape*, Corgi, London, 1969.

[2] Leakey, R. and R. Lewin, *People of the Lake*, Penguin, London, 1981.

[3] Lorenz, K., *The Waning of Humaneness*, Unwin Hyman, London, 1988.

[4] Smith, A., Wealth of nations, in Kempner, T., MacMillan, K. and Hawkins, K., *Business and Society*, Penguin, London, 1976.

[5] Ansoff, H.I., *Corporate Strategy*, Penguin, London, 1968.

[6] Porter, M.E., *Competitive Advantage*, Free Press, New York, 1985.

Further Reading

Reading is to the mind what exercise is to the body.

Sir Richard Steele

Analytical methods
Sprent, P. *Management Mathematics—A User-friendly Approach*, Penguin Books, London, 1991.
Waters, C.D.J., *A Practical Introduction to Management Science*, Addison-Wesley, Wokingham, 1989.

Change
Pascale, R., *Managing on the Edge*, Penguin, London, 1990.
Peters, T., *Thriving on Chaos*, Pan, London, 1988.
Peters, T., *Liberation Management*, Macmillan, London, 1992.

Communication
Baguley, P., *Effective Communication for Modern Business*, McGraw-Hill, Maidenhead, 1994.
3M Meeting Management Meeting Team, *How to Run Better Business Meetings*, McGraw-Hill, New York, 1987.

Conversion processes, layout and capacity
Wild, R., *Production and Operations Management*, Cassell, London, 1989.
Hill, T., *The Essence of Operations Management*, Prentice Hall, Hemel Hempstead, 1993.
Voss, C., C. Armistead, B. Johnson and B. Morris, *Operations Management in Service Industries and the Public Sector*, Wiley, Chichester, 1985.

Measuring and monitoring
Harrington, H.J., *Business Process Improvement*, McGraw-Hill, New York, 1991.
Lynch, R.L and K.F. Cross, *Measure Up—The Essential Guide to Measuring Business Performance*, Mandrin, London, 1992.

266

Organizational development
Pedler, M., J. Burgoyne and T. Boydell, *The Learning Company*, McGraw-Hill, London, 1991.
Senge, P., *The Fifth Discipline*, Century, London, 1990.
Semler, R., *Maverick!: The Success Story Behind the World's Most Unusual Workplace*, Century, London, 1993.

Problem solving
de Bono, E., *Lateral Thinking for Management*, Penguin, London, 1990.
Henry, J. (ed.), *Creative Management*, Sage, London, 1991.

Projects
Meredith, J.R. and S.J. Mantel, *Project Management—A Managerial Approach*, Wiley, New York, 1989.
Lockyer, K.G. and J. Gordon, *Critical Path Analysis and Other Project Network Techniques*, Pitman, London, 1991.

Quality
Crosby, P.B., *Quality is Free: The Art of Making Quality Certain*, Mentor, New York, 1979.
Deming, W.E., *Quality, Productivity and Competitive Position*, MIT Center for Advanced Engineering Study, Cambridge, Massachusetts, 1982.
Oakland, J.S., *Total Quality Management*, Heinemann, London, 1989.

Strategy
Ansoff, H. Igor, *Corporate Strategy*, Penguin, London, 1968.
Moore, J.I., *Writers on Strategy and Strategic Management*, Penguin, London, 1992.

Teams
Belbin, M.R., *Management Teams*, Butterworth-Heinemann, Oxford, 1981.
Belbin, M.R., *Team Roles at Work*, Butterworth-Heinemann, Oxford, 1993.
Katzenbach, J.R. and D.K. Smith, *The Wisdom of Teams*, Harvard Business School Press, Boston, Massachusetts, 1993.

Index

aims, 27
attributes, 41
control systems, 65
culture, 5, 30, 40
goals, 23, 26
health factors, 9
objectives, 8, 32, 34, 35
politics, 29
pulse points, 8
stakeholders, 27
strategy, 31
structures, 26, 121, 124, 125
systems, 29, 124
targets, 30, 35
vision, 32, 34
Outcomes, 49, 52, 97
intangible, 52
Outputs, 48, 49, 50, 53, 56
tangible, 49, 50
intangible, 49, 50

Pareto analysis, 215
People:
as a resource, 49
and work outs, 122
commitment, 127
in The Body Shop, 126
roles, 121
skills, 8, 29
teams, 23, 124, 178
Performance, 3
improvement (*see* Performance improvement)
Performance improvement, 4
and change, 155
and conversion process, 67
cycle, 133, 244
failure, 22
process, 24
and projects, 236, 239, 244
results, 23
steps to, 128–138
successful, 23, 120–127
and TQM, 85
Planning, 117
of projects, 252–259
Presentations, 171–174
Problem:
convergent, 199
definition, 198, 200
divergent, 199

Problem-solving techniques, 201
brainstorming, 205
Ishikawa diagram, 209
lateral thinking, 206
nominal group, 204
visioning, 208
Process:
batch, 96–98
conversion, 47, 95
layout, 104
line, 96–98
and performance improvement, 98
project, 96–98
Product layout, 105
Project conversion process, 97
Project managers, 243
Project organization, 246, 248
Project planning, 252–259
Project structures:
client-integrated, 249
matrix, 248
project-dedicated, 248
Project teams, 243
Projects:
definition, 237–239
life cycle, 242
and performance improvement, 236, 239, 244

Quality, 70
assurance, 84
circles, 88
control, 81–83, 119, 125
costs, 75, 80
definition, 72–74
fallacies about, 75
gurus, 90
management, 81
and performance improvement, 71
and profit, 76
steps to, 76
sources of, 76

Resource:
capital, 49, 104
conversion, 24, 119
human, 49
issues, 32
natural, 49

Semco, 120

www.iani?

www.itcon.com
www.eibacadia.nl

www.Service.beis.b.uk

Usui-E

Elsevier.com

web. lewis

www. it con. com
www. cibworld.nl

www. Service. beis. co.uk

User ⟶ E

Elsevier. Com

www. UB4U. co. uk

doublezero. co.uk